The Rebels' Hour

LIEVE JORIS

The Rebels' Hour

Translated from the Dutch
by Liz Waters

Grove Press
New York

PUBLISHER'S NOTE: *The Rebels' Hour* falls into a category—literary reportage—that
has a long history worldwide, but does not have an established tradition in the
United States. As Joris clarifies in her preface, "the facts in this book have all
been researched in minute detail, but in order to paint a realistic picture of my
characters I've had to fill in some parts of their lives from my own imagination. It
was the only way to make the story both particular and general." The end result,
as one French review noted, is a book that is "even truer than truth" *(Afrique-
Asia)*. Having had to choose between fiction and nonfiction, we felt *The Rebels'
Hour* belonged on the shelf marked nonfiction.

First published in the Dutch language by Uitgeverij Augustus, Amsterdam, as
Het um van de rebellen

The translation of this book was subsidized by **Flemish Literature Fund**

Published simultaneously in Canada
Printed in the United States of America

FIRST EDITION

ISBN- 10: 0-8021-1868-2
ISBN-13: 978-0-8021-1868-4

Grove Press
an imprint of Grove/Atlantic. Inc.
841 Broadway
New York, NY 10003

Distributed by Publishers Group West

www.groveatlantic.com

08 09 10 11 12   10 9 8 7 6 5 4 3 2 1

With thanks to the monks and staff of the St. Andries Abbey in Zevenkerken, Bruges, Belgium

This book is based on real characters,
situations, and places, without ever coinciding
with them completely.

Congo and the surrounding countries

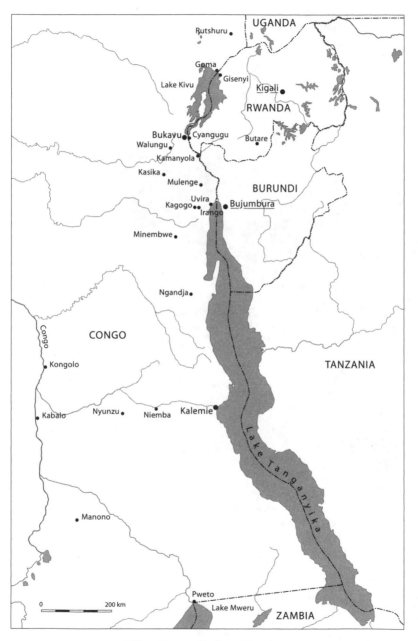

The Great Lakes Region

CONTENTS

Maps   viii

Preface   xiii

The Rebels' Hour   1

Historical Background   286

Chronology   289

Historical Characters   293

Glossary   297

PREFACE

In May 1998, in the Congolese mining town of Lubumbashi, I met the soldier who was to become the model for Assani, the main character in this book. He was a Tutsi rebel who'd arrived from the east of the country with Mzee*—"Old"— Kabila to overthrow the dictatorial Mobutu regime. He belonged to the Banyamulenge,* a people living in the inhospitable high plains of eastern Congo, close to Rwanda and Burundi. As a child Assani had herded cattle. Later he gave up his studies to become a rebel. A herdsman turned soldier: I could immediately see the outline of his life story.

The Banyamulenge originally came from Rwanda. They had a reputation for being belligerent, violent, and secretive. Along with the Rwandans they'd helped Kabila to power, but they were distrusted by many Congolese.

*Words marked with an asterisk can be found in the glossary.

There were rumors that Kabila wanted to rid himself of them and their Rwandan allies.

It was not my first trip to Congo. In the 1980s I'd spent six months traveling through what was then still called Zaire, in the footsteps of an uncle who'd been a missionary in the period when Congo was a Belgian colony. I'd experienced the Mobutu era at close quarters and written a book about it.

In the years since then Mobutu had taken his country, one of the richest in Africa, to the brink of bankruptcy. State institutions had survived in name only and an army of unpaid soldiers was terrorizing the population. By the time the rebels led by Mzee Kabila began advancing from the east in 1996, the regime was so rotten that it fell within seven months.

I'd flown to the capital, Kinshasa, in May 1997 and spent a year traveling in the country that Kabila had renamed Congo; I was working on a second book. Many people hoped the fragile peace Kabila had brought would hold, that after thirty-two years of Mobutu followed by a turbulent takeover the Congolese would be granted tranquillity at last. Meeting Assani made me realize we were deluding ourselves. He was defiant: he'd fought against Mobutu, but the revolution he'd hoped for had failed to materialize. Assani told me Kabila had turned his back on the rebels who'd helped him to power and surrounded himself with people from Katanga, his home region. He believed the regime was heading for a tremendous crash.

His style of driving, the things he said, the way he moved—in the middle of the city I was suddenly in the bush.

Beneath his hard, closed-off exterior Assani seemed vulnerable, ready to tell his story. I must follow him, I thought; by following him I'll get to know what's going on behind the scenes.

Assani's predictions proved accurate. A few months later he was in Kinshasa when Kabila ordered his Rwandan allies to leave. All Tutsi were associated with them, and in the streets of the capital they were hounded, lynched, and burned. I sat and watched it all on television. Assani was tall and slender—unmistakably a Tutsi. I couldn't imagine him surviving this. Something he'd said during our last telephone conversation still reverberated: "You don't know even a hundredth of what's happening here. We're soldiers, but we're being forced to engage in politics."

I thought he'd been killed, but some time later he suddenly reemerged, at the end of a crackling satellite line. He was in the forest, in the east of the country, where a new rebellion had broken out; I could hear the shrieking of wild parrots in the background. "Are you still a writer?" he asked. "Well, now you have a story."

In the years that followed I tracked my subject and slowly crept inside. The rebels controlled the eastern half of the country but had failed to win over the local population. They were supported by the Tutsi regime in Rwanda, regarded by the Congolese as an occupying force. Pockets of resistance by the Mai Mai*—a people's militia—were everywhere, despite repeated and heavy-handed attempts to crush them.

Meanwhile Assani was rising to become one of the most important soldiers in the rebel movement. I met him in the rebel capital, Goma, in a fortress where he lived with forty child soldiers. I saw him in the equatorial town of Kisangani, bivouacked in a hotel room with a closet full of munitions. I visited him in his native province, South Kivu, where Banyamulenge soldiers had started a revolt; he was fighting the very people he'd once chosen to defend.

But just as often I didn't see him at all: he would go off on a mission without leaving any clues to his whereabouts, or spend several months at the front. One time I came on him at an airport in the interior; he gave no sign of recognition.

His disappearance shortly after our first meeting had alarmed me. What if he was killed? I couldn't rely solely on him. I explored his environment, met his fellow rebels, his mother, an uncle, a fellow student, a former girlfriend. Although some of them were no less suspicious than he was, things they let slip now and then helped me to understand what a complicated life Assani led, what difficult choices he had to make.

I who had grown up in antimilitaristic times suddenly found myself sitting next to rebels with crackling walkie-talkies in a jeep that smelled of gasoline, young soldiers in the back, or in a house they'd seized, where a painting hanging lopsidedly on the wall was the only reminder of civilian life. My new acquaintances wore a medley of uniforms and tended to talk among themselves in a language I didn't understand, stop answering the phone from one day to the next, or vanish without a trace.

For their part they thought me an odd customer. They didn't know anything about writing—except for security service reports; they were familiar with those. I must surely be an agent; otherwise, who was paying my travel expenses? Who was financing the endless hanging about I subjected myself to?

It wasn't easy to get inside, but once there I soon saw nothing else. Back home in Amsterdam, I looked in amazement at children in the streets dressed in fashionable camouflage clothing, at boats decommissioned by the Dutch navy that puttered past my window as pleasure craft.

For days on end I scoured Web sites, peering at weaponry, and felt strangely drawn to army surplus stores. They smelled of war and were full of handy bits of gear my new acquaintances in the bush could do with: floppy hats with mosquito netting hanging from the brims, a flat thing made of fabric that folded out to form a basin, earplugs the Americans used in Vietnam to dampen the noise of helicopters and mortar fire.

Assani's forebears had come from Rwanda in the nineteenth century, along with their cows. Growing up in the high plains of South Kivu he'd barely been aware of his origins, but at school in the valley he learned he was a Tutsi. It was a loaded term in those days; in Rwanda a bloody power struggle between Hutu and Tutsi was under way that would lead to a genocide in which 800,000 Tutsi and moderate Hutu were killed.

When the Rwandan war spread to eastern Congo and

the Mobutu regime chose to side with the Hutu, Assani increasingly found himself with his back to the wall, until his identity no longer coincided with that of his country but instead with that of his people, and he crossed the border into Rwanda, where a pro-Tutsi regime was about to take power.

I traced Assani's route. Rwanda, Uganda, Burundi — I ranged across the countries of the Great Lakes region that had become involved in the Congolese war, and visited the campus where he'd been studying when he set out one evening to go to war against Mobutu.

I finally managed to travel to Assani's native region in the high plains of South Kivu in the spring of 2004. There I became aware of the hurt he'd suffered as a child and how it had made him a loner. There I understood why he'd left the high plains and would never return, why the place he came from no longer afforded him any protection, and why the new world he found himself in was just as inhospitable.

All that time Assani thought he was going to die, but he survived. In 2001 Mzee Kabila was assassinated by a bodyguard from the east. Mzee's son Joseph succeeded him, paving the way for peace negotiations that would lead to national reunification. In 2003 Assani, now a general in the reunited national army, arrived in the capital he'd fled five years before in fear of his life.

The story I wanted to write about Assani was probably not the one he had in mind. I wasn't a supporter of his cause; I wanted to understand what had made him. The contact between us was not always easy, but a mutual curiosity kept us going. No matter how intractable, suspicious, and impenetrable he could be, he felt a need to talk about the world in which he'd ended up.

In the fall of 2004, more than six years after I first met Assani, I returned to Amsterdam with the material for this book. I'd done all I could to gain an insight into Assani's life, but certain periods remained mysterious. How exactly had he become a soldier? Where did his true loyalty lie? To what extent had he been involved in the massacres perpetrated by the rebels in the east?

These were questions Assani had not been prepared to answer. He was still keeping some cards hidden. He and his fellow soldiers were inclined to obfuscate their lives, throwing up one smokescreen after another. Sometimes I had the impression that every time a fellow rebel died, they held his story up to the light and appropriated whatever suited them. How could I write a book about people who were so engaged in self-mythology?

To tell the story I'd watched unfold in the shadows, I had to venture deeper into the subterranean depths of my characters than I'd ever done before. Only after I withdrew behind the walls of a monastery near the Belgian city of Bruges did the material finally yield itself up.

The facts in this book have all been researched in minute detail. But in order to paint a realistic picture of my characters, I've had to fill in some parts of their lives from my own imagination. It was the only way to make the story both particular and general.

More than forty years after independence, the concept of the nation-state is fading fast in many African countries.

The continent is littered with tribalistic armies that sustain themselves by looting and extortion. War has become their profession; peace only exposes their shortcomings. The Great Lakes region* is one such area. The wars that have raged there since the early 1990s have cost several million lives.

Through Assani I was able to describe this reality. He went to war to defend his people, killed and saw friends killed. Somewhere along the line he lost sight of how it had all started and where it was all leading. Peace negotiations brought him to the capital, but as long as the problems in his native region remain unresolved, the thread that connects him to his country will be extremely fragile.

This is my third book about Congo. I grew up sheltered from great political dramas in a Flemish village in Belgium, but over the years I've grown familiar with the complex reality of this heart of Africa. Any reader who loses track along the way will find two maps at the start of the book: one of Congo and one of the Great Lakes region. At the end are a short sketch of the background to the war, a list of important dates and historical figures, and a glossary.

Lieve Joris, Amsterdam, 2007

KINSHASA
2003

Assani felt naked as a baby on his arrival in Kinshasa. For years he'd been driving around in the east in a pickup with eight soldiers, armed to the teeth. Now he stepped off the plane with just a few bodyguards. The sky above the city was milky white. He'd forgotten how hot it could get here — the tropical heat fell like a clammy blanket and he was struck by the sickly reek of palm oil and putrefaction. The asphalt gave slightly under his army boots.

Sirens blaring, the convoy drove the miles-long boulevard to the city center. The overpopulated *cités** with their labyrinths of narrow sandy streets were hidden behind garish billboards for Vodacom and Celtel telecom services. Minibuses shot past, so full that legs dangled from the half-open back doors and children hung their heads out of the small windows, gasping for air. One bus stopped to pick up a *maman** carrying a basket of baguettes; the passengers somehow made room for her.

Then suddenly he was in the Grand Hotel, formerly the Hotel Intercontinental, his bodyguards warily investigating the corridors while he inspected his room. Through the window he could see the Congo River, water hyacinths bobbing toward the rapids, and the skyline of Brazzaville in the misty distance. He'd recently learned to swim. In the high plains in the east of the country where he'd grown up the rivers ran fast and cold and he was always horribly sick if he had to travel by boat, but now he'd overcome his aversion to water. No more traipsing along a riverbank trying to devise a way across.

That afternoon he was driven out to Camp Tshatshi to meet the others. Some had phoned him while he was still in Goma. He had no idea how they'd gotten hold of his number, but as soon as his nomination was announced the calls started coming. People complained about their superiors, saying they couldn't wait for him to arrive. That subservient, singsong tone — he couldn't stand flattery, and nothing they said made the slightest impression on him.

The guards at Camp Tshatshi peered in through the car window as if he were a *revenant,* a ghost. The camp was in a euphoric mood. His arrival had been postponed so many times that no one really believed he'd ever turn up. He recognized some of the soldiers who flocked to greet him, men he'd last seen here five years ago when he fled the city. They were thrilled and wanted to know everything: How had he gotten away? How had he survived those first few months? This from people who would gladly have lynched him at the time.

As soon as he managed to get himself a car, he drove into town with his *kadogos**—little ones—cautiously, the way he was used to moving about, on the alert for an ambush. The signs of authority he'd been expecting weren't much in evidence. The situation felt fragile; no one could guarantee anyone else's security.

He and his bodyguards wore Burundian uniforms and big slouch hats. In the past they'd have been conspicuous dressed like that, but to his surprise the Kinois* paid little attention. It seemed they had other things to worry about. It was only when he stopped at a sidewalk café in the *cité* for a drink that a few inquisitive people came up to them. The soldiers from the east were *mibali,* real men, they said. They'd been told the soldiers were all dead, but here they were, alive and well! It was a good thing they'd come. Maybe they should take over again; those who'd stayed behind hadn't achieved very much.

Driving back, he got lost. He didn't know Kinshasa very well. He needed a map, but how could he get one? Surely it would look suspicious if a man with his history asked for one now.

He was incorporated into the reunited national army, along with other high-ranking officers. Everybody was there, and he saw Joseph Kabila again. When Joseph's father was alive they'd been young soldiers together, and even after the war broke out they'd occasionally phoned one another, but they hadn't spoken since Mzee Kabila died and Joseph stepped into his shoes. Assani had his number, but you needed to keep statesmen at arm's length; you never knew who else they might still be talking to.

The thirty-two-year-old president had bags under his eyes — presumably the presence of all those rebels in town made it hard to sleep at night. His father's friends must have told him they'd come here to kill him and that Mzee Kabila would turn over in his grave if he knew his son had made peace with his sworn enemies. Representatives of the international community who'd dragged the young president through the peace negotiations, from one compromise to the next, looked down from the podium with satisfaction. They'd saddled him with no fewer than four vice presidents.

Assani was taller than the rest, and he slumped down in his seat so the cameras wouldn't pick him out. From under his new general's cap, too big for his narrow head, he could look around surreptitiously. The transitional government was an amalgam of stones, roots, and cabbage — how could you ever make decent soup out of that? Long after the vegetables were cooked, the stone would still be a stone.

There was Yerodia. As soon as he was appointed vice president he'd rushed off to Mzee's mausoleum with a television crew, to invoke his help and to have a good cry for the cameras. He had the dazed look of an inveterate cigar smoker and he'd dressed for the occasion by tucking a silk handkerchief into the breast pocket of his sleeveless jacket.

Next to this tropical dandy, Vice President Ruberwa looked sober in his gray suit. Like Assani, he was a son of the high plains. It couldn't be easy for him to sit so close to Yerodia, who'd said at the start of the war that Ruberwa's people were vermin to be eradicated—if only because some of those people would see them together on television this evening and call him a traitor.

As the long, pompous speeches dragged on, the officers caught each other's eye, whispered, and laughed, like schoolboys forced to sit still for too long. Afterward they had their pictures taken. Another freshly appointed general, a member of the Mai Mai, clearly felt intimidated by the bustle of the city. He pulled Assani aside conspiratorially, spoke to him in their own dialect, and suggested the officers from the east should be photographed together. "Not with the others," he whispered. "Just us." To think they'd been arch-enemies over there.

It was the end of one era and the beginning of the next. No more crouching in trenches while Antonovs shat bombs and the sky lit up, like in an American war movie. No more killing, destruction, shooting at everything that moved—he felt no particular sensation.

At Camp Tshatshi, his new workplace, little had changed. A vague smell of urine hung around the corridors of the main building, rusty springs stuck out of the leather couches by the stairs, ceiling tiles were hanging loose, and some of the windows were broken as ever. They hadn't even repaired the locks on the weapons depot, which he'd forced before fleeing five years before. How could they have dreamed of winning a war from such a dilapidated HQ?

Responsible for the budget of the armed forces —it had sounded important enough, but the office he was shown to by his pre- decessor was empty. No table, no cupboard, no chair, and in this oppressive heat not even an air conditioner, only a hole in the wall where it used to be. When they toppled Mobutu in 1997 there had been paperwork, archives, but now there was nothing. How had Kabila's men worked, for God's sake—by walkie-talkie?

His predecessor was a surly man, not the type you could ask questions. He handed Assani a cell phone from the insolvent company Telecel and got him to sign for it. That was all: one phone, without a battery—when he tried for a replacement he found none was available anywhere in the city.

While he was on the way back to the hotel his wife called, as she had so often in recent days, probably to check he was still alive. When they met he was head of military operations in Goma, the rebel capital. She'd thought they made the perfect match; nothing had prepared her for the situation he now found himself in, nearly 1,000 miles from home, in enemy territory. She was much younger and the panic in her voice was starting to irritate him. "Leave me alone, won't you," he said. "Why keep calling? You people can't imagine how complicated everything is over here."

In his hotel room he turned on the television halfway through the program *Forum des Médias*. The participants were fulminating against the rebels from the east, saying they'd come to kill the president, that *he'd* come to kill the president. He sat rigid on the bed. So the people who wanted him dead were still around. They had a free hand here.

Politicians from the east, desperate to secure jobs in government—why had he followed them? Why return to a city where he'd escaped death by a whisker? What was he doing here, in this room, this hotel? He didn't like hotels. He was allergic to the wall-to-wall carpeting and the air-conditioning was making his nose clog up. He didn't feel safe in this environment of strangers and diffuse noises.

That night he was up in the high plains, walking down a narrow mountain track toward the city. The great river far below churned and thundered more and more violently, until the wash slopped over both sides of the path. A fine mist soaked his face and the current sucked his feet out from under him.

He jolted awake, groped for his wife's warm body, realized where he was, and struggled to suppress the fear that was mounting in him again. The violence was cyclical; he'd never known anything else. It had always been wartime.

HIGH PLAINS
1967

The people of the high plains in the east lived outside time; they rarely had any idea how old they were. But his mother remembered exactly when he was born: on the second day of the second month of the year 1967, early in the morning, just before the chickens started to talk. It was a blessed day, since up to then she'd had four daughters, and a woman without sons was regarded as childless by her in-laws. His birth safeguarded her late husband's cows, which would otherwise have been shared out among his uncles. She named him Mvuyekure, he who comes from afar, after his grandfather, who had also been a long time coming. Everyone called him Zikiya.

They lived in Ngandja, a hilly region of unspoiled green meadows. Zikiya's great-uncle Rumenge, who once killed a lion with his spear, had moved there around 1955 with his two wives and children. He encountered a small community of Bembe, who grew cassava and beans and hunted monkeys and wild swine in the surrounding forests. As soon as he'd befriended their chief the others joined him. Before long there were a hundred of them.

They were known as Banyarwanda* — people of Rwanda — since that was where they came from originally, although some had arrived from Burundi. This was in the days before the Ababirigi, as they called the Belgians, when there were no borders and their ancestors habitually moved westward in search of better grazing for their cattle or after conflicts with local rulers.

Zikiya was about four when rumors of rebels came blowing through the hills like an evil wind. The rebels were after their cows, which they'd promised to share out among the poor Bembe farmers; they soon won over the Bembe chief, and the first fatalities followed.

The Banyarwanda gathered their meager possessions and fled — men, women, children, cows, and sheep — escorted by armed warriors who'd left the safety of Minembwe to come and rescue them. That flight and his father's death somehow became intertwined in Zikiya's childhood memories, and he grew up with the bitter conviction that his father had been killed by Bembe rebels.

His uncles said he'd made the trip on his mother's back, but the way he remembered it he must have been able to walk, because during a rest break he wandered away from the path. His mother didn't notice until the caravan was about to move on. In a panic, she went looking for him and found him playing happily in a banana plantation. It was the first time he'd ever seen her cry.

They traveled for seven days. One moment they were walking across an open landscape of rolling meadows, the next through the forest, struggling uphill between trees with long frayed beards of lichen and fast-running streams full of slippery green boulders. Occasionally they were attacked. By the end of the journey ten people were missing, and several cows had run off during clashes with rebels.

In Minembwe they saw army trucks patrolling the hills. President Mobutu had come to power six years before, in 1965, but he had great difficulty establishing his authority in this eastern outpost. The high plains suited the rebels perfectly: they were sparsely populated, with hardly any roads, and Burundi, Rwanda, and Tanzania were close by.

The Cold War was still at its height. To the partisans of rebel leader Laurent-Désiré Kabila, Mobutu was a puppet of the Americans and the former colonial rulers. From socialist Tanzania the rebels moved into the mountains to fight his regime. They called themselves Simbas, Lions. At first the Banyarwanda tried to stay on good terms with the Simbas, but when they realized the rebels were after their cattle they turned to the government army for protection. You could kill a man, but not his cow.

In those days Mobutu's soldiers were still acting correctly. They kept a low profile and listened to the people. They supplied the Banyarwanda with weapons to defend their cattle, and if they needed a cow for food they paid for it.

A lieutenant colonel visited them at their new abode in Minembwe. Zikiya's mother gave him some milk. "Watch it, they're about to run away," the officer told the soldiers standing near the door. That was what usually happened when soldiers came to a village: first they were offered milk, then people took to their heels.

The colonel had used a Lingala* word that Zikiya understood to mean "move house." "Why are they going to move house?" he asked. The man laughed, pulled him close, and shared his milk with him. Zikiya didn't want to leave his side, and his mother, far from running off, came over to hear what he had to say. "That was a good soldier," she said afterward.

Later his family returned to Irango, where they'd lived before moving to Ngandja. Irango lay hidden behind a ridge and no one passing through would ever suspect that people were living there. The round huts—bamboo frames covered with dried cow dung and thatched with straw—were a sorry sight after standing empty for so many years, but they quickly built new ones. Now they could doze off in the evenings again to the heavy breathing of cows asleep in the grass.

Cows were sacred. Zikiya's people drank cow urine as medicine and used it to rinse out their *ngongoros*, wooden milk bottles with woven lids. A cow doesn't talk, they said, so you can't argue with her; like an angel, she won't hurt a soul. They seldom ate meat but lived on milk, maize, and beans. They had the same tall, slender build as cattlemen in other parts of Africa. If a cow died they mourned, whereas the Bembe, who were short and muscular, rejoiced in the knowledge that they'd be eating meat very soon.

Zikiya's father had been the eldest son in his family. When his grandfather died, Zikiya was given a bull and decked out in the old man's personal possessions: a white *pagne** —length of fabric—that knotted at the shoulder and was far too big for him; an ivory bracelet; and an *inkwebo,* the long iron-tipped walking stick the men always carried as they strode through the hills—you could use it to prod the buttocks of a reluctant cow or chase away nosy children, or plunge it into a stream to vault across. He hadn't held on to any of these heirlooms, but he would never forget the ceremony.

He and his older sister were both late arrivals, born when their siblings had already left home. "Don't bother about her," his mother said of his sister. "We'll marry her off when the time comes." Sons increase your own family, the saying went; daughters increase someone else's. Occasionally his mother sold a cow so she could buy things he needed for school, but she always consulted him first about which cow to sell. If she'd picked one that responded when called, or that went ahead leading the way, she'd choose one of the others instead.

Before leaving for school in the mornings he had to take the cows to pasture outside the village. By the time he got back, white clouds would be rising from the dewy straw roofs, the whole of Irango steaming gently in the strengthening sun. Inside, smoke from the wood fire hung low in the room. It stung your eyes if you weren't used to it; he'd noticed when strangers visited how their eyes always started to water. His clothes and hair would be soaked after his early morning walk in the damp mountain air. Other children had to wait to dry off naturally, but he had a towel. He'd no idea where his mother had gotten it, but it was specially reserved for him.

He sat by the fire to drink the milk his mother put ready for him, then picked up his exercise book and walked to Kagogo: down through the forest, across the river, and up the hill on the far side—a forty-five minute walk if he didn't dawdle. On the way he passed the villages where the Bembe and the Fulero lived. They had small fields of crops, and pigs and chickens grubbed about between the huts.

The school was a shabby building standing apart in a meadow, protected from wandering cattle by a bamboo fence on which the children hung their coats. Shafts of light fell through the open shutters into the crowded classrooms and soon children's voices filled the air like the bleating of young goats.

Their parents were illiterate, except for a few who'd been to mission school in the valley and returned as teachers, or had gone back to tending cattle after a couple of fruitless years at a desk, lugging the burden of their unseasoned knowledge with them. Uncle Mufunga had been taught by the Belgians. They were so pleased with him that Zikiya's grandfather feared they'd take him away to their own country and decided to remove Mufunga from school.

"You're always top of the class," the teacher told Zikiya. "But we never see your father." Zikiya didn't let on that he was an orphan. He'd hidden a stick in the bushes on the way to school and would hit Bembe children with it, convinced that his father had been murdered by Bembe rebels. When all the pupils were asked to bring their fathers to school he didn't know what to do. He tagged along behind another boy's father and asked him to be his for a while. The following year the teacher was a member of his own family and demanded he bring his mother instead. He refused — she had nothing to do with school. The teacher punished him by making him tend the soccer field for a week. Zikiya had never forgiven him for that.

Often a man would take his brother's widow as a second wife, so that she'd go on producing children for his family, but Zikiya's mother didn't get on with his uncles. They'd have preferred her to go back to her own family and leave her children with them, so they could do as they liked with her late husband's cows, but she refused to go: those cows were for Zikiya. "Your uncles are nasty," she said. They said the same about her — and before long about him as well.

One afternoon he came home from school to find his mother and grandmother resting in front of the house. They'd just finished pounding corn. Squeezing past them to go inside, he accidentally knocked over the wooden mortar of cornmeal. "Look what that orphan's done!" his grandmother exclaimed. It was as if she'd hit him in the face. He stood trembling in the doorway as cackling chickens ran toward the spilled meal and his mother twisted the mortar firmly back into the ground. "Don't expect me to cry when you're dead!" he snapped at his grandmother.

Inside he picked up a ball he'd made out of rags and hid it under his coat. He tightened the cord at his waist so the ball wouldn't fall out. Without another word he walked off into the hills with the cows.

He enjoyed driving the cattle ahead of him, the best in front, the others meekly following. He had a bull that was fabulously strong; if it saw the leader of another herd it was certain to provoke a fight, stubbornly locking horns with its opponent until blood dripped from their mouths and Zikiya had to pry them apart. He'd shaped the arching horns of some of the cows himself when they were calves, gnawing off the hard outer layer with his teeth. Blood dripped from his own mouth then.

Slowly the trembling sensation went out of his legs. When he'd climbed so high that no one could see him, he got out the rag ball. His mother had never reproached him for being an orphan, although she did say that because he didn't have a father he had no time to play.

The ball had a string attached. After kicking it he could reel it in, so he didn't have to keep running down the slope. He refused to visit his grandmother for three years after that, no matter how hard she begged.

He didn't want to be called Mvuyekure any more, after his grandfather. He crossed the name out of his school exercise book and replaced it with that of his late father. Around this time Uncle Rutebuka, who was very strict, found him asleep in the grass outside the village. Rutebuka prodded him in the ribs with his stick and asked what he thought he was doing there, all on his own. Zikiya blinked and looked up at the man towering over him in faded trousers and jacket, his weather-beaten face shaded by a felt hat. "Am I in your way?" he replied.

Blows rained down, but he shielded his head with his long arms and didn't make a sound. Rutebuka headed off to fetch his mother and aunt. Their clothes flapped in the wind as they approached. They'd hurriedly locked their huts and knotted the keys into their head scarves. "What on earth can you do with a boy like this?" his uncle asked, poking Zikiya with his stick. "He'd rather be alone than with the others." His mother said nothing; she knew better than to defend him in public — his uncles wouldn't hesitate to hit her as well.

Irango was a world of its own, accessible only on foot. Few people ventured into these parts, except for the market traders who toiled up the mountain path from Uvira, their wares on their heads, with a bit of luck arriving in the village two days later.

Zikiya was about eleven when his mother took him into town for the first time. They set off early so they could reach Uvira the same night. Before long they left the hilly landscape of Irango behind them and walked through the forest as if through a tunnel, over fallen trees rotting in the boggy ground and roots that had wormed their way up to hover above the earth like giants' feet with long toes. Then they were in the savanna again, with the fog rolling in over the high ridges all around and streams murmuring far below.

The path became narrower and steeper, stones slid out from under their feet, and his mother told him to be careful: a cow once wandered off the path and fell so far that it lay injured, unable to stand. The Bembe had to kill it and carry it up on their backs piece by piece.

The lower they went the hotter it became, as if they were walking into an oven. On the slopes he saw the round huts of the Fulero, hewn out of the thick forest, surrounded by maize fields and banana trees. Sometimes they met people on their way up, belongings on their heads or in baskets on their backs. Some had flopped down next to their loads, breathing heavily, wet with sweat. Without a word of greeting they stared mournfully into space, or sighed "*Mama-éééh*" as if they regretted ever having set out on the climb. Zikiya was walking mechanically now, as if in a dream, bending his knees, braking with his feet.

On the horizon lay a huge flat plain. When he looked more closely he saw that it wasn't land but water. "Is that a river?" "Yes," said his mother. "A very big river." The water was turbulent. "Why are there so many sheep rolling around in it?" "Those aren't sheep." He didn't believe her. He could see them perfectly clearly, some brown, others white, rolling about to their hearts' content.

In Uvira that evening he looked up at the steep blue mountains. They were like dark men with giant hats and long robes—it was hard to believe he'd come from behind their backs. Red dots shone on the hillsides; it was the beginning of the dry season and the Fulero were setting light to their fields.

His relative's house in Uvira had electricity. For the first time in his life he didn't have to blow out the lamp before going to sleep. As soon as he closed his eyes the day started all over again. He heard the tap of walking sticks on the gravel, saw the climbers grimacing with pain, felt the stones slide out from under him.

Next day they left Uvira and crossed the border into Burundi. He'd been suffering terrible headaches lately and quarreling with the village children. He was sleeping hardly at all; his eyes refused to shut at night. His mother had decided to take him to the hospital in Bujumbura.

The white doctor said it was nerves. He massaged Zikiya's head and proposed keeping him in for observation. His mother ran out of money and had to return to the high plains to sell a cow. He stayed with the doctor. It wasn't until several days later that he noticed how dirty his clothes were. People in Bujumbura wore much cleaner clothes. And that smell of smoke — why hadn't he noticed it before? His jacket, shirt, pants, and bag were saturated with it. There were no fleas here, unlike in the plains, where they crept into your bed at night, went looking for the warmest parts of your body, and left tiny red spots.

The doctor bought new clothes for him and they threw out the old ones. During the day Zikiya stayed at the hospital, where all the patients had red eyes. It was a madhouse, but he wasn't mad. In the evenings the doctor took him home, played with him, taught him to ride a bicycle, and gave him books and notepads. The doctor slowly worked out what was wrong.

Uncle Rutebuka had recently removed him from school, saying Zikiya only needed to look after the cows his father had left him — school was for poor children. Yet Rutebuka's own children went to school! His mother protested that Zikiya wouldn't learn other languages if she kept him at home. Rutebuka laughed at her. Did she want her only son to leave for the city to finish secondary school and never come back, the way schoolchildren always did? Who would look after her then?

On her return from the high plains, she was amazed to find Zikiya calmly bicycling around the courtyard of the doctor's house. "There's nothing wrong with him," the doctor said. "He wants to go to school, that's all."

When they got back to Irango he looked like a city boy in his new clothes. For years he'd been top of his class, but now he'd missed three full weeks and the cleverest girl had caught up with him. The next year she grew breasts and stopped coming to school; it was time to marry her off.

The school holidays coincided with the dry season, when the banks of cloud that usually hung over the high plains gave way to clear bright blue skies. The sun scorched the savanna until it was arid and yellow, reducing the soil to fine dust. In the late afternoon an icy wind came up, blowing the dust into your clothes, turning your skin into crackleware. People hunched down in their jackets and crept into bed at six. The cows began to lose weight and gave hardly any milk. It was time for the transhumance,* the seasonal migration.

The women stayed behind with the small children and a few cows while the men set off with their herds and walked for many days before setting up camp in a region where it still rained and the pasture was green. They'd have liked to go all the way to Ngandja, where the cows would grow so heavy they'd trample the skinny cows when they got home, but the rebels were still there and it wasn't safe for them yet.

Sometimes they were gone for up to four months. A servant had taught Zikiya to use his father's gun, a thirty-caliber. He took it with him, since the more you strayed from the inhabited world, the more likely you were to come across rebels. The Bembe wanted payment for grazing. According to local custom, endorsed in colonial times and upheld after independence, the cattlemen were subordinate to the *bami*,* the traditional chiefs. But Zikiya refused to pay and was ready to defend himself if necessary.

In the evenings they sat by fires in the huts they built during the transhumance, listening to the old men's stories. In the early evening they discussed current affairs: a cow that had calved and pissed blood ever since, a bull that appeared to be sick. They recited poems in which cows could speak, reassuring their worried masters. Or they told the story of a cow that grew ferocious after her master died, stamping her foot whenever his children came near, until someone had the idea of donning the dead man's jacket and hat. As soon as the cow recognized her master's silhouette and breathed his smell she grew docile and allowed herself to be milked.

As they talked, one man poked the fire with a piece of wood, while another absently threw a few more stripped corn cobs onto it, or picked up a glowing ember in his calloused fingers to light his pipe. The past was like a bandage you could unroll endlessly. If they sat together long enough they'd invariably get back to the time when their ancestors first arrived in these parts.

It was a history that had dissolved in the mist, but they never stopped trying to reconstruct it. Although Zikiya knew all the stories by heart, he listened as if for the first time. Later too, in the city, he cherished the smoke-ridden stories handed down to him during the long evenings of the transhumance.

The westward migration had begun centuries ago, the elders said, but it reached its peak in the second half of the nineteenth century when the despot *Mwami*—Chief—Rwabugiri tried to tighten his grip on Rwanda, demanding more and more cows from his subjects. Rwabugiri. A century later his name still sounded ominous in the high plains.

At first their ancestors settled in the central plateau, but gradually they moved deeper into the interior. At the time of their flight, Rwanda was one of the most tightly organized kingdoms in Africa, with a strong feudal tradition. After Rwanda the high plains seemed like a world where everything had yet to begin.

The newcomers went around in cowhides; the people they encountered wore hardly any clothes and admired their large cows with arched horns. The cattle became a powerful weapon in their struggle to win favor among local chiefs. "If a Bembe is hostile toward you, give him something to eat," was the maxim they passed on to their children. They persuaded people to tend the cattle and work the land for them in exchange for cows and cowhides, just as they'd done at home, or they purchased slaves at the market, brought in from the heart of the country.

In their new surroundings they lived in clans. Their language eroded and became colored by the speech of the Bembe and Fulero. Their new heroes were the men who, as they moved into the interior, had killed leopards, hyenas, lions, and wolves with their spears, or crocodiles that had dared to snatch cows drinking at the water's edge.

Despite their economic superiority they didn't own the land they lived on, but were forced to defer to local *bami*.

Since their flight from Rwanda they'd grown nervous of central government. For fear of forced labor and other sanctions they avoided the administrative centers set up when the Belgian colonizers arrived.

Elsewhere in the country newcomers eventually started marrying locals, but the Banyarwanda kept to themselves. The old men around the fire wondered what else they could have done. Their wives were used to collecting cow pies and mixing them with colored earth to decorate the walls of their huts. A Bembe girl would never do that. Bembe villages were dirty—pigs, which they regarded as unclean, wandered between the huts. And how could they let a girl marry into their families if she wasn't used to drinking milk and regarded a cow simply as a lump of meat? How could they marry one of their daughters off to a family that ate monkeys, snakes, frogs, birds, and insects—everything, in fact, apart from mud? The bride price paid by a Bembe might be no more than a rat-trap, a machete, a goat, a torch, and a set of cooking pans, whereas they were used to getting at least eight cows for a girl. Their own women didn't even eat goat's meat, because goats bleated so horribly when they gave birth—the women feared they too might cry out like that during labor.

So the gulf between them remained. The Marxist Simba rebels, who moved into the high plains after the Belgians left in 1960 and found themselves face-to-face with their impressive herds, called the Banyarwanda capitalists and regarded the poor farmers, with their pigs and chickens, as proletarians. The cattlemen had sharp noses, too, like the whites, so they must be foreigners.

His cousins had fallen asleep, but Zikiya was still wide awake. No one was tending the fire any longer, or refilling his pipe. Here and there people started to cough. The old men stared into space. They were thinking of their sons, who'd taken up arms to defend themselves against the Simbas. Some were now soldiers in the government army.

Perhaps they were also thinking about Ngandja, where they'd been happy before the rebels came. Recently a group of men, along with trained fighters, had been back to see how things stood. The Bembe were upset by their arrival, claiming that their cows would put the wild animals in the forest to flight. "We were here first," they said, "so this land belongs to us." "Oh really?" someone replied. "Is this land your child? When did you give birth to it?" That made them all laugh. The Bembe were just as stubborn and proud as the Banyarwanda, and that was why they were always fighting. "But the Bembe can't stop us from returning to Ngandja," one old man said, "any more than you can stop a cow from looking for salt."

The evening came to an end. The men sighed, stood up, and withdrew to their own huts. Zikiya remained where he was with his cousins and one of his uncles, who would stay a few weeks and then be replaced by another. The uncle slept in a bed by the fire while Zikiya and his cousins lay under a torn blanket on the ground in a drafty, uncomfortable place near the door. Smoke from the smoldering fire blew toward them all night, making them cough. The uncle took one of his children into bed with him, and the child lay there snug under a sheet and blanket, close to his father.

None of his uncles ever thought of taking Zikiya into bed
with them. Not once.

He'd been taught that if you pass a village where you know
someone, you must visit him, otherwise you're a sorcerer.
So on the way back from the transhumance he sent the cows
on ahead and went to see Uncle Mufunga, who lived with
his wife and children half a day's walk from Irango.

Uncle Mufunga could write beautiful Swahili,* although
he became a bit strange after his father took him out of the
Belgian school. He'd been forced to leave Ngandja even
before the rebels came, because he was sick. It wasn't an
ordinary illness; something was wrong in his head, and his
brothers took him into the valley for treatment. The bustle
of the city did him no good at all and Mufunga danced
through the streets of Uvira, talking nonstop. The doctor
prescribed medicine, which he refused to take. He recov-
ered of his own accord, but every year around Christmas
and the New Year it would start all over again.

Zikiya found him at home, sitting on a three-legged
stool by the fire. The door was open and as he went in Uncle
Mufunga turned to face him. He had fiery, rather alarming
eyes and he stared at Zikiya out of the half-darkness like a
nocturnal animal. His coppery skin was smooth and firm and
he'd retained a kind of youthfulness even though he was in
his late sixties, as if the sickness in his head had kept him
from aging.

Zikiya sat on the ground next to him and after they'd
exchanged news about the transhumance his uncle fired a

salvo of questions at him: He'd been to school. Had the master told him yet whether the world was created all at once or stage by stage? Or whether the water and the earth were finite or not? Or why the moon gave light and the sun's rays stung? Or whether the earth, the moon, and the sun were independent bodies and if so what they rested on? Uncle Mufunga didn't sit still on his round stool for a second, and he fixed Zikiya with a penetrating stare that frightened him a little. Every time he failed to come up with an answer his uncle sucked at his teeth disapprovingly. What was he actually learning in school? The Belgians had taught him more in two years than Zikiya had picked up in six!

Although Zikiya was easily hurt by what adults said, he sensed that his uncle was only playing a game. Deep down he must be proud that his little nephew would soon be going to the secondary school run by Italian fathers in Kagogo.

When it was time to leave, Mufunga went outside with him. He disappeared behind the house and came back with a goat and a chicken, which he gave to Zikiya. They walked to the edge of the village together and as they were about to part his uncle reached into his pocket, handed him some money and then, to Zikiya's surprise, started to cry.

The whole way home, the chicken under his arm, the goat on a rope behind him, he tried to figure out why Mufunga had wept. The tears of a man go to his stomach, the saying went, but his uncle's tears had run down his cheeks. He had wiped them away with the sleeve of his jacket, looking distraught.

His mother was standing on the path to Irango waiting for him. That evening, in the privacy of their hut, he showed her the money Mufunga had given him and asked her why he'd cried when they parted. Instead of answering, his mother began crying too. He questioned her repeatedly in the days that followed, but she refused to say anything, and years would pass before he understood why Mufunga had cried that day.

KINSHASA
2003

Gradually Assani began to move about the city more freely. Sometimes he was followed, even photographed. One afternoon he shook off his tail and drove out into the hills. Before he knew it, he was on his way to Kinsuka. This was the road they'd fled along five years before, in a long column, laden with heavy crates of ammunition looted from Camp Tshatshi, the wounded between them on improvised stretchers.

They'd gone down to the quarries beside the Congo River, until they no longer felt safe even there. At that point they were still in touch with the soldiers who'd left the city by a different route, but they'd soon be outside the zone covered by their cell phones.

One friend had chosen not to go with Assani. He claimed he was out of danger, that he had a good place to hide. How many days had he lived after that? What had they done with his body? Where was he buried? Bitterness welled up in

Assani, even though it was he who told the soldiers in the east not to look back but ahead.

They kept calling him up, asking him what to think, what to do. Some had refused to come to Kinshasa. They were frightened. If he died here in a traffic smash they'd never believe it was an accident, despite the high number of road deaths in Congo.

He was approaching the place where he'd lost one of his *kadogos* as they fled. Fortunately they'd been able to bury him. He still knew exactly where. He'd arrive at the spot if he just kept on driving. Would he recognize the place or would it be so overgrown after five years that no trace remained? Nature played tricks on your memory here; he'd seen that many times before.

The landscape was increasingly bare. Suddenly he no longer felt safe and decided to turn back. He should never have come. There were no cars on this road; he was completely alone. What if he ran into a roadblock? What should he say?

Now that his appointment was official he could start looking for a place to live. One of his wife's uncles, a wealthy businessman who'd fled Kinshasa in 1997 during the first war, had given him the title deeds to two houses. People were living there, but once he got them out he could move in.

The occupant of the first house, a walled villa on 30 June Boulevard in the city center, was Lebanese. The Lebanese! Assani knew them from the east. They were all involved in shady businesses: gold, diamonds, weapons. Unimpeded by principles, they dealt with the highest bidder. Assani phoned him. "I'm renting this house officially," the Lebanese said, in the stern tones of a man who knows he can count on protection. "I'm not doing anything illegal." When he heard who was calling he began to sound less self-assured. "We know what you people are doing here," Assani said. "Times are changing. Don't go thinking you can get away with it forever." He promised to pay the occupant a visit shortly.

The house had been confiscated by the OBMA,* he discovered: the Office of Ill-Gotten Gains, a bureau set up to return property unlawfully appropriated by the Mobutists* to its rightful owners. But the elite around Mzee Kabila had started to help themselves to anything that took their fancy. If they didn't want to move in, they rented the houses out to foreigners. A villa on the boulevard could easily bring in $3,000 a month.

Assani went to visit the Lebanese in uniform, flanked by two bodyguards. He got no farther than the terrace, but from there he could see that the house was in good condition. It had a garden at the back where his soldiers could camp.

"You'll have to move," he said. The man told Assani again about the rent he paid every month to a man from Katanga province. "You don't understand what I'm telling you," Assani said icily. "The person you rent from and the owner are two different people. If you don't leave, I'll have you kicked out. Is that what you want?" The Lebanese went on protesting until Assani ran out of patience. "Have you got a pistol?" The man shook his head nervously. No.

"Make sure you get one before my next visit. I'll bring mine. We'll see which of us survives."

The second house was a more complicated matter, since it was occupied by soldiers. It was in the chic residential district of Macampagne in the Kinshasa hills. Assani drove out there with four bodyguards—you never could tell. On the way he ran into a roadblock manned by police. He wound down his window and looked at them without saying anything. They peered suspiciously into the car and asked him where he was going. He said he was on his way to his house.

Vice President Yerodia, the cigar-smoking dandy, lived in the neighborhood, so they couldn't simply let Assani through. It was only after he'd given his name and they'd checked him out by walkie-talkie that they raised the barrier. Before he rounded the next bend the chief of staff phoned. He'd just received word that General Assani was on his way to Yerodia's house with a bunch of soldiers.

"No, no," said Assani. "I've come to look at my own house."

"What? You have a house there?"

"Yes. That is, it's *ours*. But apparently it lies within the extensive grounds of Mr. Yerodia's residence."

That made his boss laugh. They'd have to stop bothering him with such trivial matters, he said.

A dilapidated minibus was parked in front of the house, and on the black gate someone had written in chalk that paving slabs were for sale inside. Assani talked his way past the guards. To the right of the broad driveway stood an impressive house. The main terrace looked out on a garden with a swimming pool, and the city lay in the misty valley below — if he looked carefully he could make out the People's Palace.

Six years had passed since the uncle fled Kinshasa and his paradise had steadily eroded: thick trails of rust trickled down between the fine white stones of the mosaic on the side walls, the doors and windows at the back were hanging out of their frames, and wherever he looked there was a film of grimy mold. At the edge of the driveway a tap was running. He saw it was broken — the steady stream of water had worked the paving slabs of the terrace loose and caused the garden wall to crack from end to end. Inside he could hear children crying and women quarrelling.

"Who's in charge here?" he asked a group of men tinkering with an army jeep on the lower gallery, surrounded by a chaos of scattered car parts. They'd barely looked up when he came in, as if they were used to military visitors — perhaps they thought he wanted his car fixed.

There turned out to be seventeen families living on this one plot of land. The men belonged to the special presidential guard recruited in Manono, Mzee Kabila's native region, in the first few months after he took power. They were simple villagers who, after a brief period of training, had come to the capital with high expectations, only to find there was no employment for them here, nor any amenities, until someone drew their attention to this empty house. They tried to support themselves by doing odd jobs for the army.

Assani stood at the top of the steps to the swimming pool and gazed out over the city. Below the house lay a cemetery and beyond it what looked like a *cité:* low houses built of cheap materials, with occasional patches of green. His wife's uncle used to sit on his marble terrace looking out at that poverty-stricken world. While his servant wheeled a trolley of champagne and Chivas Regal, and ice cubes tinkled in crystal glasses, *mamans* down there cooked their miserable pots of food.

When Kabila's soldiers marched into the capital, the Mobutists fled en masse and the inhabitants of the *cité* scrambled up the slope. They plundered the abandoned houses, dragging away the furniture and destroying the fixtures and fittings. Then the wretches from Manono installed themselves here. They had no need of plumbing; a broken tap in the garden would do.

Assani disliked the pompous architectural style of the Mobutu years. Left to his own devices he'd bulldoze the whole concrete block. But he did like the spacious garden and the swimming pool—he could relax here if the city below became too hectic for him.

As he walked down the steps his mood turned somber. The current occupants were using the overgrown garden as a garbage dump. There were even people living in the changing cubicles to the left of the pool. They'd built a few extra walls, he noticed, to accommodate more families.

It was Friday evening. He could hear the hum of music rising up out of the valley, heralding the weekend. Plastic bags and dead toads floated in the slimy green water of the swimming pool. He stared at them, seized with revulsion. People took pleasure in wrecking things here, but when it came to constructing something you couldn't get them to lift a finger. This country, he thought, was bound to disappear.

HIGH PLAINS
1979

On Sundays his mother went to the Protestant service in Kagogo, but as Zikiya got older he often refused to go with her. Sunday was his day off and he wanted to play football.

All morning you could hear the roll of tom-toms, and hymn-singing resounded across the hills. After the service people stood outside the church to talk, then walked home merrily along the paths of trodden grass that veined the landscape.

His uncles still remembered a time when people attended Christmas and Easter services at Protestant missions run by Swedes and Norwegians down in the valley. But by the 1950s preachers were moving up into the plains and the first churches were built, initially of wood, later of stone and corrugated iron, paragons of austerity with their bare, whitewashed walls. The men's walking sticks stood in a row at the back, their hats on top, while the word of God was preached from the front.

They'd brought a belief in Imana, God, with them from Rwanda, but now God started to speak. Tales of Abraham, Isaac, and Jacob; of family quarrels and disputes between farmers and cattlemen; of wandering in the desert in search of a promised land—the stories were all about them. They prayed, sang, praised the Lord, and held nocturnal vigils, after which they walked home through the moonlit hills with so little distance between themselves and God that they could converse with him effortlessly. As time went on they colored the biblical stories with tales of their own. Old women prophesied the future, attracting an eager audience; one father decided not to send his sons to school after a prophetess swore to him the great deluge was imminent.

This was the state in which Father Paolo found them when he arrived in Kagogo in 1977. He built a mission post on a hilltop, sheltered from the sun and wind by eucalyptus trees, with bedrooms for himself and his colleague and a guest room for visiting fathers. They often sat in the kitchen–dining room, which had a wood-burning stove. The table in the reception room was set only on Sundays. On the hill opposite, Paolo built a secondary school—two low buildings flanking a meadow that served as a playground.

Paolo, an Italian, would live there for ten years and they were the happiest years of his life. He felt as if he'd stepped into the Middle Ages and intense spiritual experiences were granted him in that unspoiled countryside with its dramatic cloudscapes. With visiting fathers he sometimes walked for days in the surrounding hills, calling at other mission posts.

He never tired of the forested slopes that rolled on as far as the eye could see, the swift streams in the valley, the silver lichen that hung from the trees in long strands, like filigree.

The fathers lived simply, since all their supplies had to be brought in by carriers. In the mornings Paolo shaved at the open window, using a mirror that had been broken on the way up. In no time the courtyard would fill with nosy children, whispering, giggling, and sniveling — they'd never seen themselves in a mirror before. As he chased them away he could hear the excited drumming of their little feet on the sand. Here at well over 8,000 feet, the mornings were often brutally cold, but the children went barefoot. All year long they had damp eyes and runny noses.

Paolo was a temperamental, ambitious man in his forties who'd lived in Congo for fifteen years by the time he arrived in Kagogo. He was capable of exploding with rage if a cow or a goat slipped in through the mission house fence to munch at the vegetables in his kitchen plot. Woe to the animal's owner if it happened to find the door to the reception room open, take a turn through the house, and do its business on the stamped-earth floor. Paolo would call him a *mushenzi,* a wild man, and remind him he had an air rifle in the house, saying he'd shoot the animal if it happened again.

All too often his energy and resolve were thwarted by the conservatism of the mountain people. The fathers installed a hand pump to bring water up from the valley to the mission post through plastic pipes. The men stood looking at it, shaking their heads. As if their wives were incapable of carrying buckets of water for the fathers! They boycotted the

mill Paolo had ordered from Uvira to grind maize and cassava. Did he think they'd paid the bride price only to let
machines do the women's work for them? The flour smelled
of diesel oil, they complained, and they refused to eat the food
their wives made with it, so Paolo dismantled the mill and sent
the parts back down the mountain.

If a Bembe or Fulero woman had something to sell, she'd
walk into the yard with her basket, place it on the ground in
front of him, and start telling her story. Banyarwanda women
came empty-handed and preferred to sit indoors, out of sight
of inquisitive villagers. It would take him a while to realize
they hadn't just happened by; a casual reference to the cold
was really intended to bring up the subject of the wood he'd
need for his stove, which they'd hidden in the shrubbery near
the fence, ready for a possible transaction.

He suspected that back where the Banyarwanda originally came from, their relationship with the Hutu had been
very much like the relationship they now had with the
Bembe and the Fulero. They felt vastly superior. At first they
enchanted him with their intelligence and obstinate pride,
but slowly he became drawn to the disarming openness of
the others. During the Simba rebellion, Mobutu had supplied the Banyarwanda with weapons to defend their cattle.
They lost both people and cows but claimed plenty of victims of their own. The others had not forgotten: in the 1980s,
when the Banyarwanda began to demand political and social rights, they took revenge by saying the Banyarwanda
weren't Zaireans.

Whenever Father Paolo thought back over those years
he grew sentimental. Nothing could ever compare to his

experiences in the high plains. The pupils at his mission
school were clever in their way, although he had to admit
they lagged behind children in the valley. Their parents
failed to see why they had to do homework after school instead of chopping wood, fetching water, or tending cattle.
And what was the point of explaining the basic principles
of electricity in a region that relied entirely on oil lamps?

In 1982 Paolo went to Uvira with 180 schoolchildren to
collect cement and corrugated iron for an extension to the
mission school. It was a clear day and shortly after noon he
saw Lake Tanganyika sparkling far below. Some of his pupils
were descending the mountain for the first time, even though
many were over eighteen; he could hear them whispering and
suppressing giggles just like the children in Kagogo when he
shaved in his broken mirror in the mornings. "What's that
over there? It looks like the sky has fallen!" "Nonsense. See
how black it is? That's where they've set fire to the savanna."
Father Paolo listened and said nothing. Zikiya wisely held
his tongue as well. The water was smooth, he noticed, not
like before, when he'd thought he could see sheep.

As soon as the asphalt road came into sight, cutting
Uvira in two, the excited whispering started again. "Look
over there—a river standing still!" They refused to believe it
was anything but water until they got close enough to touch
it with their own hands. And here came the next miracle, right
on the asphalt. A Volkswagen overtook a truck. "Hey, look,
that one's outrunning his mother," one boy shouted. "He's
going to be real strong when he grows up!"

Paolo's fellow mission fathers had prepared a dormitory for his pupils at a school in Uvira. Paolo had a room at

the end of the corridor, but he couldn't get to sleep. The boys kept running up and down. Why were they so restless? After a while he could no longer contain his curiosity. As he approached the dormitory he saw the light going on and off. He looked in through a small window. One boy had stationed himself by the light switch. Every time he flicked the switch, two boys raced toward the light while the others cheered. It took a moment for Paolo to work out what they were doing. They were trying to run faster than the light.

The main thing Zikiya remembered about the journey was that he had to carry a sheet of corrugated iron back up on his shoulders. It was too heavy, and somewhere along the way he threw it into the valley. As a punishment he had to give Father Paolo a goat, but that was a price he was happy to pay.

Around the time he turned sixteen, Zikiya began to wander across the high plains with his friends. If it was market day anywhere, they'd get up early and leave together. On days like this a shimmer of enjoyment danced across the landscape. From all around, people were heading in the same direction: men with cows and goats to sell, traders from Uvira and Bukavu, Fulero women carrying barrels of homemade beer on their heads, and sightseers like the boys themselves, simply on their way from one place to another.

The older Banyarwanda had put on their Sunday best for the occasion: suit jackets, pants, shirts, wide-brimmed hats—secondhand garments that had seen better days and would have been recognized instantly in Bujumbura as hopelessly old-fashioned, but that passed as rich people's clothing here in the mountains and in fact gave them a rather stylish air. Most people were sweating under their heavy loads, but the old men adopted a nonchalant stride, hands behind their backs, walking sticks held loosely between their fingers. When they decided to quicken their pace Zikiya couldn't keep up; they shot off like arrows and he suddenly saw them reemerge two hills away. Their eyes were used to scrutinizing the distance and they scanned the horizon for familiar things: the dark-green bean fields of the Fulero on the slopes, the cows standing in tight formation on a hilltop, watching the market-goers intently as if asking themselves all sorts of questions.

The hazy patch in a far-off dip in the hills grew steadily more distinct and Zikiya could hear a soft hum, just like the swarms of bees he and his friends sometimes came on in the forest and gleefully smoked out so they could run off with the honey. On ordinary days the marketplace was a collection of flimsy bamboo structures, straw shelters, and lopsided huts, but now life and color were flowing into the empty decor.

As soon as they entered the ambulatory town a noisy throng pressed in on them. Zikiya strolled past the stands, tried on a leather jacket from a pile of clothing on the ground, bought batteries for his transistor radio, tea and sugar for his mother, salt and medicines for the cows, and then hung around for a while near the gold dealers. They used tiny pairs of scales, placing coins on one side and yellow grains of gold on the other. The gold diggers, poverty-stricken wretches with timorous expressions who lived in the over-populated mining villages of the region, crouched to watch, hurrying away as soon as they'd been paid.

Later he saw them again, in a sour-smelling section of the market set apart from the rest. It was the only place where Banyarwanda, Fulero, and Bembe sat together like brothers, using mugs to scoop *pombe*, beer made from maize or bananas, out of gourds standing between them. They had a great deal to tell each other, and the eyes of men who carried on drinking became as red as those of the madmen in the hospital run by the white doctor in Bujumbura. The gold diggers drank more than anyone else, and some lay stretched out in the grass while others abruptly nodded off against the hut where women were serving food, shrieking in protest when they were eventually dragged away.

Zikiya went across to the cattle market and squeezed past the cows, listening to men slap their animals' flanks and praise their stock. As soon as they seemed close to reaching a deal they withdrew to a patch of grass nearby. One man from Kagogo had brought a large bull to market. He sold it for two calves and a thick wad of zaires. Zikiya knew the man would exchange the money for gold as quickly as he could; the zaire had been plummeting in value so fast lately that it was impossible to keep track of its fall.

Out of the corner of his eye he could see Uncle Rutebuka, who had quarreled with his mother not long before. One of Rutebuka's innumerable sons was getting married shortly and he wanted to include a few of his deceased brother's cows in the bride price. His mother had resisted fiercely, but afterward she was so quiet and downcast that Zikiya—who'd reached an age when he'd more or less stopped speaking to his mother—asked what was wrong.

It was evening. His mother was sitting on a reed mat by the fire. "You ought to get married," she said after a moment's hesitation. "Then the cows will be yours and no one can give us any more trouble about them." This had been in the air for a while. Many of the boys in his class were married; some even had children already. He'd resisted up to now because he wanted to finish school first, but the pressure was mounting. What if something happened to him? His father's line would die out.

"Zikiya!" His friends beckoned him over. They'd flopped down in the grass with their backs to the market, gazing at the hills where the first market-goers were walking home. He slowly wandered over to join them. The traders had begun to pack up. They traveled from market to market carrying their wares on their heads, moving around the high plains for a week before returning to the valley for fresh supplies. Some became so exhausted they succumbed to attacks of malaria, dying for lack of medicine.

The humming noise dissipated and the colors that had briefly clustered together slowly spread out over the hills. When Zikiya and his friends left, it wasn't long before they saw the marketplace far beneath them, lifeless in the glow of the setting sun.

It had grown chilly and in the houses they passed little

fires had been lit. Children played in the fading light; here and there a baby cried. High in the sky a bright star had appeared.

Zikiya was quiet all the way back. He'd closed his heart to so many people over the years, but he loved his mother. He could never bring himself to disappoint her.

The world outside the high plains reached them by transistor radio. For good reception you had to climb a long way up the hill. Voix de l'Amérique, the BBC, Radio Rwanda, Voix du Zaïre—they knew all the frequencies by heart.

That summer Zikiya belonged to a group of friends that called itself Radio Vacances, after a popular program on Burundi radio. When they heard that their favorite Burundi soccer team was going to play the Egyptian club Zamalek, they sold a few goats and set off without telling their parents: first the steep descent to Uvira, then on foot over the border to Bujumbura.

Those left behind were worried. They thought the young men had left to enlist in Mobutu's army. When they got back, some people grumbled that banditry had now reached the high plains as well, but others said, "Oh, well, what else are goats good for?" His mother wasn't angry but rather curious to know what he'd seen. She was disappointed he hadn't brought a Coleman lamp back from the city—they were so much better than the Chinese oil lamps on sale in the local market.

After the match they'd walked into a studio and had their picture taken, against the backdrop of a faded panorama of Paris. Zikiya would never be so thin again, except when he returned from the front line. He would remember it as his last carefree trip, the last of the days when his life was completely his own.

"At least let me choose my own wife," he said to his mother. She agreed, and Uncle Mufunga also felt they should let him have his own way, but his other uncles had a relative in mind for him. They slapped him, said Mufunga was soft in the head, and insisted on their own choice.

She lived in a village not far away. He was seventeen now and had a hut of his own. The girl came over the hill to a roll of tom-toms, accompanied by her friends, who had thrown a *pagne* over her head to prevent him from seeing her face. The moment she walked into his hut she was his wife. In return for the bride price Zikiya had paid, she would produce children for the family of his father and uncles. It seemed unreal, as if it were happening not to him but to somebody else. Now he belonged to a world from which he'd always kept aloof; now he was shackled to what he detested most: family.

He sat in the classroom staring into space. As a child he'd fought to attend school, but now he was sometimes absent for days at a time. He was sullen, turned in on himself. Something was gnawing away at him.

That was how one of his wife's brothers found him when he visited two years later. Elias was among the first sons of the high plains to have studied in Kinshasa. He'd been a teacher in Kagogo and remembered Zikiya as a clever pupil. He knew exactly what was wrong: Zikiya no longer had time to study. He was in the penultimate year of secondary school but at this rate he'd never finish.

One day they went up into the hills together. To people who asked where they were going Elias said, "Oh, just for a walk." As soon as they were out of sight he dropped down into the grass and gestured to Zikiya to come and sit next to him. They listened to the wind as it gathered the rhythmic thumping of maize-pounders down in the valley and swept it up to them.

"Why stay here?" Elias asked after a while.

Zikiya looked at him in surprise. "What do you mean?"

"Why don't you sell a cow and come down?"

He shrugged. "And do what?"

"Just . . . just look around for a bit. You could finish secondary school. What else are those cows good for?"

The school run by the Italian fathers was a bush school — anyone wanting to pass the state exam had to complete his studies in Uvira or Bukavu. Selling one cow a year would pay for lodging with a family, or at a boarding school.

Zikiya sat up. That was a question he'd been asking himself more and more often lately: what were those cows good for, apart from counting, and worrying if one was missing? But he'd become so apathetic it hadn't occurred to him they could help him get his diploma.

"Give it some thought," he heard Elias say. "We can leave together."

"What about my cattle?"

"You've got herdsmen, haven't you?"

"Phhh . . . As if they . . ."

"How about your mother then, and your wife? Anyhow, it's not far. You can get back up here again in no time if anything happens."

Zikiya went on arguing with Elias, naming all the obstructions that had accumulated since he became a married man, father of a baby girl, and responsible for so many cows. But meanwhile he was staring at Father Paolo's church on the hill, the wooden bell tower next to it, and the mission post farther down, and he caught himself beginning to look at them from a greater distance.

By the time he got home the decision was made. That same evening he got out the papers he'd put away in a chest under his bed. Suddenly he was in a hurry, afraid the inertia and indecision of the past several years might regain their grip on him. His wife looked at him in silence. He'd never been particularly communicative with her. If she had any questions she'd have to go ask his mother.

There wasn't much to take with him. He wouldn't be needing his smoky clothes in Bukavu. "Look around," Elias had said. It sounded attractive. If he looked around and didn't like what he saw, he could always come back.

They left early. By afternoon he could feel the familiar heat rising up out of the valley. Before long a roadblock appeared out of nowhere, manned by Mobutu's soldiers. "Stop! Papers!" Elias gave him an encouraging prod in the back and whispered, "Brace yourself."

Mobutu was no longer paying his men and they were scouring the interior, foraging and racketeering. They were

insolent, cunning, entirely different from the amiable soldiers Zikiya had known as a child. They barely looked at
Elias; it was Zikiya who interested them—they could smell
the greenness on him. While one scornfully examined his
laissez-passer the other searched his bag. They knew that
village boys like him usually sold a cow before leaving for
the city. But they found nothing.

The evening before, by the light of the oil lamp, his
mother had sewn the gold from the cow into the collar of
his shirt with such devotion that he felt guilty about his taci-
turn behavior of the past few days. Surely she couldn't have
failed to recall Uncle Rutebuka's old warning that her son
would leave her if she let him go to school. Yet she'd bravely
gone on sewing and not a word of complaint had passed her
lips.

KINSHASA
2003

Assani did have one friend in Kinshasa. They hadn't seen each other in five years and he'd been looking forward to meeting up with him again. He'd have come here for that reason alone — to get a photograph of them together to show people in Goma — but now he was here he could no longer take their friendship for granted. Mwepu had worked for the military court back then. Assani wasn't sure exactly what he did now, except that he had an office job — he'd heard various phones ring in the background when he called him. Mwepu came from the rich mining province of Katanga, like Mzee Kabila. Someone had whispered to Assani that he worked for military intelligence.

They'd agreed to meet on the covered terrace of the Grand Hotel, across from the swimming pool. Mwepu was already there, at a table near the bar, his back to the wall — a place where few people would notice him but he could see

everyone. Mwepu's discretion appealed to Assani. At his
appointment as general they'd merely exchanged nods from
a distance, although they'd managed to stand next to each
other briefly when the photos were taken. It was better if
people didn't notice their friendship—he was glad Mwepu
felt the same way about that.

Mwepu watched Assani arrive. He was a head taller than
everyone else, but Mwepu would have recognized him by
his gait alone: he was lean; he slipped past people. On the
way to the terrace Assani met a minister from the east and
stopped for a chat, glancing across at Mwepu's table from
time to time. He was trying to provoke the minister, to judge
by the way he laughed at every remark.

It was almost five and the Grand Hotel was crowded.
Anyone wanting to gauge the political temperature in the
capital need only take a tour of the shops in the marble
lobby, as Mwepu had done—designer clothing, expensive
jewelry, French perfume—and then glance into the Atrium
Café and go out through the glass doors. In the covered
restaurant, at the bar, near the pool, all over the place,
people sat or stood together in groups, in an atmosphere
charged with anticipation, old acquaintances falling into
each other's arms as the air buzzed with cries of "My dear
friend!" and "Excellency!"

It reminded Mwepu of the first few weeks after
Mobutu's flight six years before, when Kabila had just arrived in the city and the men from the east were strolling
self-confidently along the hotel corridors, nostrils flaring as

they breathed the scent of victory. Mobutu's men had kept a low profile then, but now they were back. They'd flown in from all over the world, and although the anxiety of the past few years had left its mark on their faces, their suits were ironed, Montblanc pens stuck out of their breast pockets, and they were clutching brand-new cell phones, with personalized ring tones ranging from the Congolese national anthem to the barking of dogs. They'd come to see whether they could reclaim their villas in the Kinshasa hills now that reconciliation had been proclaimed. The cake was being divided up and they were determined to get a share.

Their insouciance bothered Mwepu. As if the war were over simply because they had posts in the transitional government! He'd followed the peace talks closely; as soon as they entered the tunnel it had been impossible to back out — it collapsed behind them at every turn — but the future was still uncertain. You needed to be able to see in the dark, like a cat, to guess what might happen. All those bodyguards who'd arrived from the interior with their warlords — what if they fell out and started shooting each other? He knew Assani well enough to be sure he too was worried. That was one thing they would have in common.

"Sir!" Assani saluted boyishly, shook Mwepu's hand, and dropped into a chair. He'd put on weight and at a glance Mwepu registered the Cerruti belt, the Celio watch. "I see you've become brand-sensitive too," he said.

Assani looked at his wrist and pretended not to understand what Mwepu meant. "Celio? Is that a good make?"

At the table next to them a cell phone rang. Recognizing the number, a man shot to his feet, stammered "Yessir! At your service, sir!" and continued the conversation standing up. Mwepu and Assani exchanged glances and laughed.

"How's young Kabila doing?" Assani asked. "Why doesn't he come out of his shell? We never hear a word from him."

"It's better if he doesn't say anything, don't you think?"

"What's he afraid of? Dying?" Assani sucked his teeth disdainfully. "I've got one foot in the grave all the time, haven't I? He should learn to take risks."

"People round here have short fuses," Mwepu said, discreetly eyeing nearby tables.

"And meanwhile we have to put up with being insulted every night on television!"

Mwepu was playing with his car keys, as if he might leave at any moment. His eyes smiled behind his glasses. "Don't let it get to you. At least this way we know what they're thinking."

"If they start lynching us again, it'll be the fault of you Katangese. Just as long as you realize that."

"Don't you worry; they'll do themselves in with their ranting."

It was good to hear Mwepu's pleasant, melodious voice again. Slowly Assani's recalcitrance ebbed away, but he continued to prod at Mwepu, as if to test his own strength.

"And where am I supposed to live?" He gestured at the people around him. "These guys like living in hotels. I don't. I'm trying to reclaim a house belonging to one of my wife's uncles, but it's been taken over by Mzee Kabila's fellow villagers."

"Why don't you wait a while? You've only just got here." With a hint of reproof Mwepu added, "After all, you're not the only one looking for a house."

Assani's long arm rose into the air and he rubbed his head—a bashful gesture. At first sight they were an unlikely couple: Mwepu calm, with a ready laugh; Assani impatient and temperamental, a child thrashing wildly in all directions. But Mwepu was good at calming his friend and when they'd finished bickering they started to talk. At first Assani went on casting anxious glances left and right, but after a while he'd checked out his surroundings and they did as they'd always done—they analyzed the situation, each from his own point of view, to see where the dangers lay and find the best strategy for avoiding them.

They sat there for four hours. Afterward Assani felt tired and relieved: his friend hadn't changed.

Even before he got back to his room, Assani was seized by suspicion. Mwepu was concerned about the soldiers in the east who were refusing to come to Kinshasa. Had he been sent to sound Assani out? Was that why he'd agreed to meet in public, to show the others he was doing his job?

In his room Assani forced himself to go back over the conversation and reexamine all Mwepu's questions. It was a dangerous friendship. No one knew him as well as Mwepu did—if anyone was hoping to do him any damage they'd be well advised to send Mwepu after him.

Meanwhile Mwepu was driving his black Mercedes with tinted windows up into the hills outside the city, where he lived with his wife and children. When he reached the Kintambo-Magasin intersection a black shadow suddenly dashed out in front of the car. He slammed on the brakes and gave a heartfelt sigh of relief, following the tiny figure with his eyes. It was a girl. She couldn't be more than five years old. She moved between the honking cars like an elf.

His twelve-year-old son was driven to school every morning. He wouldn't know how to cross a busy road, whereas the street children, who'd been turning up at the oddest hours and places recently, had an agility that astonished him. Assani's face appeared before him again. By the time they'd finished talking the terrace was crowded. They decided to leave separately. Assani stood up and walked to the glass hotel doors. Despite all his training, Mwepu lost track of him within seconds.

THE EAST
1986

The high school was a large redbrick colonial building on a hill covered by scrawny pine trees at the edge of Bukavu. There were better schools in town, but you had to take an entrance exam and Elias realized that would reduce Zikiya's chances. He knew the headmaster and slipped him some money, so Zikiya was admitted without any problem. The boarders slept in bunk beds, wore a blue-and-white uniform, and had three meals a day—it would leave Zikiya with a profound hatred of cabbage.

There were several other boys from the high plains and they were instinctively drawn to each other. They spoke the same language and had the same worries, the same secrets. Most were married and responsible for cattle. They had a talent for math and chemistry but were bad at languages and social sciences, probably because of the isolation in which they'd grown up. They weren't very good pupils—the difference between the city and their own environment was too great for that—but they remembered the cows they'd sold to pay for their studies and were determined to succeed.

At high school Zikiya met Rwandans for the first time. Their parents had been forced to flee Rwanda in 1959, because they were Tutsi and on the eve of independence from the Belgians the Hutu had risen up against the dominant Tutsi minority. Some still lived in the Rwandan border city of Cyangugu a few miles away, but they couldn't go to school there because there was a quota for Tutsi.

Zikiya's Rwanda was a mythical, precolonial state with customs his ancestors had brought into the mountains along with their herds, where they'd become hopelessly outdated over the years. His Rwandan classmates laughed at the archaic language the boys from the high plains spoke, and the way they talked about their cows.

Up there they'd been Banyarwanda. Here, to distinguish themselves from the Rwandan refugees, they were Banyamulenge—people of Mulenge—one of the first villages in the central plateau where their ancestors had settled when they moved west out of Rwanda. But other pupils saw only their tall stature and narrow faces and couldn't tell the difference between them.

Zikiya studied hard. He ignored the letters from Irango telling him about mutinous herdsmen and missing cows. He didn't go home at Christmas or Easter, for fear that his family would keep him there.

Despite all his efforts he didn't pass his final exams. When he got back to Irango he cried and was inconsolable for days. "You can try again, can't you?" his mother said. He looked at her in amazement. "And waste another cow?"

But the next time he passed.

He went home for the annual holiday with a light heart, taking the bus to Uvira via Rwanda, since that was the shortest route. On the Rwandan side of the border the bus was stopped and boarded by two Hutu immigration policemen, who plodded sluggishly down the aisle. "You there, Tutsi! Off the bus!" He looked around, but they meant him.

Outside they demanded his papers. He gave them the green identity card Elias had arranged for him. It was a bit tattered—he'd plasticized it meticulously. One of the policemen took a quick look, passed it to his colleague, and grinned. "We know you. Your name isn't Zikiya. You're not a Zairean; you're a Rwandan, an Inyenzi."*

Zikiya was shocked. Inyenzi—Cockroaches—he'd heard the Rwandans at school whispering about them. They were Tutsi refugees who'd attempted to overthrow the Hutu regime in Rwanda in the 1960s, shortly after independence.

"You guys going to make up your minds?" the bus driver called out, anxious to get going. Some of the passengers were mumbling that they didn't want to wait for a student whose papers weren't in order.

Zikiya felt the midday sun scorching his head. The river they'd just crossed gurgled in his ears. "I'm not a Rwandan," he stammered. "I've just taken my final exams in Bukavu. I'm on my way to the high plains. My mother . . ." He would have said more, but the policemen recognized his accent. "He's a Zairean," they mumbled, disappointed. They handed Zikiya his papers and he was allowed back on the bus.

All the passengers were shouting at once. Some cursed the driver: if something like that happened to them, would he leave them behind too? Others urged him to get moving, to make up for lost time. Zikiya sat silently by the window. He would always remember the incident at the border in fine detail: the pitiless sun on his head, the peremptory voices of the bus driver and the passengers, the face of the policeman waving his green identity card, the sound of the river in the background. But above all he'd remember what the men had shouted as they ordered him off the bus: "You there, Tutsi!" It was the first time anyone had ever called him a Tutsi. It sounded like a curse.

Zikiya waited a year in the high plains for the results of his state exam, the national test every scholar had to take after gaining his high school diploma. Irango struck him as belonging to an old, stagnant world. Whenever he went into the hills with his cows he listened to the radio and obstinately read his chemistry textbook or studied the atlas he'd brought back from Bukavu.

He was twenty-three. When his wife gave birth to a son his mother was happy. By securing her husband's issue to the second generation she'd fulfilled her life's purpose. But Zikiya corresponded with his friends in the valley and could think only of how much he was falling behind.

In the summer of 1990 he arrived in Bukavu again. His atlas had given him an idea. He enrolled at the geography department of the ISP,* the Institute of Higher Education.

Shock waves from the collapse of communism in the Eastern Bloc were felt as far away as Zaire. Universities and colleges teemed with political resistance. In the west of the country, 1,000 miles away, the political leader Etienne Tshisekedi was fighting Mobutu's corrupt regime and gaining increasing popularity among students.

Feelings were stirring among the Tutsi at the ISP as well, but they were looking eastward. The Tutsi refugees of 1959 who lived in Uganda had united to form the Rwandan Patriotic Front, the RPF, and in October 1990 they invaded northern Rwanda. The offensive failed, but it caused great excitement among Tutsi throughout the region. They started collecting money for the RPF and from time to time a classmate would disappear. Later you'd hear he'd left for Uganda via Goma.

The rise of the RPF made the Tutsi around him more confident and Zikiya was drawn in against his will. At the end of the first term only two geography students had managed to pass their chemistry exam. The tutor, a Tutsi, was furious. He claimed the students were stupid because they ate cassava, which always contained traces of poison no matter how carefully you washed the tubers. He was certain the boys who'd passed the exam didn't eat cassava, he said, and he asked them to come to the front of the class.

Zikiya walked reluctantly down the aisle; he saw out of the corner of his eye that the other student was a Rwandan Tutsi. There they stood, two Tutsi, three if you counted the tutor, solving the question in front of the blackboard—living proof that maize-eaters were cleverer than cassava-eaters. He felt the eyes of his fellow students burning into his back, and although some congratulated him afterward, they were stand-offish toward him from then on—as if that afternoon by the blackboard he'd taken sides.

One day Zikiya received a letter from his uncle Rutebuka. The men who looked after his cows had rebelled. It was fairly common for a herdsman to quit his job, since working for a year would earn him a calf and he could start his own herd after five years or so, but this time they'd all simply upped and left.

In no time Zikiya was back in Irango. He succeeded in finding new herdsmen but had to stick around to train them, a job it was impossible to delegate. Time was once again slipping through his fingers like sand. The academic year in Bukavu ended without him.

If he wanted to complete his studies he'd have to move farther away, to Kisangani, for instance, where they'd be unable to reach him if there was a problem with the cows. His mother was distraught when she heard this: Kisangani was on the equator—people died of malaria there! But he was no longer of an age when people could stop him from doing as he liked.

Again he left. Meanwhile the fighters of the RPF had established themselves in the mountains of northern Rwanda and were waging a guerrilla war. Attacks by the RPF reawakened Hutu fears of the old feudal Tutsi regime. A myth began to haunt the Great Lakes region: the Tutsi wanted to establish an empire that would extend far beyond the current borders of Rwanda. The Zaireans were afraid now as well.

On his way to Kisangani Zikiya stopped in Bukavu. He ran into a boy he'd known at the ISP. "Where have you been all this time?" the boy asked. What did people in the city know about troublesome herdsmen? "I was home, in the high plains," Zikiya said hesitantly. "There were some problems in the family."

"Yeah, yeah, that's what they all say," the student answered. He told Zikiya about an acquaintance of theirs, a Tutsi, who'd suddenly disappeared. "We won't be seeing *him* again. He was killed during an attack by the RPF." Zikiya was shocked, but the student gave him a hostile look and said, "He's dead and you've all got it coming—you too."

That boy pushed him into the arms of the RPF, he would later tell his second wife. He described to her how, at the start of his training, he'd been locked in a house for a week. "I had everything I needed," he said. "A bed, television, food; it was just that I couldn't go out." Later he was given permission to drive around in a jeep, as long as he stuck to a certain route. His freedom of movement was increased bit by bit, his capacity for obedience tested.

It was a strange story that made her think of a scene from a film she'd once seen and not fully understood. But when she tried talking to him about it later, he seemed to have forgotten he'd ever told her and gave her an irritated look, as if she were making it all up.

A year after his meeting with the student, Zikiya turned up in Bukavu again. Instead of Kisangani he was on his way to Rutshuru, where a branch of the ISP had just opened at which he could continue his studies. Rutshuru lay near the border with Uganda and Rwanda. In the autumn of 1992 it was still peaceful there, but not for much longer. There had always been a large Hutu population in Rutshuru and a small number of Tutsi; they couldn't remain indifferent to the trial of strength their peoples were engaged in over in the mountains of northern Rwanda.

Again Zikiya registered as a first-year geography student. He was no longer using his father's name and he'd taken a new forename, a common practice among members of the RPF. He now called himself Assani Zikiya.

The little clay house rented by Assani and his fellow student Pascal lay on the main road through Rutshuru: two rooms with small windows and a corrugated-iron roof. They cooked together and each contributed twenty-five dollars a month for food.

Traffic at the front, the landlord's crying children at the back, and in between the pair of them trying to study. Pascal belonged to the Nande, traders who lived to the north of Rutshuru. Assani told him about the tough life of the high plains, where his poor, elderly mother still lived. He seemed very attached to her.

Sometimes Assani went to visit his sister, who lived in a densely populated neighborhood of Bukavu. He usually traveled on from there into Burundi. He confided to Pascal that he smuggled small amounts of gold across the border to earn his keep, and once he took Pascal along to visit his sister. They would go to the high plains together one day, he promised. Nothing ever came of that.

Pascal believed Assani wasn't interested in political or military affairs and wanted only to concentrate on his studies. He didn't know that Assani was married with two children. By this time Assani's life was running on several tracks. He was capable of being close to people without letting them in on some of the most fundamental details of his life.

When Assani went home for the annual holiday his bus was again stopped on the Rwandan side of the border. The immigration police were tense. Guerrilla attacks by the RPF had increased in recent months and the Hutu regime responded each time by killing innocent Tutsi civilians in the interior. All the bus passengers paid but Assani had to come up with more than the rest, even though he was broke. The police searched his luggage and confiscated the sneakers he'd need for the climb to Irango.

In Uvira he got out and slung his bag and jacket over his shoulder. This time it was Zairean soldiers who stopped him. Looking the way he did, he must be a fighter with the RPF. He was in jail for three days. His fellow prisoners were kind to him, sharing their food and commiserating, but he felt the net closing. The Rwandan problem had crossed the border. He could no longer escape it.

Nevertheless he went back to Rutshuru after the holiday to start his second year of geography. The tension between Hutu and Tutsi in Rutshuru was mounting. The Hutu listened to the inflammatory Radio Mille Collines; the Tutsi tuned in to a radio station run by the RPF that called on them to join its ranks. Pascal even began to feel uncomfortable as a Nande. The Hutu were in a majority in Rutshuru and regarded everyone else as "immigrants." Armed with machetes, a group of Hutu students besieged two new tutors in their houses—a Tutsi and a Nande—and forced them to leave.

In April 1994 the Rwandan president's plane was shot down as it came in to land in the capital, Kigali. The president had been a Hutu. Within an hour there were roadblocks all over the city and Hutu massacres of Tutsi citizens and moderate Hutu began. Over the next few months they would spread across the whole country. Meanwhile the RPF was advancing on the capital from the north.

One night there was a power outage in the clay house Assani and Pascal shared. Assani went outside to a stand where a man sat peering across the dark street by the light of an oil lamp. He asked for a candle. The vendor turned his face away. Assani repeated his request. "I won't accept money from a Tutsi," the man said in a monotone.

By the time he got back to the house the electricity was on again, but those words would stay with him.

On a hot June evening a crowd gathered outside the door of the ISP auditorium, where a Hutu professor was due to hold a reading. "Interpretation of Events in the Great Lakes Region in Light of the Document *The Protocols of Zion*"—the title had been reverberating through the corridors for days, adding to the general buzz that had held Rutshuru in its grip since the genocide in neighboring Rwanda began. The ISP was sheltering a Hutu soldier who'd fled Rwanda. The Tutsi students regarded him with suspicion—who could say what he had on his conscience? The Hutu for their part followed every move of a man who sometimes came from Uganda by bicycle. They said he looked like a Hutu, but he was actually a Tutsi who belonged to the RPF, recruiting soldiers and collecting information from RPF spies among the students. Nobody at the ISP was interested in science any longer; everything was political now.

Groups of students stood chatting in the warm evening, excited, looking around nervously to be sure no one was listening. The professor they'd come to hear was a militant close to the Hutu regime in Rwanda. Knives were being sharpened.

As soon as the local political, administrative, and religious authorities had taken their seats in the front rows, the students poured into the auditorium. It was stifling, with the heat of the day trapped under the low corrugated-iron roof.

The professor mounted the podium, looked into the hall, and began. "I realize that the topic I'm about to speak on is a sensitive one," he said. "But I believe in freedom of expression and I hope we can have a fruitful discussion afterward."

Before long there was total silence. The recent war in Rwanda, the professor said, was part of an attempt by the Tutsi to establish a new political order in the region. "For years Tutsi in Uganda, Burundi, and Zaire have been combining forces, capital, and manpower so they can take power in Rwanda again," he declared. "Not because they're particularly interested in that small, poor country, but they need it as a base from which to dominate its neighbors."

The Tutsi were exactly like the Jews, he went on, who had revealed their plans for world domination a century earlier in *The Protocols of Zion*. He was aware that the authenticity of the *Protocols* was disputed by the Jews themselves, but the document interested him because it corresponded with reality. The Jews didn't believe in borders in the modern sense of the word. Since establishing the state of Israel they hadn't only occupied part of the Arab world, they'd succeeded in infiltrating western governments. Not even the White House had been spared.

Assani stood at the back of the auditorium. His heart was thumping and his legs felt weak, but he managed to grin at Pascal, who was leaning against a wall and nodded toward the door. "The Tutsi have infiltrated the highest political, economic, and religious spheres in Mobutu's Zaire," the professor was haranguing them. "Now they're trying to oppress the Hutu in the east." He was no longer sticking to the text in front of him. He glanced up at his audience more and more frequently, seeking support.

The buzz of voices around Assani was growing louder. A student protested that there were Tutsi in the hall. Someone pointed in his direction and some Tutsi students began to stir, but all sounds were drowned out by the Hutu students, who demonstrated their support by stamping their feet and chanting "Move the mountains, kill them! The only good Tutsi is a dead Tutsi!"

Pascal pushed the door open and slipped outside. Others followed. The smell of sweat around him made Assani feel sick, but he controlled himself. Out of the corner of his eye he took note of who was provoking the audience. He stayed to the end, when the professor's cry of "Long live academic freedom!" was met with thunderous applause and he was swept outside by the crowd. A group of Tutsi students was waiting for him. What should they do? They were no longer safe here. One of them tore up his workbook demonstratively. "I've had enough," he said. "I didn't come here to learn this sort of thing."

The next morning they went to the office of the security service to report that they felt threatened. The security men sided with the Hutu and weren't willing to protect them.

Many students didn't make it to the end of that year. The Tutsi left in small groups for Uganda. Assani wanted to take his exams first, but his results were worse than last time and he needed to retake various tests. Pascal was apprehensive about what might happen if all the Tutsi left town. The Nande would be next. But he was even more worried about his friend's fate. Assani with his tall, slim build and narrow face had the look of a typical RPF fighter. Why didn't he leave?

"Get out of here," an older Rutshuru Tutsi said to Assani. "What do you think you are, a man or a ghost? You're not immortal. What's the point in studying if you don't survive this?"

It was August 1994. The RPF had reached Kigali. In the aftermath of the genocide, a great flood of Hutu had poured across the border into Zaire, terrified of the victor's fury. They'd set up camp in the desolate volcanic landscape north of Goma, hundreds of thousands of wretched people, a mixture of fear, hatred, and death in their eyes.

Assani rode in a minibus right through the throng, heading south for Goma. A truck went past carrying bodies wrapped in gray blankets, presumably victims of the cholera epidemic the radio had been reporting for several days. He turned away and found himself eye to eye with a Hutu woman sitting beside the road staring at him in terror.

"Stop!" Two Zairean soldiers brazenly stuck their heads through the window. When they spotted Assani they did a double take. "Papers!" He said he was going home for the holiday and showed them a copy of his ISP report, but they didn't believe him. The driver, a Tutsi, managed to talk them around; three times on that journey he had to give soldiers money. By the time they arrived in Goma, Assani knew it was dangerous to go any farther.

When everyone had gotten out he asked the driver if he could sleep in the minibus and travel back north with him the next morning. The man gave him some food and found him a place to sleep. They left early. The driver had bought bread to help bribe the soldiers. Every time they were stopped Assani stuck bread through the open window, several loaves at once. When they reached the turning for Uganda he asked the driver to stop.

He was wearing jeans and a shirt, with his jacket slung over his shoulder. He didn't have any luggage — that would have looked suspicious. The man drove on, but suddenly he threw the bus into reverse, came back, took the money the passengers had paid him out of his breast pocket and gave it to Assani, zaires and dollars jumbled together.

Assani adopted a nonchalant stride, as if out for a stroll in the fields. Over the past few months he'd gradually broken loose from the landscape that produced him. He'd become so light that he blew across the border like a feather.

KINSHASA
2003

He bought a padlock for his office at Camp Tshatshi and got down to work. He couldn't afford to make any mistakes — no one would speak up for him if he failed. The job itself didn't worry him. Anybody who'd ever been in charge of cows, received a monthly salary, or commanded a group of soldiers knew how to administer a budget.

He had promised himself that those who proved corrupt would find him on their trail, but within a few months he was completely demoralized. This was a new war, one he couldn't hope to win. The system was stronger than he was. All the invoices that reached his desk were counterfeit; if he protested and asked for a genuine bill he was handed yet another fake.

He could understand why a commanding officer might take ten percent for his own needs. The whites who came to him tried to get twenty. But his compatriots took eighty percent! He couldn't fathom it. They weren't behaving like citizens of a nation; they were like fathers taking food out of their own children's mouths.

The chief of staff was a straw man, placed there to dupe the international community. The real power lay with the *maison militaire,* the "military house," which took its orders from presidential circles. Then there were the embittered followers of Mzee Kabila, who had no faith either in the straw men or in the people who were really in charge. Power drifted between the three groups. They were at each other's throats, continually trying to undermine one another. The country needed a leader who could show his people the way, but young Kabila was confined to his palace, surrounded by his black-uniformed presidential guard. The four vice presidents had entrenched themselves in their residences as well, like spiders in their webs.

They made him think of certain people he'd known in the high plains. If they found a cow pie on the path, rather than remove it they'd cover it with straw, which would blow away in the first gale that came along. They zigzagged around obstacles and seemed to feel at home in the resulting forest of impediments. Didn't they realize their behavior could mean the end of Congo? Certain countries already had plans for dividing it up and were simply waiting to implement them.

The politicians who'd arrived from the east before him weren't any better—he could tell from the clothes they wore, the champagne they drank, the furniture in their living rooms. If he made any comment they looked at him pityingly. Wasn't he satisfied with his post? Why didn't he take advantage of it? Someone had recently compared the dignitaries in the capital to goats: when they were hungry they made a great racket and their bleating could be heard far and wide. It had grown quiet of late. They were grazing.

But Assani couldn't relax, since no one believed he'd come here to manage a budget. According to the latest allegations on television he was a Rwandan mercenary who'd left the east after taking part in a meeting where a plot against young Kabila was hatched.

Meanwhile brigade commanders all over the country were phoning to ask when their soldiers' pay would come through. He begged them to be patient. First he had to find out what was going on around him.

During a tour of military camps in the city he came on a company of soldiers guarding a food depot. They had nothing: no gas burner to cook on, no chairs to sit on, not even any food. Hungry men guarding food! Naturally they bartered supplies from the depot for peanuts and *chikwange,* cassava paste. He made sure they had a kitchen; he bought chairs, a fridge, a gas cooker, and padlocks to secure everything. They were beside themselves with gratitude. But the commander of the base, who had neglected his men, accused Assani at a public meeting of supplying his soldiers without consulting him and of coming to Kinshasa to build up his own military force!

His friend Mwepu was aware of his precarious position and called him daily. That was the best way of keeping an eye on him, of course. The wall of misunderstanding between the different camps was high; at times like these it was important to have a friendship that could straddle such a wall. But Assani remained on his guard. A man is like a forest: you see the trees at the edge but not what lies behind them. He didn't drink. They wouldn't find him in the bars, or in the churches where people poured out their souls at the tops of their voices. Mwepu was the only person he talked to. If the president wanted to know what he was thinking, he'd have to ask Mwepu.

They no longer met in public. To the people around Mwepu, Assani was the enemy. It was best for them to be seen together as little as possible. One afternoon Assani walked out of the hotel without his bodyguards and Mwepu picked him up in the car with the tinted windows.

"Now I'm at your mercy," Assani said as he got in. "Now you Katangese can do with me what you'd most like to do: kill me." Mwepu laughed and said nothing. "It's like with Sankara and Blaise," Assani went on, referring to the former president of Burkina Faso and his confidant, Captain Blaise Compaoré. "When Sankara heard that Blaise wanted to kill him, he said: Blaise is my friend, I can't escape him." And Blaise did kill Sankara, as there was no need to add.

Instead he told Mwepu about the gang of Mafiosi he'd ended up among. The Katangese around Kabila always came out on top, because they held the reins. They kept a firm grip on the parallel structures they'd erected behind the presidential facade.

Mwepu listened and tried to calm him. "You need to be patient," he said. "We can't tell yet how it's all going to pan out."

'That's exactly what my chief of staff says," Assani muttered. "Meaning he doesn't even have the authority to get a box of ammunition out of the depot."

He knew Mwepu didn't have it easy as a Katangese. He disagreed with the others, but eventually he too would be made to pay for the mistakes they were making.

"Your president," said Assani, "is afraid of the soldiers from the east. That's why he's shut himself up in his palace with people from his village; if he doesn't watch out they'll end up killing him for refusing to do as they say."

They'd driven out into the hills. All around people were busy; everywhere houses were being repaired—a sign that the former owners were moving back in. Assani came here regularly to look at the house that belonged to his wife's uncle. It was still occupied by soldiers, but he was hopeful they'd soon move out.

"What have you got there?" Mwepu asked, pointing at the brown package Assani had been clutching on his lap since he got in.

"A present for you."

"Oh?"

Assani had gotten two prints made of a photo taken on the day of his appointment and had both of them framed. There they stood, he in uniform with his oversize general's cap; Mwepu in jacket and trousers, shorter than Assani, sturdier too, his tie pulled a little too tight. "It's a tainted present," Assani warned him. "As soon as you've seen it you'll want to hide it away."

A short while later there was a meeting of ministers and army officers, attended by President Kabila. The ministers, as always, said everything was fine and praised the president to the skies, obscuring their embezzlement in the clouds. When bigwigs spoke the rank and file kept silent, so Assani held his tongue, merely making a few notes on his pad.

Suddenly the president turned to him. "And you, Assani, you haven't said anything yet, what do you think?" He asked the question in Swahili, the language they'd spoken in the past, which gave his words an intimate tone.

Had Mwepu been talking to the president about him? If he had, Kabila would know he was dissatisfied and regard him as a traitor if he didn't give an honest answer. It was like a pass from the soccer player Zidane—he had no choice but to play it.

Assani inhaled deeply and said, "*Afande*,"* —commander —"I'm no diplomat, so I'll tell you what I think. These ministers are lying to you. Things aren't going well at all and they're partly to blame." He told him that soldiers in the interior were dying in droves for lack of medical supplies, that troops were not being paid even though the money was available, that 13,000 gallons of gasoline had disappeared overnight, that . . .

Once he got into his stride there was no stopping him. "One day I'll be the victim of all this myself, *afande*. Whatever

goes wrong in my department, I'll be the one charged for it.
Why should I defend people who're hastening my own de-
mise? To die in their name?" His outburst had a salutary
effect on him. He felt much calmer now. "Before long you
won't have any army left, *afande*. All your soldiers will either have deserted or died of malnutrition and disease. Then
the enemy will take you by surprise in your own house. He'll
come right up to the chair where you're sitting and you won't
be able to defend yourself."

The president had been listening seriously but now an
amused expression crept across his face. "Before they get
to me there are others they'll have to kill first," he said. He
slapped shut the notepad in front of him, asked the ministers of defense and planning to come to him the following
morning, and declared the meeting closed.

"You'd have done better to leave out that last bit,"
Assani was told afterward by the minister of defense, whom
he'd known for many years in the east. "They murdered
his father while he sat in his chair. You could scare him
like that."

Assani shrugged. "It's better to warn him."

A deputy minister stared at him in astonishment. "You're
dangerous," he said. "Attacking us in public in front of the
president, without even blinking!"

❖   ❖   ❖

After several visits from Assani and his men, the Lebanese
tenant was sensible enough to leave the villa on the boulevard. Assani moved in. He put up the UNICEF tents he'd
brought from Goma for the soldiers allocated to him and

posted two guards at the gate. Now he was finally on his own again.

In the evenings his bodyguards lay talking on reed mats in front of their tents in the garden and sometimes he went to sit with them; they knew a lot more than he did about what was going on in the city. One afternoon they spotted the woman who always dominated the conversation on the inflammatory television program *Forum des Médias*. She was waiting for a taxi right outside his house. They came and told him excitedly: What if they lured her indoors and put a bullet in her head? They could bury her in the garden — no one would ever suspect anything.

He'd been here almost four months. Christmas was approaching. He'd have liked to go to Goma for the holidays. His son Moshe was two years old, an angry child who kicked, scratched, and lashed out just as Assani had done at that age. Assani loved him. Moshe would grow up able to defend himself if attacked.

But the situation in the east was unsettled; he was afraid he wouldn't be given permission to go. Recently the second in command in Goma — a Katangese — had left with a suitcase containing the soldiers' pay. He'd been staying in a hotel and claimed the money was taken from his room. Yet there were no signs of a break-in.

The soldiers immediately started calling Assani. They'd hoped his appointment would mean he'd be able to sort things out for them. What was he doing in Kinshasa anyway? Had he been seduced by the perks of government like all the others?

What could he tell them? How could he convince them

anything good could come out of Kinshasa? The president
was no doubt afraid that if Assani went to the east now he'd
be influenced by the dissidents. But if he wasn't allowed to
leave Kinshasa, didn't that make him a prisoner?

Colored lights went up all over the city and at the head
of the boulevard Christmas trees were on sale. Should he buy
one? Or should he take a Santa Claus home, one of those fat
red clockwork men bleating their heads off in all the shops?

One afternoon, driving home after work, he saw a boy
at the side of the road holding an astonishing little contraption. It was a Christmas tree, no more than six inches tall,
but inside something was moving. He stopped. The street
vendor ran over to him. At the center of the tree was a
sphere with a little Santa Claus inside. If you shook it, snow
started falling. Assani asked the price and paid without
haggling.

That evening Mwepu called. Could he come by? He
sounded busy. It made Assani think of the years when he
worked for military intelligence: you went out hunting all
day and came home in the evening with nothing to show for
it. A rotten business. You ended up with no feelings at all.
You could be friends with someone in the afternoon and kill
him that same evening.

Mwepu flopped exhausted into an armchair. He looked
at the bottle of Amarula on the coffee table. A women's
drink. Assani liked it because it tasted of milk. "Don't you
have anything else?"

Assani pressed the remote control that operated the
kitchen bell and asked the soldier on duty for whisky and
Coke. Mwepu insisted on pouring it himself. He didn't have

much time and came straight to the point. Assani's recent outburst during the meeting with the president — Kabila had appreciated it, he said, but some of the others hadn't. "The president isn't like the Mobutists," he explained. "He's not out to enrich himself. He fought for an ideal, like you. That's why he let you have your say. Don't be surprised if he calls you for advice sometime soon."

Assani sat looking at him. Mwepu had told the president how discontented he was and Kabila had decided to challenge him in public. Now Mwepu had come to report the result of his outburst, so that Assani could tell the soldiers in the east the president didn't approve of everything that was being done in his name. His friend was dangerous, it occurred to him, because he was intelligent enough to think up this kind of thing.

Assani reached for the little Christmas tree on the table and made the snow flutter down on Santa Claus's head. He was delighted with the toy. He would put it away after the holidays and get it out again next year — if he didn't have to flee again and leave everything behind.

He had a boyish look, sitting there in his blue track suit, his legs tucked up under him. He was a general, Mwepu a colonel, but of the two of them Mwepu was undoubtedly the more levelheaded. "What do you think," Assani asked. "Would I be allowed to go home for the holidays?"

Mwepu's phone rang. He looked at the number and pressed away the call. "We'll see," he said. "Try not to take it too badly if you aren't. It's still early days."

He stood up and looked around the room: the yellow curtains Assani kept drawn all day, the yellow sofa, the little tables with photos of Assani with his wife and children, the flat-screen television with a framed photo of Joseph Kabila on the wall above it, and beyond that the table where the evening meal was getting cold in covered dishes. "You've got a nice place here," he said, smiling. "But something's missing."

"What?" Assani looked around the room, trying to guess what his friend was driving at.

"Our photo. Where's our photo?" Mwepu's eyes were still smiling. "Or have you sent it on to Goma already?"

RWANDA
1994

Assani was twenty-seven when he arrived in northern Rwanda in August 1994. The war wasn't over, bodies still lay in the streets, and there they were, the fighters of the RPF. They'd come from Uganda with high expectations only to find so many corpses in their native villages that they could think of nothing but revenge.

The stench of death and decay followed him to the capital, where people wandered the streets with vacant expressions. The Hutu had murdered 800,000 people in three months, then fled to Zaire. No buses were running, the shops had been looted, and people with luggage were everywhere — some leaving, others arriving and looking for places to stay.

In a photo album he showed his wife many years later, there was a picture of him sitting at a table in the main street of Kigali, selling cheap watches. That was right after the genocide, he said. It was his task to keep an eye on people and listen to what they were saying. He'd worked as a chauffeur for a while, too, for a British army officer at the United Nations mission sent to monitor security in the new Rwanda. One day the man saw him exercising in the garden. "Are you a soldier?" he asked suspiciously. Assani shook his head. "No, no. Everyone in Rwanda's done paramilitary training."

He didn't tell his wife exactly whom he'd been working for in those days. There were gaps in his résumé, like stains on an old black-and-white photograph. Every time she tried to piece it together she was left with bits of the puzzle that didn't fit anywhere. He was no help. He liked generating confusion — he hid behind it.

As soon as the university in the Rwandan town of Butare reopened, he registered at the geography faculty and found himself a room on the modern campus — very different from the little clay house in Rutshuru. People were doing their best to get back on their feet and forget the screams that had echoed across the hills and marshes for months. But anyone who looked them in the eye could see that death still haunted them.

"Zikiya! Zikiya!" His mother's voice broke when she heard him on the phone. Why hadn't he been in touch for so long? She'd come to Bukavu from the high plains to visit his sister. It was two years since they'd spoken. She'd thought he'd joined the RPF and been killed in the fighting.

In no time she was inundating him with news from the village. Four of his cows had calved and the calves were healthy. His wife had been forced to sell his old bull, since they needed the money. She'd bought chickens that . . .

"She's no longer my wife."

His mother held her breath for a moment. "She's had a third child, Zikiya," she went on soothingly. "A girl."

"It's not mine." All the anger buried in his heart welled up in him. "It's no more my child then I'm my father's son." There, now he'd said it. He knew he was hurting his mother, but he had to be hard; if he wasn't hard now, she'd never believe he was serious.

"Zikiya," she said sternly, as if she could force him to be reasonable simply by saying his name. She must have heard from other mothers how callous the war in Rwanda had made their sons and assumed that was why he was being so ruthless.

"I'm never coming back," he said. "If you want to see me you'll have to visit me here. I'm studying."

"I'm glad to hear that, Zikiya." Her gentle tone unnerved him. There was nothing to reproach her for; she'd done all she could. But for her he would never have gotten himself out from under his uncles' yoke. He'd still be walking behind the cows.

"You wouldn't understand, *ma*," he said, suddenly milder. "One day I'll explain." The post office clerk knocked on the cubical door—his time was up.

There was silence at the other end of the line. He had to say one last thing, but what? "Remember the keepsake you gave me before I left Irango?" It was a black rubber bracelet, a trinket, not much broader than an elastic band. "I'm still wearing it, *ma*. I haven't taken it off once."

*

Outside he blinked against the light. He decided to take a detour on his way back to the campus, not wanting to go straight to his solitary room. It had been a hot day, but now a light breeze had come up. He liked Butare: the sky was clear and the nights were cold, as in the high plains.

His outburst on the phone left a bitter taste in his mouth. Those people up in the plains — did they think he would always stick to their biblical customs? Didn't they know he'd renounced all that? They had no idea who he was. He himself hadn't known who he was until something snapped.

It had started long ago, on the day he first saw Uncle Mufunga cry and, shortly afterward, his mother. In the years that followed the reasons behind this puzzling episode had become clear little by little. The man his mother married had died in the 1950s. He'd left nothing but two daughters and a large herd of cows, which her brothers-in-law had their eye on. Afraid she'd be forced to leave her children behind and return to her own family, she went on to have two more daughters and a son by Uncle Mufunga.

In his culture, the man who paid the bride price was the father of all his wife's progeny, even if he died and she had children by one of his brothers. Zikiya had grown up an orphan although his biological father was still alive. His mother had refused to marry Mufunga, since that would make him the owner of her dead husband's cattle. The cows were for Zikiya, she'd decided. So everyone wrote him off as a mother's boy.

The day Mufunga gave him a goat, a chicken, and some money, then promptly started to cry, a crack had appeared in the universe of hard-hearted uncles in which he'd grown up. But everything quickly reverted to the way it had always been, and when he eventually discovered the truth he was all the more bitter. Things everyone around him regarded as normal — they caused him pain.

But his uncles weren't finished with him yet. They'd insisted on choosing a girl for him to marry. He did as he was told, unable in those days to imagine disobeying their orders. One night while he was studying in Rutshuru, his wife was visited by a relative. "Comfort" it was called, and it happened regularly if a man was gone for a long time. Sometimes a husband would return to the village after several years to discover that his wife had given birth to another man's child in his absence. If a student protested, his family generally managed to calm him. The offender would give him a cow in compensation and the problem was solved.

When Assani first heard that his wife had given birth to a child who couldn't be his, his whole being had risen in revolt. The news that he'd disowned her had soon reached the mountains and his uncles had reacted with disbelief. How dare he renounce his own culture? But his mind was made up. He was no longer a prisoner of the culture that had produced him; no one could force him back into that old straitjacket.

❊   ❊   ❊

One Saturday morning his friend Masasu knocked at the door of his student room. Assani was lying on the bed listening to Zairean music and reading his geography book.

He hadn't washed and wasn't planning to do so — he barely left the campus at all on weekends.

"You need to get out of here," said Masasu, smelling the sour air in the room. "I'm meeting some people in Cyangugu — I'll take you along if you want." He glanced at Assani's textbook. "You'll get to do something else than sit here surrounded by books."

They drove off the campus in Masasu's dilapidated jeep. It was the first time since leaving Rutshuru that Assani had traveled toward the Zairean border. Kigali and Butare were safe now, but the farther west you went the more dangerous it got. The Hutu army was refusing to accept defeat. It had fled to Zaire with its weaponry intact and was preparing to finish "the work," as it called the genocide.

"This isn't our country. One day we'll have to go home," Masasu said. "Even if we have to fight our way back." When Assani didn't answer, Masasu glanced around at him. "There are enough people willing to help."

Assani was only half-listening. "I'm exempted from service during my studies," he said.

"Until they need you again."

Masasu had grown up in Uvira. His father was a Shi, his mother a Rwandan Tutsi. He was younger than Assani, but he'd become involved with the RPF much earlier. He knew the Ugandan president and the Rwandan minister of defense personally.

Had Masasu ever finished high school? Assani wasn't sure. They used to play soccer together in Bukavu, but when Masasu became a soldier their paths diverged. Masasu was now his superior. That was how the liberation movement worked: those who'd been involved in the struggle longest were given the highest rank.

Until they need you again. Masasu's tone alarmed him. "If there's anything I should know, I hope you'll tell me."

"No, no, nothing special. When the time comes, you'll hear about it."

They drove into the forest. A high green wall rose on either side of the road and a spicy scent wafted through the open window. "Look how they conserve their rain forests here," Masasu said. "No one would take it into his head to chop down a tree when he felt like it. While at home . . ."

The forest at the edge of Irango had been partially felled when Assani was a child to make space for a field of maize. Beyond the edges of the square clearing, the trees had slowly been thinned out. In the dry season long beards of lichen waved sadly in the wind.

He was shocked by the clarity of the image—he could see the lichen and hear women chattering as they came home from the fields in the evening with bundles of firewood on their heads, cheerfully telling everyone they passed about the things they'd seen on the way and being told in return what to expect farther down the path. Suddenly his wife's smiling face appeared and he felt a pang of bitterness. *Around a woman lies your grave*—those words had crept into his head some time ago and he couldn't get them out.

Masasu was driving faster now. Rumors of infiltration by the Interahamwe*—the Hutu militia—were growing louder by the day. Occasionally they passed a roadblock and every few miles they saw soldiers, half hidden in the foliage, staring expressionlessly along the road. Just when Assani was beginning to wonder how often they relieved each other, a jeep stopped at a guard post and a soldier got out with a pot of food.

"Did you see that?" Masasu asked, without taking his eyes of the road. "They're being fed." He laughed. "Mobutu better not let his soldiers find out!" But from one moment to the next he stopped laughing and clenched his jaw.

Assani thought of the loaves of bread he'd handed to Zairean soldiers through the open window of the bus on the morning of his flight. A wordless transaction: he wanted to get through and they were hungry—they hadn't hesitated for a second. Now they were being bought off in the same way by the Interahamwe, which was steadily gaining freedom of movement. The story went that Zairean soldiers were even selling their weapons to the Hutu. Perhaps Masasu was right when he said they should go back to Zaire. To put a stop to all that.

He was completely unprepared for the feelings that took hold of him as they drove into Cyangugu. On the far side of the glistening blue water of Lake Kivu lay Bukavu, so close it was as if he could reach out and touch the houses. He could have found the way to his sister's house in his sleep: the long road to the Athenaeum, the broad boulevard beside the lake, then a left turn up into the hills and on toward the *cité*, which would be teeming with life at this hour.

There was the long spit of land in the lake where he used to go walking with his friends. Along the broad eucalyptus-lined avenue they strolled all the way to the tip of the peninsula. If anyone got on the wrong side of him then, Assani wouldn't hesitate to punch him out, something he wouldn't dare do in Rwanda. Here he wasn't at home.

This isn't our country. It was only now that he understood what Masasu had meant. Fellow students in Butare went home for the holidays. Even those who weren't born here in Rwanda could point to the hills where their grandparents were buried. But all these generations later, how many Banyamulenge from the high plains of eastern Congo knew where their forefathers came from, or on which hills they'd lived? They were cut off from their Rwandan past. That was why they hung around the campus on weekends and during the holidays, until lessons started again.

Masasu parked the jeep at Hotel des Chutes, on a hill with a view of the lake. He ordered a Coke for Assani and left him on the terrace. He had an appointment with the Rwandan soldiers who were sitting together in the hotel dining room. Out of the corner of his eye as they passed, Assani had seen some of them playing billiards.

Far below was the Rwandan border post. Disabled Zaireans on outsize tricycles piled high with tins of milk powder, oil, sugar, and other foodstuffs were negotiating with a customs official, gesticulating furiously. Mobutu had decided to let disabled people transport goods into and out of the country tax-free to support themselves, and they'd become extremely shrewd traders. The customs man waved them on with a weary gesture and stared after them in silence. Assani felt embarrassed. What kind of country sent its disabled out onto the streets to "fend for themselves," as Mobutu put it?

A yellow minibus sped down the hill, passed the gas station, and stopped at the border checkpoint. The passengers got out and watched with resignation as two officials searched their bags. In a flash Assani saw the immigration police who'd ordered him off the bus when he was trying to get home after his final exams. "You there, Tutsi!" On this side of the border he wouldn't have any trouble now, since the officials were Tutsi, but on the Zairean side all Tutsi were stopped, or so his brother-in-law Elias had said when he visited Butare not long ago.

He'd burst into Assani's room looking agitated and flopped into the only chair. An acquaintance of his who'd recently been to Zaire had returned with a series of ominous reports. "Those Hutu refugees are campaigning against us over there," Elias said. "The longer we stay here the harder it'll be to go back."

Assani lay on his bed listening, his pillow folded double under his head. The Zaireans no longer distinguished between Banyamulenge and Tutsi who'd left Rwanda in the 1950s, Elias told him. All Tutsi property had been confiscated, and Tutsi had been fired from administrative jobs and expelled from the country. "The soldiers are even starting to go into the high plains and confiscate cows!" But the boys up there were determined to defend themselves; they'd gotten out the weapons their fathers had used against Simba rebels. The Banyamulenge soldiers who'd fought for the RPF were secretly making their way home to help them. "More are arriving all the time."

Assani grudgingly heard him out. The day Elias had persuaded him to leave home to study in the valley lay far behind him. He was twenty-nine and these past few years he'd gone his own way, no longer dependent on anyone. His proposed thesis, "Topography of the Subsidence Basin of Lake Tanganyika," had just been approved and soon he'd be leaving for Burundi on a field trip.

When Elias had finished, Assani stared at him in silence. The expectant look on his brother-in-law's face convinced him the rumors were true: Elias was recruiting soldiers. The Rwandan Tutsi regime couldn't wait to take revenge on the Hutu army across the border and was eager to exploit frustration among the Banyamulenge, needing a military vanguard to spy out the terrain.

Assani remembered a Rwandan soldier he'd met on one of his first evenings in Kigali, in a bar where the atmosphere was both euphoric and downcast. "We haven't finished yet," the soldier said. "We'll carry on till we can shake hands with the president of Angola." Angola! That was on the other side of the continent—they'd have to cross the whole of Zaire to get there. What was he talking about? The man's words suddenly seemed less wildly optimistic than they had at the time.

"I never knew you were involved in politics," he said to Elias.

Assani's ironic smile didn't go unnoticed. "There's a time to be politically active and a time to bury your head in books," Elias replied resentfully.

"It's easy for you to talk—you've finished your studies. No doubt the Rwandans have a nice job lined up for you in Zaire."

Elias gritted his teeth. He'd always known Assani to be surly and tight-lipped, but now he'd become arrogant as well. Assani had locked his fingers behind his head. "Is that why you took me out of Irango, to make a soldier of me? You'd have done better to leave me there."

"As if you could have escaped all this if I had! You wait till your mother runs out of cows to buy off Mobutu's soldiers. They'll have her then. After that it'll be your children's turn."

Neither of them had mentioned his wife and now when Assani thought back over their conversation, he realized his obstinacy had arisen from a fear that Elias was about to broach the subject. In fact little that Elias had told him was new. The Banyamulenge students in Butare regularly met to discuss the alarming situation in the plains. Sometimes feelings ran high, and the number of students wanting to go to war immediately was growing by the day. They'd even asked for an audience with the Rwandan minister of defense, Paul Kagame, to offer him their services, but they got no farther than his aide-de-camp, James Kabarebe. He'd laughed at them: what would the Hutu students on the campus think if a large group of Banyamulenge left overnight? That sort of news traveled faster than light. The Interahamwe would be waiting for them on the other side of the border, licking their chops. He urged them to be patient. When the time came, he'd know where to find them.

The yellow minibus down in the valley jolted over the bridge into Zaire. Assani hated borders. They were a colonial invention. His ancestors hadn't needed to bother about them.

A jeep stopped in the hotel parking lot and five soldiers walked up onto the terrace. He knew one of them from his early days in Kigali running errands for the RPF. The man recognized Assani but went in through the open door without greeting him.

Meanwhile more soldiers had entered the bar. In Zaire there would have been just as many women as men by now; they'd have turned the music up to full volume and been drinking so much that all the secret plans they were concocting would reverberate through the room and be known far and wide by tomorrow. But Rwandans were discreet; they didn't raise their voices. Apart from the soft tick of billiard balls, not a sound reached Assani.

At last Masasu came out. He beckoned him with a jerk of the head. "Sorry to keep you waiting so long," he said, walking ahead of Assani to the parking lot, bolt upright, his shoulders raised slightly to disguise his short stature.

"No, no, it was good to be close to . . . to home for a bit."

"What did I tell you? This isn't our country. One day we'll go back. Yourself included." He turned around and sized up Assani's tall, lean frame. "We'll need people like you." Assani suddenly realized his friend had brought him here for a reason.

It was late and dusk was falling. "This isn't a good time to be on the road," Masasu said, looking worried. "Especially in the forest. I always prefer to wait till after dark. Between midnight and two, that's the best time." He laughed. "Then even the Interahamwe are asleep."

He drove out of town lost in thought. He said nothing about the meeting but he exuded the seriousness of matters

discussed. "The situation in Zaire is becoming untenable,"
he told Assani after a while. "Not long to wait now."

❖   ❖   ❖

Dozens of Banyamulenge were killed during demonstra-
tions in Uvira and Bukavu. Assani's sister and her family
fled for their lives and ended up in a refugee camp in
Rwanda. His mother was forced to leave Irango and move
to a place near Minembwe, where it was supposedly safer.

Then finally the waiting was over. Zaire was at war.
Officially it was an internal revolt by the Banyamulenge, but
anyone living in the region knew the Rwandan army had
invaded Zaire.

One evening Masasu showed up at Assani's door again
with an air of mystery about him. He'd come from over the
border. He glanced around the room in surprise, as if astonished to find life going on as normal. There was someone he wanted Assani to meet. "If you can be ready in two
minutes, I'll take you with me."

This time they drove to a house in a suburb of Kigali.
The place was crawling with soldiers and Masasu and Assani
were led through the back door and into a room where a
short, heavy man was standing at the center of a group of
people, talking. "Kabila," Masasu whispered in his ear.

Had he heard right? The leader of the Simba rebels
who'd driven his family out of Ngandja when he was a child—
what was he doing here? The last Assani had heard, he'd become a smuggler in Tanzania.

As soon as he saw Masasu, Kabila excused himself and
came over, grinning broadly, his skin shining with satisfac-

tion. He had a slight limp—from a bullet wound, Assani had been told, inflicted by a Munyamulenge* fighter.

Masasu must have informed him they were coming, as Kabila started talking immediately. His weight on his good leg, hands in his pockets, he said he'd been fighting the Mobutu regime for the past thirty years. It had been a long, lonely struggle, but now his African brothers—he gestured vaguely at the other men in the room—had decided to help him.

Kabila spoke the heavy Swahili of Tanzania, not the lighter variant of eastern Congo. Mobutu's army was made up of looters and thieves, he said. The time had come to put an end to the kleptocracy, which had reduced the inhabitants of one of the richest countries in Africa to beggary.

At first he'd stared into space, but now he was looking straight at them. "You'll make the Zaireans a free people again," he said. "Throw Mobutu onto the garbage heap of history." His eyes suddenly darted to Assani's face. "Didn't I know your father? Wasn't he a fighter at the time of the Simbas?" Kabila was still smiling, as if to assure Assani he needn't be afraid—that the hatchet had been buried now they had a common enemy.

It was strange to hear his own childhood fantasy so many years later from someone else's lips. "No, no," Assani protested. "That was an uncle, I think."

Kabila's eyes remained fixed on him, as if he wasn't completely convinced. "He was a good warrior," he said.

Assani took his photo album and various documents to his cousin for safe keeping; a man who'd once slept under a dirty

blanket with him during the transhumance and was now
studying in Butare. He didn't say why, and his cousin didn't
ask.

Twenty students gathered that evening in strictest se-
crecy at the edge of the campus, where a bus stood waiting.
No one had told them where they were going. Throughout
the journey Assani tried to look out into the dark Rwandan
night, but all he could see was his own frightened face in
the window. He studied his profile: his thin nose, arched
lips, and deep-set eyes—it struck him this might be the last
time he ever saw himself.

Just short of the capital the bus turned left and drove
into an army barracks. They shivered in their thin coats as
they stepped out into the evening air. The place was deserted, as if all the soldiers had been sent home. Whispering, bunched together, they went inside. What were the
Rwandans planning? What would happen to them?

The next evening they sneaked across the border into
Zaire, a total of thirty-six men. The Rwandan soldiers
among them were frightened, Assani noticed, but the boys
from the high plains cried, danced traditional dances, or
grabbed handfuls of earth to put in their mouths. Assani was
silent, as requested.

Two days later, when he still hadn't turned up in college, his cousin went to his room and knocked. No answer.
The cousin hesitated before putting his hand on the door-
knob, which turned.

Everything was still there: his workbooks on the shelves
above the table, his pajamas on a hook, his jacket over the
chair. Only Assani had disappeared.

KINSHASA
2003

The Katangese soldiers had moved out of the villa in the Kinshasa hills that belonged to his wife's uncle, but Assani still couldn't get his hands on the place. His correspondence with the authorities was increasingly complicated—he was caught in an administrative maze and every turn took him farther from his goal.

"You Katangese are bandits," he said to a government minister, an acquaintance of his friend Mwepu, at a reception. "You rent out our houses and use the money to fill party coffers. No wonder you're going to win the elections!"

He had no information about things like that—he'd thought it up on the spot—but his tone was so emphatic that the minister gave him a startled look and made elaborate excuses. Three days later a call came through from a minister at the housing department: the ownership documents were ready for collection.

That evening Assani drove to the house and visualized clearing up the devastation. First he'd get the sputtering tap at the edge of the driveway fixed, then he'd tackle the swimming pool and demolish the outhouses. He'd have the avocado tree by the gate cut down — the roots were undermining the stone perimeter wall. Some of those useless trees and shrubs in the garden would have to go too. He wanted an unobstructed view.

As he walked across the plot of land, poking about, happy to have something to throw himself into on weekends, somebody knocked at the gate, timidly at first, then louder. It was the owner of the minibus parked out front. The soldiers had confiscated it, he said, for use as a taxi-bus, until it broke down. The minibus was all he owned. He was really hoping that . . .

He was a pleasant young man. They agreed that for a modest fee he'd guard the house and clean up the mess the previous occupants had left inside and out. Once he had enough money he could get the vehicle towed away and repaired.

By the weekend the young man, who was extremely grateful, had moved into part of the house with his wife and children. Assani had found several men to help and the work was in full swing. The tap had been repaired, the garbage removed, the weeding done. Two workmen were sliding around in the big empty swimming pool, scrubbing at a persistent layer of green slime.

Soon the garden was a stark contrast to that of his neighbor, a Mobutist from Equatorial Province who'd buried himself in a tangle of giant trees, trailing lianas, and ominously creaking bamboo. Leaning over the fence beyond the swimming pool, Assani peered at a house belonging to Mobutu's widow. Someone had pointed it out to him. Until recently an army officer had lived there, but now the run-down bungalow and swimming pool looked deserted — ready to be handed back.

A colonel telephoned to ask Assani to sign a document for urgent dispatch. Assani told him where he was and soon they were walking across the garden together. The colonel was a thickset, cheerful man from Mobutu's native region. He was familiar with this kind of house. "It's going to cost you," he said, looking Assani up and down as if asking himself how he was going to lay his hands on that kind of money. "At least half a million dollars."

Assani dismissed the sum with a flick of his wrist. "No way. A hundred thousand, max. Anyhow, I'm not going to have it all done in one go."

They watched the men at work in the swimming pool. Sky blue tiles were appearing from beneath the green slime, some of them broken. "You'll have to replace that tiled floor," the colonel said. "That alone is going to . . ."

"Has peace broken out or something?" Assani laughed sarcastically. "For now I'll only replace the tiles that are broken." He pointed to the *cité* below. "We need to make sure people down there have enough to eat, otherwise they'll come up and loot everything the first chance they get."

As he said this he was aware how insincere it sounded. The document the colonel had asked him to sign was an order for military uniforms to be manufactured abroad. They could be produced for a much lower price locally, but

that would mean a narrower profit margin for his bosses.
They didn't give a damn about the poor people down there.
Assani disapproved, but what could he do? If he resigned
they'd say he was boycotting the peace process. He had
signed the document without comment.

One of the workers had dug a trench to access clean
sand, which he was spreading neatly across the dark earth.
"We don't have peace here yet," Assani said, more to himself than to the colonel. "But that shouldn't stop us from
getting things done." The yellow soil brightened up the garden, as if someone had turned on a lamp. "Look," he said
with satisfaction. "Life's starting up again."

❁   ❁   ❁

In the corridor outside his office at Camp Tshatshi, Assani
ran into a messenger who told him all high-ranking officers
were expected at the People's Palace to celebrate the first
anniversary of the signing of the peace accords. The invitation pressed into his hand stated that the president would
be in attendance. Would he like to add his own name? It
hadn't been filled in yet. When a second invitation arrived,
he noticed the president's name had been removed, but by
then everyone was in a state of feverish anticipation and
Assani drifted outside with the rest.

The People's Palace, built by Mobutu after a state visit
to China, was surrounded by so much empty space that
anyone who got close was overwhelmed by a sense of his
own insignificance. In the immense parking lot, cars shriv-
eled into pitiful heaps of tin and the building loomed over
visitors like a drab, oversize coat. Years of damp had made

the gray floor coverings bulge and ripple, paint was flaking off the walls, and the faded curtains—which must once have been green—had slid to the ends of their rails and gave off a musty odor.

People in charge of presidential protocol had brought several busloads of citizens to the palace for the occasion. They'd been plucked off the streets without warning and were making no attempt to conceal their surprise at the unexpected turn their day had taken. From the wings of the main hall they stared brazenly at the diplomats sitting in the front rows with deadpan expressions, and at the hastily drummed-up officers ranged behind them.

Everything was bathed in uninviting neon light and despite all those frenzied efforts the room was still less than ten percent full. Now the great wait could begin. Congolese dignitaries, like pop musicians, made it a point of honor to be late.

Suddenly a man with a broom appeared onstage. Not a uniformed janitor ordered to remove a bit of dust someone had spotted, or to right a spilled vase of flowers, but a shabby servant who'd crawled out from some dark corner of the building. Without even glancing into the hall, he began sweeping listlessly. The dust he worked free from the floorboards wafted toward the diplomatic corps. Assani put up his hand to protect his eyes and looked at the man sitting next to him, a Katangese officer who seemed no less embarrassed than he was.

Then nothing happened again for a while, until Vice President Yerodia, the tropical dandy with the cigar, appeared. He was dressed in one of his trademark sleeveless

jackets—this one printed with an image of Mzee Kabila for
the occasion—and he kicked off right away with an homage
to his hero. He recounted his battles as leader of the rebels,
acclaimed his heroic march on the capital to overthrow
Mobutu's dictatorship, and described the sudden horror that
had gripped everyone when Mzee, in the middle of realizing
his great plans, fell victim to a most cowardly murder.

At this point in his story Yerodia began to cry, right in
front of the dusty diplomats in the front rows, the entire
general staff behind them, and the fascinated audience in
the wings. Through his tears he announced the end of the
period of mourning for Mzee Kabila, switching to Lingala
in mid-sentence and meandering back via Kikongo* into
French again—but such pompous French that Assani, although he understood every word, couldn't grasp what
Yerodia was talking about.

His fellow officers shifted uncomfortably in their seats.
Why did they have to listen to this? Some began to whisper
and glance at the exits, although they knew that if they left
now they'd cause a diplomatic incident. One officer excused
himself, saying he needed to go to the toilet, and six others
took the opportunity to disappear with him. Yerodia's la-
ment went on and on. He was engaged in a private conversation with the dead Mzee, apparently no longer aware of
his audience.

Assani had already exchanged knowing looks with the
disgruntled Katangese officer next to him, who'd only just
arrived in the capital. "This city is the abode of Satan," the
man whispered suddenly, with a vehemence that took Assani
by surprise. "These people are bad. If it was just one group

that was no good, we could exclude them or try to change them, but they're all rotten."

Afterward the members of the general staff stood at the top of the steps, discussing the five years of war that had divided them. The chief of staff recalled one particular defeat the government army had suffered in the east, near the Katangese town of Kabalo. "I hear General Assani was on the other side at the time," he said. "Perhaps he can tell us exactly what happened."

Assani pulled in his head defensively. People had been killed in that battle, maybe even relatives or friends of the officers who were looking at him so expectantly. But when the chief of staff insisted, he said, "We had the feeling there was no one in command on the other side. They had tanks, mortars, antiaircraft defenses — they were firing everything off simultaneously and it all landed behind us. We were shooting at them with machine guns from less than five hundred yards away!"

An almost imperceptible smile played about his lips. That morning the Rwandans had said, "Let's go; we're off to eat the enemy's breakfast." They didn't find any food, but they did pick up mortars, which they later fired at the government army.

"We must learn from situations like that," the chief of staff said, but the face of the officer who'd been in charge that day darkened. He'd since been promoted to general and Assani had recently seen him walking around self-importantly, holding a report for the president. His eye had

caught the word "east" in the title. "Aha—you lot conspir-
ing against us again?" he'd said teasingly, at which point the
general had no choice but to show him the document. It was
full of nonsense about how they ought to have Congolese
army planes fly over Bukavu and Goma to terrify the dissident soldiers who were still there. "I'm afraid they won't be
impressed by that in the east," Assani had told him. "They're
more likely to try shooting them down."

Some people weren't thinking about how to build a
better army, they were simply out for revenge. The chief of
staff was different. He'd once taken Assani aside and said,
"It seems one of the dissidents is a good soldier. How can
we persuade him to come over to our camp?"

The anniversary of the signing of the peace accords ended
with a reception later that day. Assani learned that all high-
ranking officers would soon have to line up in combat gear
for the visit of a South African military mission. Apparently
he wasn't the only one who hated squeezing into the stiff
uniform with cap, long socks, and boots—he could hear
protests from all sides. It had been a pleasant evening and
he'd even managed to arrange for someone to deliver fifteen
free bags of cement to his villa in the hills.

In the car on the way home it struck him how varied
life in Kinshasa was and how provincial the east seemed
by comparison: out there, the only news tended to be that
a rebel warlord had headed for the mountains with his men
or was about to emerge from them. The capital was great.
He was beginning to understand why people became so

full of it that they completely forgot about the wilderness they came from.

At home he turned on the television and saw a disheveled bearded man sitting on a stool while a doctor looked into his mouth with a little mirror. Saddam Hussein—the man who'd spent years announcing he'd make the Americans bite the dust! The Iraqis had toppled his statue in front of a cheering crowd. Sooner or later the same could happen to old Kabila's mausoleum. Then the pathetic Yerodia would have to find another place to weep for his hero.

THE FIRST WAR
1996

The first man he shot flew into the air, arms outstretched, like an injured bird flapping wildly as it plunged to the ground. That futile, jerky leap—he saw it again and again in his dreams during the nights that followed, until he stopped dreaming altogether because his *kadogos* kept him awake.

Most of them had been recruited by young Masasu, who gave impassioned speeches in every conquered city about the new Congo that would wipe away Mobutu's Zaire. The stadiums were packed; boys looked up at Masasu's glowing face, his ironed uniform, his shiny boots, and dreamed of following him. Mothers sent him their most difficult children in the hope he'd teach them some discipline—and leave a share of their $100 monthly pay with them.

A group of inexperienced *kadogos* assigned to him immediately got involved in a firefight. Afterward Assani heard one of the soldiers crying. His young friend rushed over to

him and began sobbing as well. They bent over the bodies
of two enemy soldiers they'd just killed and broke into a
display of grief.

Assani pointed to the guns slung over their shoulders.
"Shoot them," he said. They looked at him uncomprehend-
ingly through their tears. "Didn't you hear what I said?" The
others walked over and watched as the two young soldiers
hesitantly shouldered their Kalashnikovs and fired, shocked
by the thuds that made the dead bounce.

"Where are your bayonets?" With a nod Assani ordered them to lunge at the bodies. From then on the recruits
no longer wept when they saw soldiers killed, although
sometimes they were unable to sleep, afraid of the dead
men's ghosts, or woke up whimpering from nightmares.

✽　✽　✽

Kabila came to inspect his troops in an eastern town at the
front. They prepared chicken with rice for him in their improvised field kitchen, but while Mzee was making a speech,
his bodyguards went around to the back and unthinkingly
ate everything.

Kabila was furious. He demanded the culprits come
forward and ordered them to be beaten. Assani didn't understand. Those boys had left their fathers and mothers to follow him, the army had become their family, Mzee was their
father—how could he have them beaten up in public for
something so trivial? One of them was in a bad way. Was a
bodyguard to die for a chicken, Assani thought, when there
were so many chickens wandering about? They cooked a
fresh meal, but Kabila was still angry. If he got so upset

about a chicken here at the front, what might he do when
they arrived in the capital?

It was an ugly war, and death was all around him. A colleague he discussed strategy with in the morning was gone
by afternoon. Every time he lost a friend it seemed as if
part of his own history had been wiped away. He expected
to die but he survived. It was strange and frightening. Why
he and not his friends? Was there some kind of meaning
to it?

He'd been promised administrative duties, but the war
gained such momentum that he regularly had to interrupt
his intelligence work to serve at the front line. The Hutu
camps in the east had been cleared after heavy fighting.
Many refugees had gone back to Rwanda, but hundreds
of thousands had fled deeper into the interior of Congo,
vengeful Rwandans and a growing army of recruits giving chase.

The soldiers of the Rwandan Patriotic Army became
less sure of themselves the farther they went into Congo,
and they called on him more and more often. Some couldn't
speak Swahili, or couldn't understand the local variant, and
Assani knew how to read a map. He was deployed on secret missions, changing his name several times, until after a
while he started to feel invisible. By the time people started
to get to know him he'd already moved on. At one point he
found himself in Kisangani, he later told his second wife, but
he didn't say what he'd done there.

Was he one of the men sent to dismantle a Hutu camp called Biaro, just outside Kisangani? The air was thick with mosquitoes and the tens of thousands of pathetic refugees were more dead than alive after trudging nearly 400 miles. The soldiers sealed off the camp from the outside world and set to work.

Around that time a young Tutsi soldier walked into a restaurant run by a Congolese woman in her sheltered back garden in Kisangani. There was a dazed look in his eyes, his boots were covered with mud, his uniform was stained. He was hungry, but he pushed away the meat the woman served him. After what he'd seen the past few days he couldn't eat meat, he said in a barely audible voice. He stared into his glass all evening. As he sat there looking so alone and defeated, the restaurant owner felt sorry for him, but the sickly smell that clung to him scared her. Rumors were going around that in Biaro, on the other side of the Congo River, terrible things were happening.

The cries from the rain forest were a strangled echo of the screams that had resounded across the hills and marshes of Rwanda three years before. Later, where the camp had been, aid organizations found only torn plastic sheeting, rag balls, extinguished fires, soaked scraps of cloth—and amid the wreckage an old woman left for dead and a dying child wailing feebly. Where was everyone else? They fled, the soldiers told them.

Not far from the camp was a patch of disturbed ground. A digger requisitioned from a Belgian timber merchant had been working the earth. The road leading to the spot was guarded by soldiers — until the forest began to grow over the sandy soil and the secret that lay beneath it.

On arriving in Lubumbashi — the capital of the rich Katanga province — Assani saw Mobutu's soldiers dashing away round a corner. When the Rwandans lost a man, they angrily pulled off their shirts and went on the attack, shrieking, but the morale of the Congolese collapsed as soon as one of their number was hit. They reacted like sheep when a lion approaches — a shudder ran through the herd and before you knew it they'd vanished. If you managed to get hold of one of them, you'd find he'd studied at a military academy and had traveled all over the world, but as soon as the shooting started he fled.

Once they'd taken Lubumbashi, Assani resumed his work for military intelligence while the others marched on. He'd been expecting the war to last five years, but they reached Kinshasa within seven months. The country fell into their hands like ripe fruit and the only eligible leader was Kabila, a prickly man who was prepared to make a scene over a chicken.

"Who's going to be the new chief of staff, by the way?" Assani once let slip. The Rwandans regarded that as a suspicious question and he was reprimanded for it.

It wasn't long before Kabila declared himself president and Assani saw the new chief of staff on television. It was James Kabarebe, who'd laughed at them and sent them home when they came to offer their services during their student days in Butare. He'd been aide-de-camp to the

Rwandan minister of defense, Kagame, at the time, and he was later put in charge of the rebel army. But the *kadogos* around Assani were interested only in Kabila's security adviser, the man standing next to James. He was twenty-seven, flushed with pride, staring confidently into the camera with his shoulders slightly raised — a posture Assani remembered. The *kadogos* cheered. It was Commander Masasu.

LUBUMBASHI
1997

Claudine scanned the tables. It was seven o'clock and the first guests had arrived. The garden lights were on, a Congolese rumba by Carlyto filled the air, and a gentle breeze brushed her arms. It was already getting colder in Lubumbashi and soon diners would start asking her to put *mbabulas*, earthenware pots of glowing charcoal, around the tables.

Behind the open-air bar, Victor was polishing glasses, but before long the restaurant would fill up and he'd be run off his feet. The whites were starting to come out to test the temperature of the new state of affairs. They'd hidden in their houses for days, afraid Mobutu's soldiers would go on the rampage, but there'd been hardly any looting, and relief flickered between the tables.

Restaurant La Paillote had closed for only five days and since then it had been busier than ever. On high stools at the bar, people drank aperitifs as they waited for tables.

Under the straw lean-to roofs you could hear the cheerful popping of corks from bottles of South African wine. As she wandered back and forth greeting the guests, asking if everything was to their liking, Claudine noticed several Americans who'd arrived in the wake of the rebels. They were mining specialists, hoping to breathe fresh life into the bankrupt state enterprises Mobutu had left behind.

The inhabitants of Lubumbashi hadn't known who to fear more: Mobutu's plundering soldiers or Kabila's rebels, who'd swept across the eastern part of the country like a typhoon. The Rwandan Tutsi had given full vent to their anger at the genocide, taking it out on the Hutu in refugee camps and the Congolese who'd sheltered them, but even the Banyamulenge seemed to hate the population in the east and weren't bothered by a few more deaths here and there. Claudine's Greek brother-in-law, who ran an import-export business in Bukavu and had sent her sister and the children to Europe for safety, told her that his Congolese employees called them not Banyamulenge but Nyamamulenge: "beasts from Mulenge."

But in Katanga, the new president's native province, the Tutsi seemed to have fewer scores to settle. Here the danger came from a different quarter. Robbers were exploiting the uncertainty of the situation, seizing every opportunity, often using weapons acquired from deserters. The Katangese soldiers were increasingly audacious too. Victor the barman, who lived in the *cité*, said they sat drinking all evening in *ngandas*—local bars—but refused to pay. They were relatives of Mzee Kabila, they shouted—everyone owed them some gratitude.

"Madame . . ." A waitress hurried up to Claudine, all but tongue-tied, her usual reaction when nervous. "Two soldiers . . ." She indicated them with her eyes. "They went and sat at an occupied table. They're refusing to leave."

They were Tutsi soldiers, newcomers who didn't know the unwritten rule of the house—you didn't just go and sit down at a table with strangers. Lacking a menu, they leaned back in their chairs and peered quite shamelessly at the food on the neighboring table. People were doing their best to pretend they hadn't noticed, but the conversation had stopped and Claudine could see other guests discreetly looking their way.

"*Excusez-moi.*" Everyone assumed she'd briskly resolve the situation, but the older of the two soldiers looked at her so coldly that the words froze on her lips. With the Congolese you could easily make jokes in circumstances like these, but the soldier didn't look as though he had much of a sense of humor. Nor did he look Congolese, come to that. He made a remark to the man sitting across from him in a language she didn't know. Only then did it occur to her he couldn't speak French. He must be one of those Rwandans who'd grown up in Uganda. They were the worst, her brother-in-law had told her. They were cold as fish.

The other soldier was not only younger but more agitated too, although no less stony-faced. "We're fine here," he said. "We're not bothering anyone, are we? Just bring us the menu." It sounded like an order.

"You can wait at the bar until a table becomes free," said Claudine, nodding encouragingly to the couple next to them. "It's not the custom here to . . ."

The younger soldier stood up abruptly. "Bunch of racists," he muttered, switching to Swahili. "Why not just say that whites here don't like sitting at the same table as blacks?" Did he think she wouldn't understand what he'd said? Couldn't he see she was a quarter tone, as they called it here? I was born in this country, she wanted to say. I've had my own problems with whites here, my grandmother being Congolese, and now you're calling me a racist? She bit her lip. He was already on his way to the door, but the other soldier stopped him and they went to the bar together.

The silence was stifling. "What are we in for next?" whispered one of the guests. "Nothing," Claudine said soothingly. "Don't worry; it's over." As she walked to the bar she rubbed her bare arms—she had goose bumps.

She offered the two soldiers drinks on the house and personally made sure they got a good table. It was best to keep on friendly terms with the new men in charge. The way the younger one had flown off the handle—the idea that blacks and whites couldn't sit at the same table! Where on earth did he think he was?

But during the meal he must have looked around and realized he was wrong, because when it came time to pay he said, "Sorry about that. I thought . . ."

"It's OK," Claudine interrupted him. "It's your first time here, I think."

"We're rebels," he said. "We've spent seven years in the bush, we're not used to mixing with civilians. But now that I'm stationed here . . ."

She calculated in a flash: 1990. That was the year a truck belonging to her brother-in-law had been shot up as the RPF invaded northern Rwanda from Uganda. So he'd been a rebel right from the start. His Swahili was unmistakably that of eastern Congo. Was he a Munyamulenge perhaps? Some people called them mercenaries, *Militaires Sans Frontières*.

Claudine put on her most charming smile. "Welcome to Lubumbashi. We have, well, occasional problems with soldiers here. Of course we're hoping the situation will remain calm so that everyone can get back to work."

The younger man shook her outstretched hand. "Commander Assani. We're here for your security. You'll be seeing more of us." The other soldier looked toward the door and said nothing.

His jeep smelled of sleep, sweaty feet, and trodden grass. "You guys could have opened a window," he grumbled at the *kadogos* in the backseat, who struggled upright as soon as a gust of cold outdoor air blew into their faces. Boni muttered something about mosquitoes. Assani looked at him in the rearview mirror. "What? Have you suddenly become afraid of mosquitoes?"

The main street with its high colonial facades was virtually deserted at this hour. Lubumbashi was a pleasant town to find yourself in after so many months in the bush. Although the mining companies had seen better days, everything still beat to their rhythm: early each morning the siren went off and people bicycled to work. With a bit of luck, life could start up again here. But we never do have any luck, he thought bitterly. The man who's proclaimed himself president isn't a leader.

After he'd dropped Charles at the house where he was staying with fellow officers of the Rwandan security service, Boni climbed into the seat beside him. Boni was his best soldier. The boy was a perfect judge of his moods and never got on his nerves the way the others sometimes did, asking questions when he didn't feel like talking.

During the war Boni once came to inform him at the end of an exhausting day that a Rwandan *afande* wanted to speak to him urgently. Assani hadn't eaten since the night before and he felt so wretched and gloomy that all he wanted to do was to crawl into his sleeping bag facedown. "Tell him I'm too tired," he said. Boni disappeared and came back with a little bag folded from a piece of brown paper. Inside was a bit of sugar he'd saved. Assani put the bag to his lips, pulled his boots on again, and walked like a zombie to the Rwandan camp, an hour away.

Now he was thinking about the incident in the restaurant earlier that evening. What was the owner called? Régine? Claudine? She'd seemed nice. The work he did — it changed you. You began to see all civilians as enemies. It was good she'd pointed that out.

He took the turn for the barracks. The boys behind him had curled up and gone back to sleep, but Boni was still awake. He wouldn't nod off as long as he was sitting next to Assani. Not Boni.

❊   ❊   ❊

A woman in a floral print dress and head scarf was standing outside the hospital where he'd just been to visit a *kadogo*. There was something about her style of clothing that attracted his attention. Her face seemed somehow familiar as well. *"Amakuru?"* — How are you doing? — he asked in Kinyarwanda.*

"Ni meza." — Good. A younger version of his mother, he thought when she smiled. Softer too, without the worry lines time had carved into his mother's face.

"Are you waiting for someone?"

"My son's supposed to come and pick me up," she said hesitantly. "But I think I'd better . . ."

"Can I offer you a lift?"

"In that?" She pointed to the camouflaged pickup in the parking lot. In the back were eight *kadogos*, Kalashnikovs between their legs, in a medley of uniforms with headgear ranging from cowboy hats to caps and berets. The sight of them inspired fear and loathing in the average Congolese, but she wasn't afraid, he noticed. She allowed Boni to help her in.

She was called Justine, and she came from Rutshuru. "I was at school there," said Assani, glad to have found someone who knew something about the world he came from. She'd followed her husband, she told him. He'd moved to Lubumbashi in the 1960s to work as a mining engineer. "All my children were born here."

He drove as if still in the bush. Even in the city center he kept up the same speed and people crossing the road jumped back. "Could you slow down a bit?" Justine asked anxiously.

He braked and went on at walking pace, grinning teasingly. "Better?"

He was a Munyamulenge. She recognized the accent. Her son had made friends with a few of the soldiers and they spoke exactly like that. "Can I offer you a glass of milk?" she asked as they turned into her street. His face lit up. Her children barely knew the difference between a cow and a horse, but she'd noticed the Banyamulenge were sensitive to anything to do with cows.

He inspected her apartment with interest, taking it all in: the china in the glass-fronted cupboard, the crocheted mats on the living room table and over the backs of the chairs, the crucifix above the mantelpiece. "It's good to be among civilians from time to time," he said. "Does this house belong to the mining company?"

Justine nodded, pointing to the paint on the walls, which had faded over the years and was covered with dirty fingerprints. "It needs some fixing up, I'm afraid."

"No, no. Compared with the rest of the country everything in Lubumbashi is in pretty good shape."

Now that he was no longer surrounded by soldiers she could see he was almost shy. He flopped down on the sofa, legs stretched out rather awkwardly. He ran his hand over his short hair and seemed unsure what to say next.

She heard the back door slam. That would be her daughter Aimée arriving home from the university. Assani looked up as Aimée walked in. She had a high forehead and large eyes in a narrow face — she might not be the prettiest of Justine's daughters, but she had a natural radiance that men fell for. Assani made some remark and Aimée turned to her mother for help. "I don't speak your language," she said.

"What? You're a Tutsi and you don't speak Kinya-rwanda? One day you'll be sorry."

"Why should I be sorry?"

"Who says you'll always be safe here?"

Justine watched as they continued bickering, Assani amused, her daughter smartly sticking up for herself. Aimée would finish her studies soon, but she was still close to her mother and of all the children she was the most home-loving. Perhaps that was why the new soldiers were so interested in her. They'd had enough of the women they met in bars during the war. They were looking for a different kind of girl. One Rwandan officer had even come to ask for Aimée's hand.

"Who says the enemy won't chase you out, like they did us?"

Adui—enemy—it was a word from over the border, from Rwanda. Her son's soldier friends were always using it.

"That's how Hutu and Tutsi refer to each other," Justine said cautiously. "But this isn't Rwanda. In Congo so many different people live together, how can we call any-one our enemy?"

A shadow passed over Assani's face. "Kabila, the man you've put all your hopes in, is bad," he said harshly. "His men killed my father and shot my mother in the stomach when she was pregnant with me. Luckily it was only a flesh-wound, otherwise I'd never have been born. He used us to seize power, but now he's trying . . ."

He stopped abruptly. While he was still in the east he'd come upon some well-thumbed papers in an office of the security service; they showed that Kabila still bore a grudge against the Banyamulenge who'd fought against him in the high plains in the 1970s. Secret documents — he wasn't supposed to . . . That was the treacherous thing about mixing with civilians. Before you knew it you'd said something you'd have done better to keep to yourself. He glanced at his watch and stood up, his eyes on Aimée as she disappeared into the kitchen, calling over her shoulder that she wasn't interested in politics.

"My mother used to offer milk to strangers," he told Justine. "It's as if I've found a mother in this town."

Justine went outside with him. "You're always welcome here," she said softly.

The *kadogos* had taken up positions at all four corners of the house and they dashed to the jeep as soon as they saw Assani coming. He adjusted his red beret in the wing mirror. "Sorry about that just now," he said to Justine. "We've been at war, maybe there's something wrong with us, but you . . . We aren't living in the same reality. You people don't know a tenth of what's happened here."

❊   ❊   ❊

"I need to talk to you," Mzee Kabila whispered in his ear when he arrived at Lubumbashi airport. The president. What did Mzee want with him? What had he been hearing? Had someone told him about what happened while they were still in the east? The incident with the chicken, then the papers at the security service office — Assani had quickly come to dislike the old smuggler so much that he'd said to a close colleague, "Give me a revolver and I'll kill him while I still can. Soon it'll be too late." The man had given him a strange look

and informed their Rwandan commander, who had Assani
locked in a dark cell. He'd thought his life was over.

Two days later he was summoned to see the commander. "Contriving a plot against the leader — don't you
know that carries the death penalty? What got into
you for God's sake?" Assani stood in front of him, head
bowed. "Kabila killed my father," he said. The Rwandan
frowned; he'd grown up in Uganda and knew nothing of
past conflicts between Kabila and the Banyamulenge.
Assani said his father had died in Ngandja, shot by Kabila's
men when he was a baby. His mother had bound him to
her back and fled.

The Rwandan had cold eyes that betrayed no emotion,
but at the end of the interrogation he signaled that Assani
could go. Charles was his name. They'd been working together ever since.

At a quarter to six in the evening — Assani had already
passed all the checkpoints on the way to the presidential
residence — Kabila called to remind him of their meeting.
"How could I forget a meeting with you, *afande*? I'm right
outside the door."

Kabila shook his hand, laughing, and pointed to a chair
on the other side of his desk. He dragged one leg and was
fatter than before, which made him look smaller, as if his
own weight were pressing him down. "Do you know who I
am?" he asked in a heavy, drawling voice, leaning back in
his chair, fat fingers linked at his chest, his eyes on the ceil-

ing as if he could read the answer to his question there. "I'm the *raïs*—president—of Congo!"

Assani felt his blood race. He peered at Kabila's bodyguards—fellow Banyamulenge. Did they have orders to shoot him?

"What do you want to drink?"

"Fanta," Assani said timidly.

"What? You're sitting here with the president and you ask for a soft drink?" Kabila turned to the guards at the door. "Bring whiskey."

He'll get me drunk and shoot me dead, thought Assani. He cautiously sipped at his drink, his face twisting into a grimace. Kabila called for someone to bring Coca-Cola to mix with the whiskey.

"I've received a report about you." Assani's heart missed a beat. This was the end, then. "You've done some good work here."

Had Kabila been told how he'd had all the drunken Katangese soldiers in the *cité* arrested one evening, or how his soldiers had shot dead two armed men who'd robbed a white businessman? The whole town knew about that; even Claudine had brought it up one time in La Paillote.

"There's a lot of crime in Kinshasa," Kabila said. "Mobutu's soldiers are leading our men astray, but in Lubumbashi . . . I'm pleased with you." He continued smiling, staring beatifically up into space and drinking neat whiskey in great greedy gulps, his eyes steadily clouding over.

"Are you married?" Assani shook his head. "Do you have a car? You don't! Did you come here by jeep?" Kabila leaned toward him and went on in a whisper, "What car do you drive when you visit women?" He laughed conspiratorially. "A commander like you must surely be a great success with the women."

He summoned his half brother Georges, the local head of security, asked him which car he'd come in, took the keys, and gave them to Assani. Then he called for more whiskey. "Not a bottle!" he shouted when the guard came back. "A case! I'm the president!"

As Assani was about to leave, Kabila felt in the pockets of a Tanzanian tunic hanging from a hook on the wall and pressed a wad of notes into his hand, which Assani quickly stashed away inside his jacket. Two guards followed him outside with the case of whiskey. Assani kept looking around. Were they going to shoot him dead as he walked to his jeep? His head was spinning, even though compared with Kabila he'd only been pretending to drink. He waited while they loaded the whiskey into his vehicle, then ordered one of his bodyguards to follow him in Georges's car.

On the way home he stopped and sent his *kadogos* away. The money Kabila had given him was burning in his pocket. He'd noticed it wasn't local currency but dollars, and that there was at least one zero. They were $100 bills.

Alone in his bedroom — he no longer lived in the barracks but had his own house — he counted the money three times. Kabila had slipped him $5,200 with that casual gesture of his. The tunic on the hook in his office was his bank!

Assani gave his soldiers $200 and ordered them to be especially watchful. He barely slept; he spent the whole night going over the meeting with Mzee, trying to decide if he'd missed something, if it was a trap of some kind. The next morning he called Georges to check whether he was angry that his car had been confiscated. "No, no," he said airily. "That's what Kabila's like: he gives you something, then he takes it away again."

❊   ❊   ❊

The road leading to the security service building had been fenced off on both sides. Men were walking around all over the place, doing their best to look intimidating, hunched in their leather jackets. Kabila's half brother Georges had mended car tires for a living before his appointment as head of security and now he'd recruited all his friends from the *cité*. Charles and Assani had a hard time getting past all the barriers. They clearly weren't welcome, but the soldier in detention on the first floor of the security building was charged with being a danger to the state, and they were from military intelligence, so after some persistence they were led upstairs. Finally they were shown into a room where a crowd of people stood bunched together.

The room was airless and there was an unpleasant smell of sweat. The men had been laughing at something, but when Charles and Assani walked in, silence fell and every-one moved back. Now Assani could see the man around whom they'd been standing. He was handcuffed, although he was clearly in no position to run away.

It was Commander Masasu — or what was left of him. He barely looked up when he saw Charles and Assani, but pride and arrogance showed through his apparent indifference, as if he still had something up his sleeve.

Kabila suspected Masasu of trying to stage a coup. Since his arrest he'd been moved time and again. He would have rotted away between the damp prison walls if his guards — most of whom he'd recruited himself — hadn't helped him escape. But by then he'd grown so weak they were able to recapture him, after a furious chase.

"Get them to remove the handcuffs," Charles said to Assani in Kinyarwanda. "We can't interrogate him like this."

Georges had come into the room briefly and then disappeared again, no doubt to call Kabila to ask for instructions. Assani looked at Masasu. A soldier must always observe the situation closely; for every two steps forward he should take a step back. If you'd been on television once, you'd better try to stay off camera the next time. But Masasu had been acting like a celebrity; a television crew had even filmed him receiving a group of musicians at a villa he'd requisitioned from a Mobutist. He'd gotten above himself and walked into a trap with his eyes open.

When Georges unlocked Masasu's handcuffs the leather-jacketed security men left the room. In the middle of the interrogation there was a knock at the door. The judge of the military court had arrived from Kinshasa to preside over the trial of Masasu and a number of other suspects. He walked over to them, smiling, and introduced himself: "Colonel Mwepu." He had intelligent eyes behind metal-rimmed glasses. His handshake was firm.

"I see you working all the time," Mwepu said one evening as Assani drove him back to his hotel after a meeting with Masasu. "Don't you ever sleep?"

"I sleep when the job's done," Assani said.

They drove on in silence. The phone Mwepu was clutching in both hands rang. It was Kabila. While they were talking, Mwepu kept looking furtively at Assani to see if he was following the conversation. Mwepu was rumored to have orders to sentence Masasu to death. The way Masasu sat in the courtroom, slumped in his chair, a picture of shattered pride, it was hard for Assani to look at him, knowing he might be about to die. He'd been allowed to keep his uniform, but his army boots had been confiscated. He wore cheap orange flip-flops.

Mwepu received a steady stream of calls from Kabila. It would have gone to other officers' heads, but Mwepu merely seemed worried.

At first Assani had been suspicious of the emissary from the capital, but gradually he grew fond of him. His fatherly manner toward Masasu in the courtroom, the way he called the *kadogos* to the front one by one — he reminded Assani of the lieutenant colonel he'd met as a child in the high plains, the man his mother had said was a good soldier.

Mwepu had served in the army under Mobutu and had graduated from college. He wasn't like the Katangese around

Georges, who wanted to burn Masasu at the stake and would enjoy warming their hands at the flames without any thought for the consequences. Mwepu was aware of the heavy burden Kabila had laid on his shoulders.

When the call ended, Assani looked at him. "And? Good news?"

Mwepu sighed. "If only." In silence he peered out over the dark boulevard. "What do you think will happen," he said after a while, "if we can't save Masasu?"

Assani had already taken the turn for Hotel Karavia. "All the soldiers in the east will rise in revolt," he said. "Masasu recruited them; he's their hero. Has Mzee forgotten how easy it is to start a war in this country?"

❊   ❊   ❊

Mwepu managed to get the death sentence commuted to twenty years' imprisonment. After the sentence was passed, Assani took Masasu to jail. He felt crushed. It was as if everything he'd once believed in was finished. Kabila had turned his back on the men who'd helped him to power and decided to rule by himself. He'd been given a dinner service but didn't know how to set the table — he'd smashed all the plates instead.

Before long Mzee Kabila summoned Assani to Kinshasa. He was barely given time to pack. An aircraft was waiting at the airport and he had to leave immediately. This was exactly how Masasu's odyssey had begun, with an invitation from Mzee that had ended not in a meeting but in prison. During the trial Masasu had repeatedly brought up the subject of his missed rendezvous with *papa* Kabila.

Those were the only moments when he'd abandoned his pose of indifference, desperately referring to the struggle they'd waged together—as if Kabila wanted to be reminded of that!

In the plane Assani racked his brains for two hours. Not long ago Charles had told him that Kabila had secretly started training Interahamwe militiamen and Hutu soldiers from the old Rwandan army. The evidence was so overwhelming he'd no choice but to believe it. Had Kabila found out he knew about this? Was that why he'd sent for him?

At Kinshasa airport, anxiety grabbed him by the throat, as if he'd stepped into a room where the air had been sucked out. Joseph Kabila's black Mercedes jeep stood waiting for him at a discreet distance from the aircraft steps. As he walked over to it, followed by the seven *kadogos* he'd brought with him from Lubumbashi, he felt the asphalt give slightly under his feet.

The stink of rotten fruit mixed with the heavy, rancid smell of palm oil—from then on it would always remind him of the first time he arrived in Kinshasa. What would his mother think if she knew he was nearly 1,000 miles from home? She swore by the climate of the high plains and worried even when he went to Uvira that he'd be laid low by an attack of malaria!

It was evening and however hard he tried to look out through the tinted windows of the jeep the city refused to reveal itself. The driver wanted to take him to a hotel, but Assani told him to go to Joseph Kabila's house. He'd brought a tent with him, intending to sleep in the garden with his *kadogos*. They'd be safer that way.

"You should never have gotten involved in politics," he'd told Masasu as they drank Fanta together at the end of a day in court. Masasu had looked at him expressionlessly. "Me today," he answered. "You tomorrow."

Joseph greeted him warmly but Assani was on his guard. Joseph had been good friends with Masasu and rumor had it that Mzee resented their friendship. Did Joseph know that Assani was on the point of sliding in the same direction as Masasu?

They were of the same generation—they'd all been Mzee's children. Joseph was the least experienced of the three and Assani appreciated his modesty. He'd never boasted about being Kabila's son and occasionally even seemed annoyed by the way his father used him to do all kinds of jobs.

Joseph had once been sent to a small town in the east where a mutiny had broken out. He'd wanted to take soldiers from Kinshasa with him, but Assani said, "No, no. I can't command them; I've got my own men here." On arrival Joseph had hung around at the airport for hours, listening to stories from anyone and everyone. He'd grown up in Tanzania and he reminded Assani of the Muslims who sat outside the doors of their houses for days on end, watching life on the street, fiddling with their prayer beads.

"What shall we do?" Assani had asked eventually.

"You've been here longer than I have," said Joseph. "You know best, don't you think?" And he'd let Assani make his own decisions.

Assani settled into an armchair in Joseph's reception room and examined the unfamiliar surroundings. The air conditioner hummed and the lamps on the coffee tables threw a gentle light. There were two separate seating areas, and glass doors opened onto a terrace with a swimming pool. The garden was well tended, he'd noticed on the way in. His *kadogos* reported that they'd erected the tent, but Joseph laughed in surprise when Assani got up to go join them. "You can sleep there," he told him, pointing to a sofa.

"No, no, I'm used to staying with my boys," Assani said.

❊   ❊   ❊

Mzee Kabila was not in a laughing mood this time, nor did he raise his eyes to heaven and announce he was the president of Congo. He didn't even say why he'd summoned Assani, who was told only not to leave the city without the president's permission.

"What if the unit I'm attached to moves elsewhere, *afande*?" he asked. "Am I to report to you then?" He, a simple soldier! "In that case get in touch with James," Kabila said gruffly, making it clear that the audience was over.

Army leader James Kabarebe gave him a check for $600 to get himself settled in. "Did you bring your own soldiers with you?" Assani nodded. "That's good." In no time he was outside again. What was going on? Why had James asked if he had his *kadogos* with him?

There wasn't any time to think about it—Mwepu summoned him immediately. He could use him as a court inspector. "Inspector?" Assani stammered. "But I don't know anything about military law."

"Don't worry," Mwepu said in a fatherly tone. "I'll show you the ropes; just stick close to me."

Was Mwepu taking his orders from Kabila or from James? Did he know why Assani had been transferred from Lubumbashi? There was no way to find out. Mwepu gave him a car and sent him off on various errands. He drove prisoners to court and back and in doing so discovered that a lot of the soldiers from the east were in custody. He learned to appreciate Mwepu. He was well paid and had all kinds of privileges, but while other officers were partying and doing all they could to maximize their personal gain, Mwepu was deeply concerned about the situation. "If we're not careful," he sighed one time, "Kabila will get us into even more trouble than Mobutu."

All the same, Assani had reservations. People who thought positively didn't know what to do when disaster struck. He always thought negatively, which helped him to handle setbacks.

In his free time he explored the city. He would drive along the avenue that followed the Congo River until he got to a roadblock, then loop around to go farther downstream. He'd stop at clandestine harbors, where workers loaded heavy sacks of flour into pirogues,* and gaze at the skyline of Brazzaville on the far bank. Or he might decide to investigate the arterial roads leading out of the city, drive into the hills, and suddenly find himself on the way to Lower Congo. He hardly ever used the car Mwepu had put at his disposal, borrowing a friend's instead, in case anyone tried to track his movements.

❊   ❊   ❊

Justine's daughter Aimée was now in the capital as well. Soldiers had offered her a lift on a plane to Kinshasa, where she was hoping to find work as a biologist. Her father had told her to wait. "I'll wait if you promise to pay for my ticket," she'd said, knowing he couldn't afford it. "Otherwise I'm leaving right now." It was the first time she'd ever disobeyed her father.

Aimée had moved in with a young woman who had an apartment on the boulevard, and Assani often visited her after work. Her boyfriend lived in the same building but as an acquaintance of the family Assani wasn't bothered by that. If her boyfriend wasn't good to her he'd kill him, he said.

It wasn't the first time he'd made a remark like that, so she realized he had a rough side to him, but during the evenings they spent talking she got to know him as a man wounded inside, an orphan who'd suffered from the unjust way he and his mother had been treated by his uncles. He'd fought to go to school but had to break off his studies to fight a war whose outcome he found far from reassuring.

He was a prisoner in Kinshasa, Assani told her. She didn't know what he meant by that and hesitated to ask. The country Kabila had taken over was just like an old jacked-up truck, he said. He'd removed the jack without fixing the tire, so the truck was slewing all over the road, impossible to steer.

She knew little about his private life, although she assumed he had girlfriends, like all the soldiers she knew. Every time he returned from the front during the war, he'd once told her, he needed a woman to make him feel alive, to reassure him that he wasn't dead yet.

One morning Assani turned up at her door. Could she come with him? He looked so upset that she didn't ask questions but grabbed the key to the apartment and followed him. They drove out into the Kinshasa hills, where he had a room at a friend's house. There Aimée encountered a woman Assani must have picked up the previous evening in one of the innumerable soldiers' bars in Kinshasa. She'd installed herself in the living room and was refusing to leave.

Assani had insisted he had a girlfriend, but she'd laughed at him. Where was she, then? She was sure Assani wouldn't dare confront her with another woman, if only because the woman would scratch her eyes out. "I told you I had a girlfriend," Assani said. "Well, here she is. This is the woman I love." The Kinoise* subjected Aimée to a stream of expletives, then fled to the kitchen.

Aimée gave Assani an apprehensive look. The language that woman had come out with! She could only guess at the meaning of some of the words. And what was she doing in the kitchen? Heating a saucepan of oil to pour over Aimée's head?

"Come on," said Assani. "We're leaving." He ordered the *kadogo* on duty to send the Kinoise away; otherwise he'd murder her—and him.

"Around a woman lies your grave," he said as he was driving Aimée home. "It's better to keep clear of them altogether."

"What about me?" she asked. "Aren't I a woman?"

Assani laughed. "No, no, you're different."

That evening he turned up again. He looked rattled. "Hasn't that woman gone yet?" she said. But he seemed to have forgotten all about the morning's incident. Something was up. He was no longer safe here and soon she wouldn't be either. That was all he could tell her.

He fell exhausted onto the sofa, clutching his walkie-talkie in one hand, his phone in the other. After a moment he said, "Long ago in the high plains where I lived, they used to burn the savanna grass in the dry season, but they could never burn it all off in one go. The ground under the grass would still be damp. They had to set it alight a second time. It's the same with Kabila's war. It's only touched the surface; the roots are unaffected. There's another war coming."

Aimée was shocked by his tone of voice. "Hey, you're frightening me."

He gave her a fierce, slightly disapproving look. "You mustn't be frightened," he said. "I'm never frightened."

❊   ❊   ❊

"*Allô?*" He didn't need to say his name; Claudine recognized his voice immediately. It was the man who rang her at the most ridiculous times, even in the middle of the night if something was bothering him and he couldn't sleep. The rebels' hour, she called it.

She was in her restaurant in Lubumbashi. He could hear the innocent chatter and laughter of people who didn't realize their world was about to fall apart.

"How's it going over there?" Claudine asked.

"Not good," he said. "We're in the army, we're always the first to feel things coming."

The voices in the restaurant sounded more distant now. Claudine had walked to a quieter spot to speak to him. He could imagine where she'd be standing: in the garden, one eye on the guests, ready to rush over to them. "What things?" she asked, sounding worried. She was a businesswoman, alert to change, and she knew how the ground could shift here — she'd seen it happen often enough.

"We're being drawn into politics," he said. "We never wanted to get involved, but we . . ."

"You're mumbling," she said. "I can barely hear you."

He laughed apologetically. "It's congenital; I can't help it."

"You mustn't close yourself off, you hear me? Keep the door open — I think I told you that once before."

Civilians! They didn't know anything. Why did he bother talking to them? And yet he'd felt a need to call Claudine. Perhaps so he wouldn't disappear without trace.

"I understand what you're saying," he said. "I'll think about it." He broke off the call without saying good-bye.

❊   ❊   ❊

The city was full of rumors. People were saying the Rwandans had looted the Mobutists' houses as soon as they arrived in Kinshasa, packing suites of furniture, cabinets, crystal chandeliers, and brand-new cars into planes bound for Kigali as war booty. Then they'd infiltrated all government departments, putting their own men in top positions, often Banyamulenge—so-called Congolese who danced to the tune of the Rwandan president, Kagame. Even then they weren't satisfied. The latest story was that the chief of staff, James Kabarebe, had tried to stage a coup and Kabila had reacted by replacing him with a Katangese.

One evening Mzee appeared on television in uniform, thanked the Rwandan soldiers for their help, and ordered them home. As always at times like these, people all over the country started calling each other, and it wasn't long before the cell phone companies were unable to cope. "What should I do?" asked Aimée when she finally got through to Assani. "I hear all the Tutsi have to leave." It was silent at the other end. "Why don't you say something?"

"I couldn't even advise my mother in a situation like this," he said reluctantly.

Assani was on his way to the airport to see the Rwandan soldiers off when Aimée called a second time. She sounded so panicky that he instinctively turned around and drove back to the boulevard. "Try to stay calm," he said sternly. "What's the matter?"

"The neighbors . . . They asked my girlfriend whether *the Rwandan* in her apartment had left yet; otherwise they'd know where to find her." Aimée was close to tears. "Me, a Rwandan! I've never even set foot in Rwanda!" Her friend was afraid that as soon as the Rwandans had left, the remaining Tutsi would be rounded up. "I can't stay here. She says it's best if I disappear for a while." Aimée was speaking in short, nervous bursts. He could hear her walking around the room — she was packing her things. "Couldn't you come and pick me up?"

On the way to the airport Aimée talked nonstop. He'd miss her, but where would he be himself? How long could he stay here? I warned you, Assani wanted to say. Don't you remember me warning you the very first time we met? But you refused to listen; you said you weren't interested in politics. Biology was more important. Look at me, I was determined to study to be a geographer until everything started to slide out from under me and I . . . But all he said was, "In Kigali everyone speaks Kinyarwanda. How are you going to manage?" Aimée fell silent then, embarrassed.

"What about you?" she asked after a while. "What are you going to do? Why don't you leave?"

He laughed bitterly. "What about my soldiers? Do you want me to abandon them here?"

The airport was in chaos. Eight hundred Rwandan soldiers were waiting to be evacuated and a large number of frightened Tutsi civilians had joined them.

James, the deposed chief of staff, had lined up with his men. It was obvious he hadn't slept much over the past few days. As soon as he caught sight of Assani he handed his service pistol to a bodyguard, who passed it on to Assani.

Driving back from the airport Assani was hungry, so he stopped at a restaurant in the center of town. He'd only just found a table when four members of the presidential guard came in and stationed themselves at the four corners of the room. Before his order arrived, he stood up and left. The men came out after him.

He drove to the military court and told Mwepu he was being followed. The new chief of staff, a Katangese, was crazy. He was still partying to celebrate his appointment; you couldn't expect anything from him. James called to say he'd arrived in Rwanda and was about to travel on to the border town of Gisenyi. "You'd better go home and stay indoors," James advised him.

Soldiers unknown to him were patrolling the streets around his house. Assani ordered his *kadogos* to pack their things and arranged for them to be taken to Camp Tshatshi, where they'd be safer. Toward evening it was time for him to leave too. If he didn't get out of here soon they'd come and get him. After he finished packing he took a last look around the room. His eye fell on the stereo installation the grateful businessman in Lubumbashi had sent him as a thank-you gift after Assani's *kadogos* shot dead the robbers who'd attacked him. It was a modern piece of furniture with little doors and a built-in television set. Assani had never seen anything so beautiful. He'd grown attached to it. That was the dangerous thing about possessions: they gave you the feeling everything was normal—they lulled you to sleep.

He got into his jeep and drove to a friend's house near Camp Tshatshi. The phone didn't stop ringing. Tutsi were being detained all over the place, civilians as well as soldiers.

❋

The Rwandans refused to accept defeat. They'd left the west but redoubled their grip on the east, and soon it was clear a new war had begun. All Tutsi in government-held areas were now suspect. Perhaps the Rwandans had left them behind as a bridgehead. They might act as a fifth column and help to bring down Kabila's regime.

In the interior, small groups of Banyamulenge soldiers who'd refused to disarm now rose in revolt. The soldiers in Lubumbashi were surrounded, holed up in their commander's house. They kept calling Assani—as if he didn't have his hands full in Kinshasa! A distant cousin, a gullible pacifist who'd never wanted anything to do with the military, had gone into hiding at a friend's house and didn't dare venture out on the street. Couldn't Assani take him to the French embassy? His friend was refusing to leave with him, not yet convinced of the gravity of the situation.

"My clothes are still at the Hotel Intercontinental. Can we pass by and pick them up?" Assani's cousin asked as soon as he got into the jeep. Assani hit him in the face. "I'm risking my life to save you," he shouted. "Don't you understand that the time for picking up clothes is over?"

While the *kadogos* who'd been left behind in Kinshasa were calling him anxiously by walkie-talkie, his phone rang. It was Mwepu, again. He was attempting to stem the flood of rumors reaching him. He wanted to check Assani wasn't slipping away.

"I hear you guys intend to take the airport," he said, a trace of irony in his voice.

"Idiots," Assani shot back. "Our men are moving away from the airport; they're coming this way."

"Where are you?"

"Heading for Camp Tshatshi. We're hoping we'll be safer there."

But as soon as they'd assembled at the camp it was surrounded. The Kinshasa military commander ordered them by phone to lay down their weapons. Assani didn't trust the situation and refused. Without weapons they'd die — like women. He called Joseph Kabila, who was in China. "We're not going to let ourselves be disarmed. I'm sure you understand," he said. Elsewhere in the city executions of Tutsi had already begun. "I'll be with you in three days," Joseph promised. As he was speaking the first shots rang out.

"You're in danger," James Kabarebe had said a few days before leaving. "Fight like soldiers and die like soldiers if you're attacked. Don't get taken prisoner."

"We're not attacking; we're trying to defend ourselves!" Assani shouted at Mwepu when the firefight at Camp Tshatshi broke out. There was shooting around his house now too, he heard by walkie-talkie. A friend had been killed. The others were forced to leave his body behind as they retreated. It was one message among many, but it hit him like a bullet. He'd spoken to the man earlier that day.

"*Afande!*" Boni tugged at his sleeve. Shooting all the way, they reached the arms depot. While they were breaking in, Mzee Kabila called. He ordered Assani to end the occupation of Camp Tshatshi immediately. "You're not my president any more," Assani told him. Kabila offered him money. "My father owned cows when your father had nothing," Assani responded. "I was wearing pants when you were still in rags. Why would I let myself be bought off by a man who's only just got his hands on money?"

They fought all night and managed to hold the camp for several days. They laid out the dead in a room, their own alongside the enemy. "What are you going to do?" James asked on the phone. "Fight," said Assani, "to the last man." "If you can get out of there with a hundred men, you'll make it," was James's assessment. "I don't know of a single unit capable of taking you on."

With the weapons and money they'd seized they left the camp early one morning, in a column 150 strong. They were rebels again, but the Kinois didn't know it yet, so they could still move around freely. Assani had ordered the soldiers front and rear to shoot if attacked. Those in between carried the ammunition and the wounded.

"Don't try to follow us," Assani warned a Katangese soldier who phoned him. "A snake in his lair—you've no idea what he's capable of."

As they were approaching the Kintambo-Magasin intersection Kabila called again. The rebels had fired mortars at the Marble Palace, his presidential residence. He'd been forced to move out and take shelter elsewhere. "I'll send the Simbas after you," he thundered. "They'll bring me your head on a plate. I'll display it in the museum!"

Assani had difficulty making out what he was saying— they were in the process of raiding a medical depot. A woman soldier who'd trained as a nurse had come up with the idea. They'd be needing medical supplies along the way.

Then they were in the hilly, virgin landscape of Lower Congo, beyond the rapids of the Congo River, marching straight across fields of crops and vegetable plots, trampling the soil with their boots.

They marched in a column, as if out on reconnaissance, but they didn't look like a patrol. Lugging crates of ammunition and boxes of medical supplies, the wounded on stretchers between them, they were such a dreadful sight that the *mamans légumes* cultivating their gardens dropped their baskets in terror and fled.

KINSHASA
2003

Whites were dangerous. Anyone clever was afraid of them. Blacks were easily discouraged; if something didn't work out they might try one more time but then they gave up. Not whites — they dug in their heels.

One evening all high-ranking officers were summoned to a reception — at the last minute as always. They were hurriedly crammed into minibuses. The Belgians had decided to send military instructors to Congo and they'd just arrived in the capital, along with a government minister.

Assani walked around observing them all evening. The Congolese had driven the Belgians out after independence, raping their women and looting their houses, but now they were back, determined to play a role. They didn't show any undue enthusiasm; they were actually quite unassuming. We left Congo, they seemed to say, and now we're back. As if that were the most natural thing in the world.

Assani got into a discussion with a talkative Belgian who used to live in Congo. It was when Belgium cut off military aid to Zaire in 1990, he argued, that everything went wrong with Mobutu's army: the soldiers' pay stopped and the looting started. But thanks to the military partnership the two countries had recently entered into, the Congolese army would . . .

As he was talking, the man beckoned a passing waitress, took a glass of wine and grabbed a cracker from the plate she was carrying. Assani declined. Receptions were the ideal opportunity to poison someone. Half-listening to the Belgian, he ran his eyes over the other guests.

"Why do you wear that?" The Belgian had spotted the gold pendant around his neck.

"Oh, this . . ." Assani said. It had been sent to him by an Israeli he'd met while he was working for Mwepu as court inspector. In the prison he'd happened on a group of soldiers from the east who were being held for no apparent reason. When he got back he stormed into Mwepu's office and shouted, "How can you work with Kabila, a man who wants to do to the Tutsi what the Hutu did to them in Rwanda?"

He was so angry he barely greeted Mwepu's visitor, but the man listened attentively, and months later a letter arrived by a roundabout route. Assani's story had moved him, he wrote. The Jewish people had been through the same experience. In the envelope was a gold chain with a pendant. Assani examined it closely: two triangles laid crosswise on top of each other to form a six-pointed star. Someone told him it was the Star of David, the symbol of Judaism.

He'd worn it ever since, just as he'd once worn the rubber bracelet his mother had given him.

The Belgian was still looking expectantly at him. He's a security service man, thought Assani. He looks inoffensive, but he works in intelligence. "I don't know what it is," he said, hiding the gold star under his shirt. "I bought it at the market. I liked the look of it, that's all."

On the way back from the reception Assani said to his fellow officers, "Have you seen the Belgians? They're here again. We sent them away, but they're back." The others didn't know what he was talking about. Some had drunk more than was good for them and were dozing off in their seats.

"Why would the Belgians be interested in us?" the driver asked gloomily. "Everything here's wrecked and no one can be bothered to fix it."

In his villa on the boulevard Assani walked restlessly from room to room. He should call someone, but who? Claudine, of course. By the time he finally got through to her, he was in bed. "The Belgians," he said. "They're dangerous people."

"What are you talking about?" she asked, laughing.

He told her about the reception. "They're so tenacious! They never stop. They just stand there, laughing to themselves, not looking much interested. But meanwhile they're back."

"You should go to Belgium sometime," Claudine said. "Then you'd understand where they get it from."

"No, no. I don't like going abroad. During the peace talks in South Africa I felt weak, like a drowning man."

She heard him yawn. "Where are you?"

"I'm in bed. Watching hate-television." Some time ago a pastor had taken to haranguing people from the east. Théodore Ngoy. Assani had added the name to his list of sworn enemies. He always watched the show; it helped him stay alert.

After the pastor was finished he picked up the remote control for his music center. Every evening he put three CDs into it and by the time they were over he was asleep. The husky voice of the South African singer Brenda poured into the room. He used to dance to it with a friend who was killed as they fled Kinshasa. If he closed his eyes he could see him: laughing, happy, waving his long arms in the air.

THE SECOND WAR
1998

They were 150 soldiers all told, and everywhere they went people fled. Sometimes they found food abandoned on cooking fires and needed only to share it out. Or they might creep silently into a village and ask the inhabitants to prepare a meal for them. They tried to reassure people, paying for any goats they slaughtered.

More often than not they found nothing at all, or too little to go around. The cassava they ate gave them headaches; fortunately there was sugar beet in the fields. The owner of one farm they descended on was nowhere to be seen, so they slaughtered all the chickens and left a note promising to make good the damage.

The farther they went the harder it became to carry the wounded. "We'll have to finish them off," someone said. Assani hesitated—wouldn't that be bad for morale? Who'd want to fight if he knew getting hurt was a capital offence? "At least let's do it on the quiet, then," he suggested. But when he pointed his pistol at a wounded soldier who'd fired on the Marble Palace, he couldn't bring himself to pull the trigger.

They heard on the radio that the Rwandans had established an air bridge to the nearby military base in Kitona in an effort to create a second front to attack Kinshasa. James was close by! How could they let him know where they were? How could they reach him? First they had to cross a wide river. Only four of them could swim and government soldiers were guarding the bridge. They traipsed back and forth along the bank for several days before finally managing to overwhelm the guards.

By that time they were half starved, their uniforms torn, their boots falling apart. The rebels from the east came to meet them. They had tanks and plenty of ammunition, even stocks of food. Someone handed Assani a package containing a uniform and a pair of boots that Charles had sent from Kigali. Charles—he'd been thinking of him in the midst of all this!

They were given one day to catch their breath, then turned around and advanced on Kinshasa. By the time they arrived Kabila had gained the support of Angola and Zimbabwe. They were stopped at the edge of the city and forced to retreat—before they knew it, they found themselves fleeing through Lower Congo again. This time they headed south and occupied the airfield at Maquela do Zombo just over the Angolan border. They were seriously weakened by

the time the Rwandans came to pick them up. Assani had
lost everything along the way, except for his photo album
and the pistol James had given him.

❀   ❀   ❀

When Assani arrived in Kigali the Rwandans congratulated
him on the way he'd led his men out of Kinshasa and told
him he'd been appointed second in command of military
security for the rebel army. He was given $3,000 to get
settled in, then driven across the border to Goma and
thrown into the war again.

He hadn't had time to recover from the privations he'd
suffered after his escape from Kinshasa; exhaustion gnawed
at his bones and fogged his brain. He was no longer used to
eating and had no appetite — he lived on Fanta and sponge
cake and grew so weak he could barely hold a pen.

Now that he was back in town, news was pouring in
about what had happened while he was away in the bush.
All over Congo, Tutsi had been arrested, executed, lynched.
In the streets of Kinshasa, those left behind had been roasted
alive, burning car tires thrown around their necks to jeers
from onlookers. In the military academy in the Katangese
town of Kamina, Kabila loyalists had shot all the Banyamulenge cadets. By the time the eastern town of Kalemie
fell, seventy-eight Tutsi had been killed, most of them
Banyamulenge. Of the thirty-six soldiers who'd secretly
crossed the border from Rwanda with Assani at the start of
the first war, fewer than ten were left.

The bodies of the victims from Kalemie were brought
to Uvira, where the rebel movement reburied them in an

official ceremony. As weeping relatives threw themselves
onto the coffins, the authorities made speeches. The bishop
of Uvira said they must pray not only for the Tutsi but for
others who had fallen in this war. The relatives of the dead
mustn't allow hatred to lodge in their hearts, he told them.
Now more than ever, the Congolese needed peace.

What the bishop said meant little to Assani. For hours
he stood in the scorching sun, sickened by the smell of sandy
soil mixed with the odor of decomposition that hung around
the coffins. He tried to make a list of the victims he'd known.
He kept losing count.

A western journalist filmed the funeral. Where did he
know him from? Where had he seen him before? Suddenly
he remembered: the Canadian journalist who'd followed
Masasu's trial in Lubumbashi. They'd sat chatting by the
swimming pool one evening at Hotel Karavia. The Canadian
had been particularly interested in Rwandan-Congolese relations. He'd asked some tricky questions, which Assani
answered with his usual vagueness, but the Canadian turned
out to be very well informed about Rwanda and he wasn't
going to be thrown off track—you had to watch it with
guys like that.

Assani kept half an eye on him. The journalist had
spotted him too and after the funeral Assani walked over.
They shook hands. Seven months—was it as recently as
that?

The Canadian had been in Kinshasa a couple of weeks
earlier, he told Assani. "Really?" Assani immediately
thought of Mwepu. "Do you remember the president of
the court?"

"Mwepu? Sure. He's been arrested too now."

Assani was startled. "Why?"

"No one really knows." The journalist shouted an instruction to his cameraman, who was filming the commotion that followed the ceremony. While the officials were getting into their waiting jeeps, relatives crowded around the large pit that had been dug for the burial of the coffins. They held handkerchiefs to their faces or pinched their noses.

"You journalists are always better informed than you let on," said Assani, towering over the Canadian, fixing him with a penetrating stare.

"You know how it is in Kinshasa. People tell all kinds of stories. Some say Mwepu was too close to the Rwandans— supposedly he wanted to inspect the bodies of Tutsi soldiers who'd been killed, as if he was looking for someone."

Assani's heart missed a beat. Had Mwepu been trying to see whether he was among the dead? Mwepu had begged him right up to the last moment to keep his men in check and now the buck was being passed to him!

"Kabila's bad," said Assani. "It doesn't surprise me that Mwepu couldn't make a go of it with him in charge."

"But you brought Kabila to Kinshasa yourselves, didn't you?" Assani recognized the journalist's devious smile—he was fishing for information again.

"No, no, not me. I was always against him." Assani could see Mwepu sitting in court, patiently listening to the *kadogos* with their childish, muddled stories. Mwepu was human; he talked to everyone—unlike he, himself, who was full of shortcomings, introverted, a loner. "Mwepu is a man of justice," he said. "If he was president of Congo I'd be as gentle as a lamb."

The journalist was surprised. "Watch out for Assani," someone had whispered to him during the trial. "He's mean." He was in intelligence—it wouldn't be difficult to trace his background. The security service of the RPF had been as sophisticated as it was merciless; agents were closely supervised for a long period and repeatedly put to the test.

Earlier that afternoon he'd instantly recognized Assani's inscrutable face among the authorities at the ceremony. The Rwandans liked hard men—he wasn't surprised to see that Assani had been promoted. The Banyamulenge suffered from tunnel vision, somebody once told him; they counted only their own dead, indifferent to those of the enemy. But the news about Mwepu had clearly affected Assani. For the first time the journalist detected something behind the tough pose that he wasn't sure what to make of. They were still standing in the sickly smell at the edge of the mass grave and Assani was staring at the men who were beginning to fill in the pit.

"Mwepu," he said. "Even in my coffin I'll feel a bond with him."

The Canadian television journalist was making a long journey through rebel territory. On the plane from the Rwandan capital to Goma he'd sat next to a soldier. "Are you working for your own nation or for a foreign country?" he'd asked, in an effort to strike up a conversation.

"You mean am I Congolese or Rwandan?"

"Exactly."

The man gave a haughty laugh. "You mean there's a difference?"

Congo had once had the reputation of a tiger, but these days everyone knew it was merely a cat. Rwanda and Uganda called the shots in the east; the Congolese rebels were puppets on a string. The journalist took lifts on military aircraft. Between Goma and Kisangani they flew via Kigali to refuel.

The rebels now controlled about half of Congo, but their popularity had dropped to less than nil. In the small eastern town of Kasika they'd recently been ambushed by Mai Mai fighters, community-based militiamen opposed to the Rwandan presence on Congolese soil. The rebels had lost several important officers and in revenge they'd murdered everyone for miles around. Kasika—the name hung in the air like a bad omen.

The Congolese felt they'd been occupied. In Kisangani people came up to the journalist to tell him they hated the Tutsi. "The Rwandans came to Congo to hunt for the people who murdered their relatives," the Congolese manager of a textile factory said, "but pretty soon they discovered they were in the Garden of Eden. At that point they halted their search and started picking the fruits of paradise."

Diamonds, gold, coltan—they were all being flown out of the country. The leaders of small, densely populated Rwanda had begun to regard eastern Congo as their backyard. They irritated the journalist. They were so damned arrogant and clever. Militarily they were strong and might have a chance of winning, but he feared that if they did the Tutsi would be slaughtered again a few years down the line.

After their meeting in Uvira the journalist saw Assani several times in Goma. One evening, as he was walking out of a restaurant with his cameraman, Assani drove past in his jeep and stopped to talk. With him was the particularly unpopular head of security who ran his own private jail, Chien Méchant, where he had people tortured.

The security chief was on the phone with a woman. He was clearly drunk. In the backseat a couple of men sat talking and laughing. They'd emerged out of the night like ghosts and seemed to be having a lot of fun.

"Any news of Mwepu?"

The question caught the Canadian by surprise. "No, no," he laughed. "I have just as little contact with the other side as you do, Commander Assani."

It surprised him that Assani had asked after Mwepu again. He wasn't sure what to make of that. Assani, such a militaristic Tutsi—he hadn't expected him to be worried about the fate of a non-Tutsi.

*   *   *

"Zikiya . . ." No one pronounced his name the way his mother did, as if a little bird had gotten caught in her throat. She was well into her seventies, but as she sat here next to him in the grass, straight as a rod, wrapped in a pagne and wearing a head scarf, he could see she was still strong.

As soon as she heard that her son was in Goma she'd flown in from the high plains in a military aircraft. She liked the house he'd been allocated as number two in security. It

had a big garden with a high wall around it—they were
completely cut off from the outside world. But why did the
main gate give on to the busy street instead of the lane at
the back, and why did his soldiers have to sit at the entrance
with their walkie-talkies? If it weren't for them, no one
would know he lived here, and that would be far better.

"But *ma*, we're not in the high plains here!"

He'd never had a house to himself before. It wasn't far
from Lake Kivu, in a district where a lot of Mobutists once
lived. The owner had fled abroad, but a local agent was
keeping an eye on the place. Assani had planted banana and
papaya trees, and behind the house his soldiers had sown
beans.

At first he wasn't sure what to do with his mother. He'd
changed. He'd been through things she couldn't even imagine and he was living with about forty *kadogos*, who slept in
wooden barracks in the garden. But after a while he realized he liked coming home and finding her there.

He felt grateful. He was her only son, but she didn't
complain that he'd chosen to be a soldier. She'd never treated
him like a child; he'd been her confidant since he was small.
She silently accepted that everybody called him Assani and
didn't ask where the name came from; she just started using
it whenever other people were around. As soon as they were
alone he became Zikiya again.

"Have I changed since you last saw me?" he asked her.
"Do you think I've changed?"

She thought for a moment. "You're calmer," she said.
"You used to be much more restless. And you're thinner.
You were always thin, but I've never seen you like this.

You wash as quickly as ever, though. You're done in two minutes."

He knew she'd come to talk about his stranded marriage. The subject often hovered uneasily between them — as it did right now. He'd come home earlier than usual and was lying beside her, on his stomach, absentmindedly tugging at the tough grass that grew in this region. He'd given his phone and walkie-talkie to Boni, who was sitting a short distance away with a group of *kadogos*. From behind the house he could hear the chatter and laughter of soldiers slicing cabbages for the evening meal.

"It's like an orphanage here," she said.

He gazed at his boys, who were playing with a black goat he'd brought back from his latest trip into to the interior. "They seem like children," he said, "but they've forgotten everything they learned at home. First they have to sit in the back of a jeep for two years, riding over terrible roads, and then . . . Would you be able to stab someone to death?"

"Zikiya!" she said, severely.

"If you could, you'd never be the same. Do you think they'd obey me if I didn't have a whip handy? They know they need it; if I lost it they'd make me a new one."

Boni was younger than the others, but no one else was allowed into Assani's bedroom. Every morning he made the bed, got the breakfast things out of a high-sided cardboard box, and put them away again.

"That boy there," Assani said, pointing at Boni. "He's seen everything. He knows why I'm so thin." Assani avoided thinking about those weeks in Lower Congo, but now that his mother was sitting next to him, so calm and protective, it suddenly seemed a good idea to tell her something about it.

"Boni survived, but I lost two boys." He looked up to see if she was following him. "I miss them," he said. "It's strange; the sense of loss doesn't go away. They're children, but when you're on a military operation with them they're not children any more."

He'd turned to lie on his back, looking at the blue sky through half-closed eyes. "I was down to eighty-eight pounds," he said dreamily.

His phone rang. He heard Boni say, in a voice that sounded like his own, that Commander Assani wasn't there.

"I put you back into God's hands a long time ago," his mother said resignedly. "I just wish you'd give me one more grandson."

She'd outwitted him. He'd been trying to distract her, but she'd simply waited for the right moment to bring up the subject.

"But I haven't even got a wife!" he protested. His mother had been here for several weeks. She'd probably thought he smoked, drank, or had women hanging around, like other soldiers, but she hadn't seen even one.

"What about the mother of your children?"

"That's over, *ma*," he said wearily.

"What's supposed to happen to her kids?" He'd arranged for his own children to leave the high plains. His daughter was living with his sister in Rwanda, his son in Bukavu with Elias.

"The ones she had after me? They're not mine."

"Mufunga says she's every right to conceive as many children for the family as she likes, that they'll perpetuate his oldest brother's name, that your cows will remain with her as long as . . ."

"Mufunga!" he exclaimed indignantly.

"But whose children are they then?" she asked, with a catch in her voice. "Who's going to take care of them in the future?"

"They'll be fatherless," he said, unrelenting. "Like me." He saw that his mother was crying.

Boni had noticed too. The next time the phone rang he came over and handed it to him. "*Afande* . . ." Assani stood up, brushing the grass from his track suit pants. "Leaflets, you say? Just shake him up a bit, I'm coming." He looked at his mother. "They're calling for me," he said apologetically.

By the time he'd got changed his *kadogos* had jumped into the back of the pickup, but his mother was still sitting in the garden, bent forward slightly, plucking vehemently at the tough grass.

The next day the air had cleared and his bitterness had receded. His mother had been thinking the matter over as well. "Take another woman, then," she said.

They sat facing each other in a large living room that was bare except for a modest sitting and dining area. He decided to play along.

"Can she be a Rwandan?"

She had no objection to that.

"Or a Ugandan?"

"No, no, they've all got AIDS."

"A Congolese?"

"As long as she's not a Bembe."

"From one of the other peoples then?"

"Yes—provided there aren't any hereditary diseases in the family."

"But what would I do with a woman here, *ma*?" he said, with a sweep of his arm. "I can't even bring my own children to live with me. The situation isn't stable. I might be called away at any moment. The work I do is extremely difficult. If I start to drink, smoke, or go out with women I might put myself in danger." She was quiet, listening, so he went on. "What if I remarry and die at the front? We're rebels, *ma,* and this house doesn't belong to me; if the others decided my widow couldn't stay here, where would she go?"

Twilight fell. All he could see was the red light of his walkie-talkie flickering on the coffee table. "*Wéwé!*"— You!—he shouted. Boni came running and switched on the light. The seating area was bathed in a weak yellow glow.

"You understand, *ma*?"

She nodded.

In the weeks that followed he was off on one mission after another, sometimes staying away so long that his mother got tired of waiting and went to visit her daughter in Rwanda. But she was usually there when he got back. He would find her in the living room, the floors shining, the floral curtains drawn, the key to his bedroom tied into the corner of her head scarf.

He was hoping she wouldn't return to the high plains, but she talked more and more about a cow that was about to calve, about her goats, even about the chickens that couldn't manage without her. He found room for her on a plane to Minembwe. From there she would walk home.

Before she left he spent a whole afternoon with her. They went shopping together; he recorded her voice on tape and took photos of her in the garden. But when he had the film developed it was blank. He called his *kadogos* together and asked for an explanation. The boy who'd been minding the camera raised his hand timidly. *"Afande . . ."* While he was playing with it he'd pressed a button and a little door had flicked open. It had been hard, he admitted, to rising giggles from the others, to get it to close again.

❊   ❊   ❊

The way people looked at him as he drove toward Uvira in his pickup, dressed in combat gear, twelve soldiers in the back—he could feel their hatred. This war might be good for the Rwandans, who'd wanted to secure their borders against the Interahamwe in the inhospitable hills and extensive wildlife reserves of the east, but for the Congolese it was a disaster.

They'd just passed Kamanyola, where Mobutu won a battle with Kabila's rebels in the 1960s and had himself immortalized in a bronze short-sleeved uniform, head erect, arms akimbo, binoculars at his chest. But Mobutu had since been pulled from his pedestal and was lying on his back in the gravel. Sometimes Assani would stop there with his boys and they'd crowd around the statue as if on a school outing, planting their boots in Mobutu's face, kicking his ribs, and posing for photos with tough-guy expressions, weapons at the ready. There was no time for that now—he ought to have reached Uvira ages ago. The Mai Mai had mounted an attack on a fishing village on Lake Tanganyika, south of Uvira. Rwandan, Congolese, and Burundian soldiers had been killed and trucks were on their way out from Uvira with reinforcements. Bad news. Yet more bad news.

It was the afternoon of New Year's eve. The streets of Goma and Bukavu were festively lit and despite the war the *commerçants*—local retailers—had decorated their shopwindows. The bars and restaurants were busier than usual. But he was traveling farther and farther away from all that— in the wrong direction.

He passed a village where *mamans* were selling oranges and bananas from roadside tables. There were so few cars here that people walked in the middle of the road. He yanked the steering wheel right and left so that they ran, startled, onto the roadside verges. It was a trick he'd learned from a Ugandan soldier. It worked—even the chickens scuttled out of the way, cackling. A goat crossed the road unexpectedly and rammed his pickup. He heard a dull thud, looked at Boni, let out a shrill high-pitched laugh, and forged on.

Toward dusk he arrived in Uvira. The sun was setting behind the mysterious blue mountains he'd walked down with his mother as a child, but he didn't see them.

Hotel de la Côte was full of soldiers. It had once been the best hotel in town, but each time he visited it had gone farther downhill. Food was no longer served, there was no hot water, and if a lightbulb blew it wasn't replaced. The soldiers hardly ever paid their bills, so the manager was letting things slide, hoping to discourage his unwelcome guests.

"Is my room available?"

The woman at the reception desk nodded, took the key from the hook, and went ahead of him to the end of the corridor. She had an unsteady gait, and a penetrating hospital smell clung to her —*cinq cents,* a cheap alcoholic drink poor people distilled from maize or cassava.

His room smelled musty. The bare bulb hanging from the ceiling cast a feeble light. As he opened the door to the terrace the room filled with noise: a sputtering moped passing on the main road, muffled male voices, a child crying in the distance. He threw back the bedclothes; the synthetic sheets were unwashed. His cell phone rang, and there was an incoming call on the walkie-talkie at the same time. He sighed. They knew he'd arrived.

Early the next morning a Munyamulenge soldier knocked at his door. Assani glanced along the corridor to check no one was watching and let him in. He'd been receiving people most of the night, meanwhile taking phone calls and listening to the walkie-talkie. He already knew the reprisal had gotten out of hand.

Deo was dirty and had a groggy look in his eyes. He smelled of sweat and gore, and he flopped into the chair by the bed without asking permission. He started talking in a toneless voice, sometimes interrupting himself and peering furtively around as if the enemy had followed him here.

The Mai Mai had fled into the hills after the attack, but the local population supported them, of course, so the soldiers had taught them a lesson. Assani could imagine the rest: the smoke billowing from the houses and huts, the screams of villagers locked inside, people trying to escape through windows and back doors and being shot as they fled.

"It isn't over yet, *afande*," Deo said. "When I left they were still at it." The hotel room seemed to have a sobering effect. The tension had fallen away and he suddenly looked deathly tired. He probably hadn't slept much the past few nights.

Assani thought of the Canadian journalist traveling through rebel territory, his sharp eyes scanning his surroundings, always searching for information. What if he heard about this? Local human rights organizations and church groups with contacts abroad would spring into action immediately too. They didn't give a damn if Tutsi were killed, but when one of their own was hurt they screamed blue murder.

"Has the area been sealed off?"

"Of course, *afande*."

That afternoon Assani drove out to the fishing village. At the first roadblock the soldiers were still standing in excited groups, fired up by the adrenaline of the past few days, but farther on they wandered past the smoldering houses in twos and threes as a guilty silence set in.

Deo had told him how they'd tricked the fleeing inhabitants. They grabbed a boy and ordered him to shout *"Amani!"*—Peace! It was an old tactic used by Rwandans and Burundians, but people here were so isolated that they'd fallen for it and left their hiding places, glad it was all over and they could get back home before their meager possessions were stolen. They lined the street, several rows deep, looking expectantly at the soldiers, who started shooting at random.

They'd killed hundreds of people in three days and now they were disposing of the evidence in their own bungling fashion. A soldier pulled a wounded baby out from under its mother's body and carried it to a latrine behind the house. Two soldiers lugged a body to a truck.

In the stench of smoke and rotting flesh, Assani stared at Lake Tanganyika in the distance. Then he turned around and walked resolutely back to his car. This must never be pinned on the rebels. He knew what he had to do. They'd be needing more trucks.

❁   ❁   ❁

When he got back to Goma he drove past his own house twice. In the evening he tried to call someone and discovered he could barely read the numbers. The doctor said he was exhausted and prescribed strong painkillers. He stayed home for three days, lying in bed most of the time, sleeping, listening to the radio, or watching Canal France International. To anyone who called he said he was suffering from a *maladie imaginaire*.

On the third evening he looked up all Claudine's numbers and called them one after the other. She was in Belgium. There was a crackle on the line and a slight delay; her voice echoed through the metallic silence. "Don't you have a restaurant to run?" he asked.

"I do, why?"

"Why aren't you in Lubumbashi, then?"

"I needed to get away for a bit." She laughed. "Your life changes all the time; mine doesn't." There was silence at the other end. "And you, where are you?"

"In Goma. I haven't been out of the house for three days."

"Are you ill?"

"No. I'm lying here thinking."

He sounded much less confident than a few months ago, when he'd called her from the bush to say he was on his way to Kinshasa to get rid of that damned Kabila. Her brother-in-law had told her that resistance to the rebels was increasing by the day. "What's happening at the front?" she asked cautiously. "From what I hear nothing's really moving."

"It's a good thing nothing's moving," he snapped. "Last time it went much too quickly."

"So what are you lying there thinking about?"

He mumbled something she didn't catch. "You're alive," he said finally. "You can't imagine what it's like here." His voice was barely audible, as it always was when he wanted to say something but at the same time didn't want to. "I've been through three wars. I'm not normal any longer. We never see anything here but corpses. I'm a living corpse myself. We shoot, we're shot at, we kill each other."

"But you go along with all that. You do all those things yourself, don't you?"

"No, no, I never chose this life. If I hadn't become a soldier I wouldn't be alive today. God himself wrote this history. I shouldn't have been born a Negro."

She was getting to know him. He was good at holding his tongue, but once he got started she found herself privy to the entire interior monologue he always seemed to be carrying on.

"They should colonize us again. We don't know how to live. Van Bilsen was right when he said we needed another thirty years, but poor Lumumba . . . He wanted independence right away."

Professor Jef Van Bilsen — she'd learned about him at the Belgian school in Lubumbashi; he'd suggested in 1955 that Congo should become independent within thirty years. She was surprised Assani knew who he was.

"We should mix with other people. Africans among themselves . . ."

"And you? Are you so different then?"

"No, no." He hesitated for a moment. "At this moment, yes. I'm reasonable now. Ten percent of me is good, but the other ninety percent . . . And I'm one of the best. At least I know violence won't . . ."

His voice fell away. "Assani?" she said, but he didn't answer. Four thousand miles away he'd fallen asleep in mid-sentence.

*   *   *

Whenever he thought the downward spiral had finally bottomed out, fate had yet another blow in store. During a military meeting with the Rwandans in Kigali, Felix, a Munyamulenge soldier, made a remark and a Rwandan officer barked at him, "Shut up, *igicucu*, who asked you?" throwing his car keys in Felix's face.

Assani hunched his shoulders as if he were the one who'd been hit. Felix ducked and picked up the keys with barely concealed rage. *Igicucu*, blockhead; *m'jinga*, ignoramus; *nyamaswa*, barbarian: the Rwandans had plenty of abusive terms for the Congolese and used them at every opportunity.

"They'd better not try that again," Felix snorted as they drove back to Goma.

"Come on," Assani said soothingly. "You have to rise above insults like that or you'll never get anywhere. Aren't the Rwandans right? Aren't we idiots who ought to be ashamed, coming from a country so much bigger and richer than Rwanda and not even able to find ourselves a leader?"

Felix sucked at his teeth disapprovingly. "It's their fault we can't find a leader. They've got their own plans for Congo; they're just using us; they turn us against each other and then rush to the rescue! If they get their way the Congolese will be feuding among themselves for ever."

The three Banyamulenge soldiers in the back said nothing, but Assani knew they agreed with Felix. As if their problems had started when the Rwandans got involved!

"Just you wait," Felix said fiercely. "One day we'll give them a taste of their own medicine."

"That's exactly how Kabila thinks," Assani sighed. "If we want to be better than they are, we should learn from their mistakes."

"It's easy for you to talk." That was all Felix said, but Assani knew what he meant: *They've got you dancing to their tune and you sure don't want to lose your privileges.*

They were approaching the border. The Rwandan customs official peered into the vehicle and was about to ask for their papers, but Assani gave him such a stony look that the barrier was raised immediately. On the Congolese side of the border several *commerçantes* were locked in animated discussion. They fell silent and watched them pass. Five soldiers with narrow faces in a jeep, coming from Rwanda—it wasn't hard to guess what the women were thinking.

The resistance to the Rwandans was like a forest fire, spreading steadily. A Rwandan colonel got into an argument with four Banyamulenge soldiers in Uvira. His attempt to arrest them ended in a firefight, with dead and wounded on both sides. The Banyamulenge managed to escape and flee into the high plains with their bodyguards.

The Rwandans were furious and demanded that Assani go after them. "Why don't you leave the kids alone?" Assani said. "What have they got out there in the bush? No money, nothing. They're hiding with their families—do you want me to go in there and smoke them out? How could we explain that to our parents? We'd only be making enemies." But the Rwandans didn't understand. They suspected him of siding with the insurgents.

Every day more soldiers deserted, strengthening the ranks of the Banyamulenge who'd left for the mountains to protect their families against attacks by the Mai Mai and the Interahamwe. Assani traveled back and forth along the eastern border in an attempt to stop them from leaving.

In Kalemie he ran into Deo, the soldier who'd burst into his hotel room during the massacre in the fishing village. "So you're a rebel now too," Assani said. Deo merely shrugged. "The Rwandans are our enemies," he said. "I don't understand why you still support them."

"Is this why we went to war?" Assani asked sternly. "To carry the humiliations we've suffered into the mountains like rocks and go back to where we came from?" It struck him that he sounded just like a priest. Deo was unimpressed—Assani no longer had any authority over him. Deo had been a small fish, but his status as an insurgent had given him an aura of invulnerability. Assani thought of the dull look in Deo's eyes on the morning after the murders in the fishing village and wanted to say: What do you have to offer your country? You're simply a village boy, driven by hatred for one person today and another tomorrow.

But he restrained himself. "Instead of turning our fire on Rwanda we should clean up the mess in our own backyard," he said. "The Rwandans are strong; we're no match for their strategic ingenuity. As long as we're weak and divided the best we can do is learn lessons from them. We've got nothing to fall back on, everyone's against us: Interahamwe, Mai Mai, Kabila loyalists. Maybe one or another faction is ready to do a deal with you, but what if your alliance falls apart? Who will you turn to then?" He stared intently at Deo. "Tell that to the others."

Deo's face was dark and expressionless; to him Assani was a traitor who'd started believing the paranoid tales of the Rwandans. Assani was trying to rectify things, but the others were bent on destruction. He'd run up against a stubborn streak in his people, a result of the isolation in which the Banyamulenge had grown up and their aversion to rules from elsewhere.

Yet as he was driving back to the guesthouse where he was staying he began to doubt everything he'd said. Maybe Deo and the others were right. Maybe he should disappear into the bush again. What about James, though? If James hadn't dredged him up after his flight from Kinshasa he'd never have gotten out alive. And now he was going to betray James?

He didn't feel safe in the remote town of Kalemie. Had the Rwandans sent him here to get rid of him? Would the Banyamulenge decide to punish him for his treachery? Everyone had weapons here — it was so easy to make someone disappear.

The others went into town after dinner, but he stayed behind, alone in his room. He was dizzy with exhaustion. Three days' sleep hadn't been enough to recuperate. His resistance was low and every time a new problem came up he panicked. He'd left Boni in Goma, afraid of losing him in a shooting incident, but now he missed him. With Boni around he wouldn't have felt so alone.

Should he call Aimée? What if their calls were bugged? No, it was better not to involve her. He tapped Claudine's number. "*Allô*?" It was good to hear her voice. When he phoned her in Lubumbashi she'd sometimes sounded nervous—in Belgium she could speak more freely.

"You feeling better?" she asked.

"Who told you I wasn't feeling well?"

"You did!"

"Sorry. I'm still overworked, I think." He could hear her waiting for him to go on. "This war is far more difficult than the first war," he sighed. "Everyone's against everyone else. How can I relax in a situation like this? I look death in the eye every day. Even right now, talking to you."

"You should get away for a bit. Doesn't a soldier have a right to a holiday?"

He laughed at the thought. "No, no, not yet. I live one minute at a time. If I started thinking I'd have to ask for asylum abroad. Galileo was condemned for saying the earth went around the sun. That's just what it's like here: anyone who wants to change anything is finished." He had no idea whether she understood any of this, but at least she was listening. And she wouldn't hold what he said today against him tomorrow.

"I reckon you need a rest," she said.

"I'll rest when I'm old—but a man like me doesn't live to be old."

"Why shouldn't you live to be old?"

"Because pretty soon they'll shoot me."

"Why?"

"First because I'm an African, second because I'm a Congolese, third because I'm a Tutsi, and on top of that . . ."—he let out a high-pitched, joyless laugh—"a Munyamulenge!"

At the other end a tense silence fell. No harm frightening her, he thought—give her a sense of how it feels to be in a godforsaken town like Kalemie with no idea whether or not you'll make it through the night.

"No one who tries to do any good can survive here," he said. "You can't think logically in a land of barbarians."

"You used to believe in what you did," she said hesitantly. "What happened? What's changed?"

"No one wants us here. We still have weapons, but when supplies run out we'll have to flee. Fortunately I've got a pistol. The last bullet is for myself; they won't throw a burning tire round my neck like they did with the Tutsi in Kinshasa."

"Where are you?" she asked, worried.

"Somewhere in the east," he said reluctantly. "Not far from Uvira."

"How come you're alone?"

"The others went out." He looked around. "Do you want me to describe the room I'm in?" He didn't wait for an answer. "On the table in front of me are two pistols, a walkie-talkie, and, wait a moment . . ."—he pushed some papers aside—"Two chargers and a box of bullets. Against the wall is my rucksack, plus a Kalashnikov, a grenade launcher . . ." Halfway through his description he broke into a ghostly laugh. "What a bunch of wretches; we're living corpses!" Then, as if struck by a sudden inspiration, he said, "I know where I'll be able to rest."

Here it comes, thought Claudine. Now he's going to ask me to help him get a visa. That's why he keeps calling. Of course. He's trying to keep a line open in case he needs to flee the country. "Where?"

"In my coffin. Doesn't that seem like a good place to rest? I'll be at peace there, with no one to disturb me."

"What about your son?"

"He'll be an orphan, just like me."

He was no longer an ordinary soldier who could hide behind his superiors or keep his head down until things blew over. He was under surveillance. If he decided to pull out, others would follow his example and the Rwandans would have lost a valuable pawn. One false move and he was done for. He knew the Rwandans—they thought nothing of removing their opponents.

One afternoon he was in Kigali for a meeting. He was going to see Aimée afterward, but he noticed he was being followed. Sooner or later they'd knock at her door and start asking questions. That was the last thing he wanted. She had enough problems already: her whole family had been picked up at the start of the second war and interned in a camp on the outskirts of Lubumbashi.

He called her from his car. "Sorry," he said. "I can't come."

"What's the problem?" she asked, disappointed. It was the weekend and she'd been looking forward to seeing him.

"Oh, nothing. I've got another appointment, that's all."

"Who with?"

He looked in the rearview mirror at the jeep that was following him and said nothing.

"Off to get your latest orders from the Rwandans, no doubt," she said resentfully.

She shouldn't have said that. He broke off the call and for days he refused to answer the phone when she tried to reach him.

But the Rwandans were clever. They left him to his own devices until he'd calmed down, then promoted him to battalion commander at a small town in the interior. Kabalo! He'd been there before. It had nothing to offer besides mosquitoes, but it was a strategic spot on the road to the mining towns of Lubumbashi and Mbuji-Mayi. Off to the front line again, to war. He'd rather have crept back into his mother's womb. But he had no choice. It was a long time since he'd been a free man.

KABALO
1998

Mwansa was in the Katangese town of Kalemie, on Lake Tanganyika, when the Rwandans invaded. Everyone said "the Rwandans," since they were in charge, but there were Congolese troops among them—and Banyamulenge, looking just like Rwandans. The soldiers needed someone to drive a train into the interior. Mwansa's colleagues said he was their man; he'd accompanied Kabila's soldiers two years before. They came to his house to fetch him. His wife and children wept, but he went along. At least then he could make sure the soldiers didn't run off with railroad property.

Mwansa was an imposing man with an amiable personality. His dark skin shone as if polished and he was invariably dressed in a caramel-colored safari suit that gleamed from too much ironing, a blue ballpoint sticking out of his breast pocket. He was the type of man you kept coming on in the interior, making you believe Congo had good things in store for it after all. Despite repeated setbacks he went on doing his job. He was concerned about the future of the railroad company even though he'd received hardly any pay the last few years.

Mwansa's father had worked for Air Congo after independence and some of his family lived abroad. This country produces things it can't consume, he used to say: an intellectual earns two dollars a month. He'd tried to leave once, to move to Ghana, but the positive answer to his job application arrived six months late because the postal service wasn't working.

Mwansa was chief engine driver on the sixty-mile journey from Kalemie to Niemba, hauling seven carriages full of soldiers and munitions, plus a multiple-rocket launcher that made an incredible noise. The Rwandans used it to scare the enemy—you could hear it a dozen miles away. Throughout the trip Mwansa asked himself why the war had started again, just when the railroad staff had begun receiving their pay. He'd been in Kinshasa a few months back and the atmosphere in the city had seemed fine.

But the soldiers around him cursed Kabila. He was an idiot, the Rwandans said. He supported their enemies, the Interahamwe. The Congolese rebels called him a tribalist, saying he'd given preferential treatment to the Katangese and especially the Lubakat from his native region, Manono. Just look at his soldiers, the rebels scoffed; they're all deserting. Who wants to fight for Manono, other than people who come from there? Nobody. Among the rebels were many soldiers who'd served under Mobutu, men the Rwandans had fought against alongside Kabila! No, there wasn't much logic to any of it.

The villages the train passed through were ominously empty. Civilians had fled, especially the Lubakat, who'd felt protected by Mzee and pinned all their hopes on him, even though they had yet to receive anything in return. Mwansa belonged to a people that lived higher up the Congo River — he didn't feel threatened.

In Niemba the rebels crossed the river in pirogues. The bridge had been down for years. Mwansa needed to get a pump trolley normally used for track maintenance across the river. He had the trolley dismantled and the parts loaded into pirogues, then reassembled and rolled to Nyunzu stacked with munitions and food supplies. The Rwandans had no railroads at home and they found the pump trolley pretty nifty — just like a car, they said.

Kabila had sent soldiers to Nyunzu to defend the town, but they'd found a wagonload of beer at the station and settled in for a drinking spree. The Rwandan commander, Satellite, found them all completely drunk. In Kabalo two planes had landed carrying freshly trained Katangese soldiers who'd been ordered to stop the renegades from running away. They shot the commander of the fleeing battalion and proceeded to the hospital, where they killed the wounded. They had little weaponry and no communications equipment; nor did they have much knowledge of the terrain — in a panic, they killed several of their own men. They looted Kabalo and then it was their turn to flee. At that point Commander Satellite appeared on the scene with his men and took the town.

But Mwansa heard about all this only later. He stayed a safe distance behind the soldiers and rolled the pump trolley into Kabalo at night. It was too dangerous by daylight, since Kabila and his Zimbabwean allies had started bombing the city. At Kabalo station Mwansa found a freight train with sixty heavily loaded wagons. It had been waiting for an engine, which was now on the other side of the front line. Rice, dried and salted fish, palm oil — it was a warehouse full of food supplies for the soldiers. In the security service building, sacks of rice were piled high; a consignment had just arrived, intended for Kabila's men.

All the Lubakat had left Kabalo. The women had buried their sewing machines and the wealthy merchant Tip Top, whose name was displayed on several shop windows in town, had bricked up his wares in his cellar. But the people who'd stayed behind gave away his hiding place and the rebels broke into the cellar, hauling the contents off to their headquarters.

Kabalo was bombed in daylight by MiGs and at night by Antonovs, horrible birds that howled as they flew over, dropping homemade bombs full of rusty bolts, nails, and bits of metal that people collected as souvenirs.

Between bombardments Mwansa explored the town. Kabalo had once been at the center of the granary of Congo, when railroad cars of cotton fiber traveled along a dedicated track to the cotton factory farther upriver, and in the shops of the busy Arab quarter Pakistani and Indian merchants sold pagnes, powdered milk, and porcelain.

Now the stylish colonial station was black with damp, the station clock had stopped, and the marshaling yards and warehouses were full of discarded railroad supplies. Everything around here was getting rusty and moldy, even the people. They'd landed in the garbage bin of history, rotting away in a depot. Only the mango trees from Belgian times had survived the battle against neglect. They were tall, casting shade along the broad streets, the wind blowing the fruit to the ground in the rainy season.

The Rwandans had set up their heavy artillery at the hospital, which had once been run by the White Fathers — surely no one would bomb that. When their multiple-rocket launcher started rattling away, the women of Kabalo would wet themselves in terror.

The soldiers set up camp under the mango trees in the fathers' garden. In the sisters' mission house, hidden away in a grove, they'd established their own hospital. They shredded the exercise books they found there and chopped up the school benches so they could make fires to cook on and keep the mosquitoes at bay in the evenings. The statue of the Virgin that had once stood in a niche in the courtyard lay headless and chipped in the tall uncut grass.

Mwansa put people up in the houses that belonged to the railroad company, afraid they'd otherwise be looted or de-roofed. The soldiers needed corrugated iron to build makeshift accommodations and they'd had so much practice they could strip the roof off an unguarded building in a few hours. Sometimes they sold the corrugated iron to civilians, who used it to make cooking pans. Next the doors would disappear, then they'd start chiseling out stones here and there. By the time the rainy season was over, ferns, palms, and marram grass would be shooting up out of what had once been a living room, like plants in a broken flowerpot.

There were Ugandans in Kabalo as well. They didn't agree with the Rwandans on how to divide up the loot, Mwansa noticed. The Ugandans had found a large amount of money in the bank in Kalemie but hadn't wanted to share it, a Rwandan told him. From a Ugandan he heard that the Rwandans in Kalemie had found cars and immediately sent them to Rwanda without telling the Ugandans. The Ugandans were not at all happy—after a while they left and Mwansa didn't see them again.

Congolese soldiers were in the habit of stealing everything they could lay their hands on—Rwandans stole only the most important things. At the station depot in Kabalo they took gasoline, diesel oil, mopeds, and a generator, but anyone who turned up with the right papers was allowed to take his property with him there and then—the Rwandans couldn't stand the harassment the Congolese soldiers were so famous for. A soldier who took a bicycle or a radio from you would be beaten up in public. For taking a goat he might be shot.

Even so, Mwansa didn't like the Rwandans. They spoke Kinyarwanda when he was with them, although they knew full well he wouldn't understand. They were distrustful, even of each other, drinking their beer straight from the bottle for fear of being poisoned. It wasn't long before they started insulting the Congolese soldiers they'd come with, calling them idiots.

*

The soldiers kept streaming in. Sometimes as many as eight planeloads arrived in a single day. Eventually there were two brigades in Kabalo: one Rwandan, one Congolese—a total of 11,000 men.

Why would Rwandan officers be willing to die in the interior of Congo? At first Mwansa couldn't work it out. Then he heard that they received regular rations, even cigarettes; their monthly salaries were paid into accounts in Rwanda, and they were given loans to build houses. Congolese soldiers had long since forgotten that such privileges existed.

The Rwandan officers were amazed by everything they saw. Children eating mangoes and pineapples—rare and expensive fruits in Rwanda. Congo was rich, they said, but the people were poor. If they stayed here for ten years, the country would be as prosperous as Belgium.

Many ordinary Rwandan soldiers had been lured to Congo under false pretences, Mwansa discovered. Some thought they were on their way to Lubumbashi and had brought bottles with them to store diamonds. When they heard that Lubumbashi was 620 miles away they were shocked. Others asked for directions to the nearby gold mines, or thought they were already in Kinshasa because they'd seen a train for the first time in their lives.

There were both Hutu and Tutsi among the Rwandan soldiers, and Mwansa met one soldier who was half-and-half. Terrible things had happened in Rwanda, this soldier told him. The Hutu had massacred the Tutsi, but vice versa too—only they weren't allowed to talk about that in this country.

On the radio Mwansa heard that in neighboring Zambia a cease-fire had been signed by the warring parties, but in Kabalo it had no effect. The day after the arrival of the new battalion commander, Assani, no fewer than six MiGs flew over. The town emptied and Assani was forced to hide in the forest like everyone else. Mwansa looked optimistically into the sky. Now for the paratroopers, he thought, but nothing happened. One bomb hit a railroad car of palm oil, which burst into flames with a fantastic explosion. A thick cloud of yellowish smoke hung over the station for days.

*   *   *

Mutombo had been forced to leave two railroad wagons full of dried fish at Kabalo station when he fled into the bush with his family. Eight hundred sacks, worth $30,000—he'd brought the relevant documents with him. Those papers were all he owned in the world right now. His three children were hungry. His mother-in-law sat whimpering softly from morning to night; she'd received an ugly burn on her leg before they fled and his wife was using leaves to treat it. The leaves had turned into a green sludge and the flesh underneath was bubbling and fermenting.

All Mutombo could think about was his dried fish. He knew the wagon numbers by heart. The cargo had come from Kalemie and had been on its way to Kasai. In the small hut where he slept on a couple of dirty mats with his family and countless other refugees, he sat brooding every evening, hardly able to breathe. If the engine hadn't taken so long to get here, if the war hadn't started again, if the Rwandans hadn't advanced so quickly, if . . . And so on until he fell into a shallow, fitful sleep.

Mutombo had been an army captain under Mobutu, but in 1980 he'd decided to quit military life and become a businessman. He had peanuts loaded onto the train to Kalemie, where they were transferred to a boat for shipment across Lake Tanganyika to Uvira. On the return journey he carried salt and secondhand clothes. Sometimes he bought gold from local diggers and traveled to Burundi to sell it. He had contacts everywhere, and although he was no longer a soldier, everyone still called him captain.

After his umpteenth sleepless night, Mutombo decided to go and size up the situation in Kabalo. Near the station he came on a Congolese soldier he knew from the old days. "Captain Mutombo!" the soldier exclaimed in surprise. "What are you doing here? Come to join us?"

"No, no," he answered, looking around nervously. "I'm only here to see if my house is still standing." He said nothing about the dried fish, afraid of giving the soldiers ideas; his wagons might fall prey either to Kabila's bombs or to hungry rebels.

He walked on toward the station with the soldier — he was better off sticking with him, since there were soldiers everywhere. As soon as he spotted the freight train his heart started thumping. Some cars were burned out; others had had their locks forced. A jeep standing on a flatcar had just been hit and was still smoldering. Mutombo searched feverishly. He knew exactly where to find his own cars. They were still intact.

For weeks after that Mutombo hung around the station whenever he could. Sometimes he chatted with the stationmaster, Mwansa, who was watching over his rusty railroad supplies like a museum director and who held out little hope for the cargo of fish. Mutombo kept running into soldiers he'd known in the past, so he was able to move around Kabalo with increasing freedom. The Rwandans had antiaircraft guns, antitank grenades, artillery, machine guns, and mortars, he noticed, and they'd moved into the abandoned houses on the outskirts of town. The Congolese soldiers were farther away, in trenches.

One time Mutombo was caught out in an aerial bombardment at the station, but again his two cars survived. Bombing runs that weren't followed up with a ground offensive—what was Kabila playing at? Did he simply want to ensure that if he had nothing, the rebels would have nothing too?

In the evenings Mutombo returned to the bush. He and his wife had sold their clothes and were doing odd jobs for the villagers to earn enough to live on. The only thing he was unable to part with was his radio. The antenna was broken and the battery flap had come off, so he had to wrap a strip of cloth around it, but it still worked perfectly.

Mutombo relied on international broadcasters for news about how the war was going, since he couldn't pick up any Congolese channels, except for a private station run by a civil servant who'd fled to the government-held zone. His voice cracking with emotion, the official appealed to people in the east to poison the rivers so that the Rwandan occupiers would die of thirst. What about the local inhabitants? Didn't they need to drink?

No one said anything about the silent war in the interior, about his mother-in-law with her festering leg, the children with their swollen bellies, the babies dying of malaria. So Mutombo began writing a book, for his children, to make sure one day they'd know what had happened. He wrote on large sheets of paper and kept them in a grubby folder. His eyesight was failing. Fortunately his late father-in-law had left him a magnifying glass. He held it to one eye as he wrote, squeezing the other eye shut.

The bush around him was alive with rumors. His colleague Tip Top was so worried about the goods in his bricked-up cellar that he sent a couple of spies to investigate. The catastrophic news they brought back so shocked Tip Top that he died of a stroke the same night.

"That's nothing," said a teacher who shared Mutombo's hut. He'd joined Kabila's army, lured by the promise of $100 a month, but when the second war started there'd been no time to flee. He'd become a rebel against his will.

The Rwandans were fearless, the teacher said. They weren't like the Congolese, who were used to digging in. No, they fought standing up and lost many men as a result. They took revenge by locking civilians into their huts before setting them ablaze. The huts were only made of clay, they said. The survivors would just have to build new ones. Sometimes they shot someone dead on the road just because he couldn't answer a question they put to him, or refused to give them the goat he'd taken along when he ran from his home. He'd done the same himself. What else could he do? This was war. The Rwandans said the Congolese didn't know what they were fighting for. "Fools," they sneered. "You passed up Kabila's hundred dollars to get zero dollars from us." They were right about that: the Congolese sometimes fought for three days without eating. That was why he'd run off as soon as he grew tired of the killing.

The teacher was in awe not only of the Rwandan government army but of its enemy the Interahamwe as well. They fired with a gun in each hand, he said, and could transform themselves into bats: they suddenly popped up behind you, or broke your weapon in half from a distance.

Mutombo wrote everything down and also committed his own opinions to paper, because although he'd become a businessman he still had the eye of a soldier. The rebels had headed for the mining towns of Lubumbashi and Mbuji-Mayi in such haste that they'd bypassed pockets of resistance in the interior. Thousands of soldiers were at the front line in Kabalo, but the country behind them wasn't by any means under their control.

In the mountains, forests, and wildlife reserves of the east everything was bubbling and fermenting, just like under the green leaves on his mother-in-law's leg. Right in the middle of rebel territory a group of Interahamwe had set up camp around a gold mine. Elsewhere a battalion of soldiers had refused to surrender and had become Mai Mai. If Kabila's soldiers didn't want to fight then they would, they said, from the inside out.

In a village north of Kabalo the rebels had stolen some goats. A *maman* who protested was shot dead. In desperation the population turned to the Mai Mai for protection and soon there were Mai Mai everywhere. They claimed the Rwandans wanted to make slaves of the Congolese. That struck a chord with the fishermen, who were unable to take their boats out because of the new war with *commerçants* and smugglers, who depended on the trains running, and with village chiefs, who were forced to watch their ancestors' land being desecrated. Even the pygmies, who used fetishes to survive in the forest, sided with the Mai Mai.

The Mai Mai had *dawa,* traditional medicine, so bullets couldn't touch them. They relied heavily on supernatural powers, since they had no communications equipment — when they were attacked they sometimes had to bicycle dozens of miles to call up reinforcements. They refused to let anyone go into Kabalo to buy salt, sugar, or soap. People traveling back and forth were treated as spies. The Mai Mai sprinkled everything they ate with a liquid they carried in plastic bottles. It was their *dawa* against poisoning by potential enemies, they said, but the story went that the bottles contained a salt solution for seasoning their meals.

The Rwandans in Kongolo set out in pursuit of a fugitive chief who was suspected of joining the Mai Mai. One of his followers had been arrested and — under torture — revealed that the chief was hiding in neighboring Tubundu. The soldiers sent a letter to the village saying they'd shortly be conducting a census and everyone was expected to be home. Refugees passing through Tubundu said it was a trick, that the Rwandans were coming to kill them. Some villagers hid in the bush.

The next Sunday morning those who'd stayed behind went to mass. There were different versions of what happened next and Mutombo felt obliged to write each one down. The villagers said that when they got back to Tubundu they found Tutsi soldiers there, who asked them where the fugitive chief was hiding. They told them he'd left a long time ago. The soldiers said that on their way to Tubundu they'd encountered resistance, which meant their chief was still in the village and the inhabitants were protecting him.

There were twenty-five soldiers, according to the people who managed to escape. They forced the villagers to line up, women and children on one side, men on the other. The men were roped together.

They arrived at eleven o'clock and the killing started at twelve. By three they were done. They set fire to all the huts as they left. Then there was silence. The villagers who'd run away stayed in the bush until morning. On their way back to the village they saw four bodies. In the village square they found the rest.

The local Red Cross came to bury the corpses. A priest blessed the ground to placate the evil spirits that would otherwise haunt the village, but the survivors no longer wanted to live in Tubundu. Two miles away they built twelve huts and settled there with the smoke-ridden belongings they'd salvaged from the fires. They made a list of the 135 villagers who'd been killed, noting their names and ages. Then they tried to remember the names of the people passing through who had been in Tubundu that Sunday. Somewhere along the line they lost count.

No one could name the men who'd carried out the massacre. The survivors talked of a soldier called Chinja Chinja, Cut Cut, but that was probably only a reference to the many throats he'd slit.

The story of the massacre in Tubundu surfaced repeatedly in one form or another in the months that followed. Mutombo heard about two boys forced to carry luggage for the Rwandans who had run off leaving the bags behind unattended. The infuriated soldiers had gone back to the village to find them. The boys took a roundabout route home and when they got there they found not a soul left alive. Only when Mutombo heard that the village in question was called Tubundu did he realize they were talking about the same massacre.

But the Mai Mai misbehaved too. Gervais—who called himself *mufuma,* the invisible, or *docta,* doctor, and who signed his letters King of the Sorcerers—knew all about fetishes because he'd once been a gold digger. He'd become a Mai Mai for want of better employment.

Some stories about Gervais were put about by his own men to convince people he'd stop at nothing, whereas others were so persistent and served up with so many salient details that Mutombo felt they must be true.

When Gervais didn't have enough goat meat to feed his men, he mixed it with human flesh. This produced a change in his followers. They forgot what compassion was and no longer respected anyone—they even hit their own mothers.

Gervais heard that Rwandan soldiers on the way to Kongolo had stopped in a village where a merchant of Arab origin had served them hard liquor, so he sent his men after him. The *commerçant* fled, but Gervais's men caught up. He begged them to spare him and promised to reward them with gold, but they cut his throat, buried his head, and carried the rest of his body back to their camp. That evening they roasted him. Gervais ate a leg; the others consumed the rest. The *commerçant* had been plump and light-skinned. It was just like pork, they said later—it tasted delicious.

Gervais set up his headquarters in the bar the *commerçant* had owned. He hung one of his enemy's arms from the straw lean-to roof to cure. He wore a military uniform and laughed when people asked if he was afraid of the Rwandans. The enemy couldn't do anything to him, he said. He could transform rocks into rocket-launchers. He only had to say the name of a village thirty miles away and he'd be there in an instant.

The rebels had used young village boys as carriers to get their food and munitions to Kongolo, Gervais heard. On arrival each carrier had been given one of the bicycles the Rwandans had found at the station depot. One boy had returned to the village. Gervais's men pointed out where he lived.

Mutombo didn't know what to make of what he heard next, but the man who told him insisted it was true. The news that the carrier would be tried in public was murmured through the village. The Mai Mai broke his legs and carried him to Gervais's headquarters, followed by his anguished father, his brother, and a crowd of onlookers.

The boy was laid on a reed platform in front of the house. His lips were cut off, then his penis, hands, feet, and head. His heart was removed from his chest. This all happened right in front of his father and brother, while spectators clapped their hands and a choir from the next village danced and sang.

They were still at it when they heard gunfire in the distance. The Rwandans! In no time the crowd vanished. Gervais and his men switched their uniforms for civilian clothing and fled so fast that they left their guns behind. Some mothers even forgot their babies.

It was an attack led by the new battalion commander, Mutombo learned afterward, not a Rwandan but a Munyamulenge who was determined to finish the Mai Mai off.

The younger brother of the dead boy died of a heart attack in the bush a few days later. The mutilated corpse was left lying on the reed platform. The wind blew through it in the dry season; the sun desiccated it. When the family returned they found the remains and arranged a burial.

Gervais had little credit with the villagers after that. He'd made the Rwandans come back, they said. He couldn't be a real Mai Mai.

While Mutombo was writing all these stories down, the people around him were becoming increasingly emaciated. They hardly dared move, afraid the Mai Mai in the interior or the Rwandans in town would accuse them of spying. Nothing was moving these days, except for the air, and the birds.

Eight hundred Interahamwe soldiers fleeing the rebel army arrived in the village where Mutombo and his family were staying. The Rwandans were advancing, they said — they killed people and cut them to pieces, they were famous for it; everyone had better go along with the soldiers to the government side.

Mutombo looked at his three children, who were starting to look like little old men as the months went by, and at his wife, who spoke less and less these days, and then at the wriggling maggots in his mother-in-law's leg. He decided it was time to leave.

The next morning a long caravan of men, women, and children set off with a battalion of Interahamwe on the journey to government-held territory. Mutombo didn't have much luggage: a bandaged radio, a folder with his account of the war — plus of course the documentation for his 800 sacks of dried fish.

❊   ❊   ❊

On the plane to Kabalo, Assani felt his stomach tighten. He was used to operating in the shadows; from now on he'd be uncomfortably visible. Whatever had happened to the time he was responsible for only eight soldiers? As battalion commander he'd have more than 1,000 men under his command.

They were approaching Kabalo airfield, a meadow with a grimy airport building that you could see clean through, since a bunch of barbarians had made off with the roof, doors, and windows. These people — they were capable of demolishing their own bridges to make cooking pans. He grinned at Boni, who'd been watching him throughout the flight. Boni knew how he felt.

That evening they were swallowed up by the electricity-free darkness of the interior, the intense silence broken only by the hum of mosquitoes—until the heavy engines of an Antonov ripped through the soundless air, followed by the rattle of antiaircraft fire and the whine of falling bombs. Not far away, near the railroad track, something burst into flames. He stared at the brilliant, idiotic glow lighting up the night sky. A sour smell filled his nostrils.

Many Congolese commanders were incapable of separating work and leisure—they wanted to make themselves comfortable wherever they were. When they moved from one place to another they caused all kinds of fuss. First they installed themselves with full ceremony, choosing a woman to cook and wash for them; then they began to receive people and the palavering* could begin. Every evening there were drinking sessions, and of course they couldn't possibly sleep without women.

Assani didn't like all those rituals. Before long you found yourself not wanting to engage the enemy because the *maman* you'd employed hadn't finished cooking. A leader should set an example. If he slept late he couldn't expect his soldiers to be disciplined. Assani never went looking for a woman at the front. Where would he find one? Women in the interior were dirty. And how could he punish a soldier for sleeping with women if he did so himself?

He set up his headquarters under a mango tree at the edge of Kabalo. His *kadogos* built a hut for him with a loophole to shoot through. He slept on a thin mattress, under a blanket and a mosquito net. There was nothing else he needed. He wore the uniform Charles had sent him after he fled Kinshasa. He wasn't superstitious, but he had the feeling it protected him.

The first few weeks he moved along the front line visiting his men, on foot, in a jeep, or in a pirogue. He rarely slept two nights at the same place. In some areas the enemy was so close that the soldiers bathed on opposite banks of the same river in the morning; by afternoon they'd be trying to kill each other again.

In Lusaka, the Zambian capital, a cease-fire had recently been signed. It was supposed to lead to the withdrawal of foreign troops and to a dialogue between the warring Congolese parties, but the accords had already been violated on innumerable occasions. It was good to test the enemy's strength from time to time, to find out where his weaknesses lay.

Assani didn't wait for orders from higher up before going on the offensive or responding to provocation. He didn't want to become like Dallaire, the Canadian UN general who kept waiting for decisions to be made in New York during the genocide. After the war he'd gone crazy with remorse.

Before combat everyone was afraid. Assani too felt as if a weight were pressing in on his chest. But as soon as the first shots were fired you got into the mood and the shooting sounded like the rumble of tom-toms—you only had to follow the rhythm. One soldier might feel afraid, another angry with the enemy, a third happy, even euphoric. The last thing you wanted was a homogeneous group, with everyone either terrified or reckless — that would be certain to end in catastrophe.

Boni was seventeen now and no longer as docile as he used to be. On the third day of the battle the enemy began to tire and Assani said to him, "You take over." Boni looked at him doubtfully. "Didn't you hear what I said? I'll stick around; no need to be afraid." A little later he heard Boni shouting orders in a voice indistinguishable from his own. A man is a parrot, he thought. But it also occurred to him that Boni was growing up. He'd been a bodyguard long enough. It would be good for him to have a different job soon.

Sometimes they took prisoners, Congolese as well as Zimbabweans fighting for Kabila. Enemy morale was extremely low, they discovered during interrogations. If they chose they could push right on to Lubumbashi, but this was a political war. The Lusaka cease-fire agreement had been signed under the auspices of the UN Security Council. The great powers had decided there would be no real winners or losers.

Assani's men brought him a female Hutu soldier they'd captured. After interrogation they wanted to kill her, but Assani decided to spare her and have her join his battalion. She turned out to be pregnant, so before long they had a baby with them at the front.

Assani had developed a habit of making notes: about the belligerence of some peoples and the indolence of others; about the palm oil press a chief in a village not far from Kabalo had invented; about the hut another chief had built near the entrance to his plot of land—there were two clay lions in it, one big and one small, with ferocious faces and outstretched front paws, and every month the chief slaughtered chickens inside so that the lions would protect him.

During a trip on a pirogue a *kaɗogo* dropped Assani's notebook into the water. The boy fished it out and instead of drying it in the sun he hid it, afraid Assani would see what had happened. By the time he found out, the whole book was soaked and there was nothing he could do but throw it away.

One afternoon Assani was sitting resting in front of his tent with one of his *kaɗogos*. A few tents farther on a boy was cleaning his gun with the barrel pointing toward him. "What are you doing for God's sake!" Assani shouted, and flew at him. As he did so he heard a tremendous bang behind his back. Where he'd just been sitting a mortar bomb had blasted a crater in the ground. Next to it lay his *kaɗogo*, dead.

When Assani was in Kabalo he made daily tours of inspection in his jeep to see that his men had enough to eat. His predecessor had never bothered about that; sometimes he hadn't shown up for weeks on end, so it was only natural that his soldiers went out robbing and stealing.

Assani always traveled at different times and tried to change his route every day, knowing the Zimbabweans were on the lookout for him, but gradually he fell into a routine and became less watchful. One afternoon he was driving

from one army post to the next along a path overgrown with
elephant grass. Suddenly he felt a huge blast and it was as
if a giant's hand picked him up, vehicle and all.

When he came to he was lying at the side of the road
with gunfire all around. He crawled to his jeep. They'd driven
over a mine. Three soldiers were lying dead in the grass, but
the others managed to fight off the enemy. Assani scrambled
to his feet and examined himself. He found nothing, not a
scratch.

After assessing the damage he got out his camera and
asked a *kadogo* to photograph him. There he was, next to the
overturned jeep at the roadside, a tall, skinny soldier in dusty
trousers and a camouflage T-shirt, with sunken eyes in a
gray, ghostly face.

That evening he went looking for a satellite phone at
Rwandan headquarters in Kabalo and called Aimée. His voice
sounded thin and long silences fell. "Why don't you say something?" she asked. "I've got nothing to say," he told her. "I
just wanted to hear your voice."

The Rwandans had been hard on the Katangese at first,
associating them with Kabila, but since the emergence of the
Mai Mai they'd realized they should try to win over the local
population. They were too far from home to survive in hostile surroundings. During an attack they'd seized a walkie-
talkie, so now they could listen in on the enemy's frequency.
They taught men to dig trenches behind their houses and
warned them when planes took off from the government-
held town of Kamina to bomb Kabalo.

They tried to establish a new civil administration in the areas they controlled and called on refugees to return to their villages. A deserted village was dangerous; the enemy might move in. But some people had no clothes and didn't dare leave the bush. Most local businessmen had fled, so the Rwandans persuaded the Shi, a trading people from eastern Congo, to come to the interior. The Rwandans bought maize and beans from the villagers, who in turn bought pagnes, secondhand clothes, sugar, salt, and batteries from the Shi.

The pump trolley traveling back and forth along the railroad between Nyunzu, Kabalo, and Kongolo was showing signs of serious wear and tear. The Congolese commander, Benz, a technical genius, proposed making a train by installing a truck engine in an open wagon. All he needed was a bogie—a swiveling undercarriage with wheels and axles. He knew where to find one, in Niemba, but it weighed three tons and Niemba was in the middle of an area controlled by Interahamwe.

The Rwandans sent the stationmaster Mwansa to Niemba, accompanied by over 100 soldiers. "What do I get in return?" Mwansa asked. "When we reach Lubumbashi, we won't forget you," said the Rwandans, but that wasn't enough for Mwansa, so they allocated him a Rwandan officer's monthly ration: beans, rice, salt, oil, washing powder, and cigarettes. "If Mwansa doesn't survive this operation," the Rwandan commander said to his soldiers, "none of you need bother coming back." On their first attempt they ran into an ambush and Mwansa was wounded, but the second time they managed to drive out the Interahamwe and roll the bogie down the track to Kabalo.

Children must go back to school, the Rwandans said. When their parents protested that they didn't have any money, a Rwandan commander paid the school fees for 500 pupils. Another gave money for seed so that a group of women could start cultivating the land again.

Encouraged by these reports, Mutombo decided to leave the village in government-held territory where he was living with his family and return to Kabalo. He found his two railroad cars of dried fish completely burned out. Commander Satellite asked him to join the rebel army but Mutombo refused and instead became the trainer of his soccer team. There were now eight teams in Kabalo—every self-respecting Rwandan commander had one.

Even Manono, Kabila's native region, came back to life. There were tinstone and coltan over there, the Rwandans told the Shi, who got on a plane with their wares and put the people of Manono to work. First they had the roofs taken off all the villas belonging to the former tin company to make pans for mining. Then whole families went into the mines. The children dug, the women carried, the men sieved. The Shi paid for the minerals and loaded them onto planes bound for Bukavu or Kigali.

Assani was promoted to brigade commander and made longer and longer tours of inspection of the front lines. He got to know his country. The complexity of it! During the first war he'd had no idea what his own country was like. No one can ever take this knowledge away from me, he sometimes thought euphorically. At other times, walking in

the pouring rain from one village to the next without knowing where he would sleep, he thought of the district known
as Coltan City on the edge of Kigali that was built with the
money from Congolese minerals. High walls protected the
villas from inquisitive stares; gates whooshed open as luxury
jeeps with tinted windows drove up. That was where the
Rwandan elite lived, keeping the war going while staying
out of harm's way.

Meanwhile the Congolese were living in terrible pov-
erty. People walked through the bush with only leaves to
cover them. And in the midst of all this the Mai Mai had
taken root. They were village soldiers, just like Assani's
Banyamulenge brothers who'd gone back to the high plains.
They had no notion of a Congolese state; they regarded
even the inhabitants of a neighboring village as strangers.
The government camp provided them with weapons and
food at secret airstrips. They had no idea what the Mai Mai
did with the supplies, since they had no control over them
and knew nothing of the traditions that were dragging
them back into old times, setting up little kingdoms built
on hatred. Didn't Kabila realize that the Mai Mai would
be the first to turn against him in a reunited Congo?

After his promotion Assani transferred his headquarters
from Kabalo to Kongolo, higher up the Congo River. There
had once been a Greek community, to judge by the facades
of the merchants' houses in the main street. He moved
into a house belonging to the former cotton company and
stuck cardboard over the windows. It was right behind the

residence of chief Kyenge, who had been appointed local administrator by the Rwandans.

Kyenge was a shrewd businessman who was glad to see life starting up around him again. He'd heard that the Rwandans were interested in antiques and along with a few friends he bought a much sought-after artwork and sold it at a considerable profit. Kyenge owned the exploitation rights for a large forest outside Kongolo. That's a multi-million business, a Rwandan commander said—he could easily find an investor for it in Rwanda.

Kyenge was guarded night and day in case of an attack by the Mai Mai. When Assani was in Kongolo he visited Kyenge every evening, along with a Rwandan colleague. "You're a traditional chief," said Assani. "Your people are everywhere; they can move around freely. If you don't want the Mai Mai to attack Kongolo you should send your men across the Congo River to find out where they are."

So Kyenge sent third-class traders in torn clothes and worn-out shoes across the river with a little soap or salt, or jerricans of palm wine. If one of his informants reported that a group of Mai Mai had arrived in a village, the rebels would stalk through the scrub until they had them surrounded. By the time the Mai Mai were ready to attack, they'd be blocked on all sides.

Assani sometimes felt sorry for the Mai Mai. They'd been tricked by their leaders. They approached the rebel army singing and laughing, clapping their hands, their bodies festooned with feathers, amulets, and plastic bottles of *dawa*, convinced bullets couldn't touch them. They went down like flies. The survivors were brought to Kongolo where, after a dose of reeducation, they were incorporated into the rebel army.

"What kind of a man are you out there?" Aimée once asked him on the phone.

"Lonely and vicious," Assani said. "I try not to think."

Kyenge's friend Vautour had once run a successful bar near the station in Kongolo. The sign reading "Au Petit Repos Chez Vieux Vautour" had faded in the sun, but Vautour declined the Rwandans' proposal to set up a small business selling palm oil, afraid of going down in history as a collaborator. All the other local traders followed his example. So the Shi came and took their place.

Vautour discovered that Assani liked Fanta and sometimes brought him a bottle. Assani was a fussy eater. The pungent smell of the bush meat people ate here made him feel sick. Part of him was still a baby, used to drinking milk, but in Kongolo they'd never even heard of milk powder. Those little bottles of soft drink were a godsend. Where Vautour got them was a mystery, but he always managed to lay his hands on Fanta.

Despite his dire financial straits, Vautour lived like a king on his plot of land, with his three wives and eighteen children. He always dressed in neatly pressed trousers with a shirt and tie, a cream-colored cap on his head, his clever eyes looking out searchingly from beneath its shade. Vautour was the head of the Kongolo notables, whose palavers under the straw lean-to roof in his yard lasted for hours.

At meetings with the military, Vautour dominated the conversation. One time, on behalf of the town's leading citizens, he complained about the many Mai Mai who were dying on the far side of the Congo River. They were only children, he said. They . . . "Oh?" the Rwandan commander interrupted him curtly. "You claim we kill your children? Show us where." The man glared so fiercely that Vautour could feel his heart thumping in his throat. At that very moment a Rwandan soldier barged in, saying he'd lost several men on the other side of the river. He was furious. "Just you wait," he shouted. "I'll kill the lot of you. You haven't seen anything yet. I'll show you how we kill." Vautour sat down. He had nothing to add. The soldier had said it all.

Kyenge and Vautour knew Commander Assani had been born in Congo, but he worked so closely with the Rwandans that they regarded him as one of them—except that no one was there to meet him when he arrived at the airfield in Kongolo or came from Kabalo by pump trolley. He was the highest ranking Congolese commander in the region, but you could watch him walk from the station past Vautour's old bar to the main street, followed by two *kadogos*, and around the corner near Kyenge's house. The whole of Kongolo could see that Commander Assani had arrived, and the Rwandans, who had three jeeps, hadn't come to pick him up.

"What do you think?" Assani once asked Kyenge. "Would I be allowed to marry a girl here?"

"Of course," he answered. "Why not?"

"How many cows would it cost me?"

Kyenge laughed. "No cows. A few goats would do."

Assani didn't believe him and later asked Vautour the same question. "Do you really mean that?" he pressed him. "You people wouldn't object if I took one of your children to be my wife?"

One evening Kyenge and Vautour paid him a visit and found him sitting at the table with his head in his hands, almost in tears. He must have argued with someone earlier in the day, although he didn't say who or about what. "I'm a Munyamulenge," he said. "What's going to happen to me after the war? The Rwandans and the Congolese both want me dead. Everyone hates us. The best thing I can do is go to the front and die there."

❊ ❊ ❊

When he got back from Kabalo, Assani drove through Goma like a zombie, cautiously, as if he were still in the interior with danger lurking around every bend.

He was overwhelmed by the noise of the city. Cars, mopeds, and big wooden scooters squeezed through the narrow streets. A moped chugged past, sighing under the weight of three adult passengers. The streets lined with little shops teemed with people. Why were they screeching like that? Didn't they ever calm down? Every time he stopped, boys would race over to him. "Cigarettes, *afande*, cigarettes!"

He was startled by the lights that popped on everywhere as it began to get dark. On one street corner a party was under way. Cars were double-parked, music boomed from a house, guests thronged at the door. He drove slowly past. "See that?" he said to Boni. "The people of Goma eat meat."

Leaders of the rebel movement were building houses, he noticed, and driving big cars, while the soldiers at the front line went hungry because less than a third of the promised rations ever reached their destination. That was something the Rwandans were scrupulous about, at least: their soldiers always received supplies on time.

One afternoon he stopped at a little shop near his house and bought dried milk, bread, jam, washing powder, and vitamins. He was deathly tired; he felt as if he hadn't slept for ten years. It was time for another attack of his *maladie imaginaire*.

At home he ordered Boni not to let anyone in. He went to his bedroom, turned on the television, and laid his pistol under his pillow, his walkie-talkie, remote control, and cell phone next to it. Other soldiers had lived in this house before him and they'd tortured people in the bedroom — how else could you explain those big pale stains on the walls? Aimée had walked into the room once and said in disgust, "What happened here?" "Not what you think," he said soothingly. "That was done by the previous occupants." She didn't believe him, so he felt forced to add, "I have one rule: I only kill people in battle. I won't hurt an unarmed man. Or I'll hand him over to someone else."

At the front he'd lived on automatic pilot, but since his arrival in Goma his brain had been churning constantly. He was angry with everyone. This wasn't a life — this was merely survival. He'd been risking his hide every day while here they spent all their time partying!

He'd been so happy to get leave, but now he could think only about what it was like back there: the mosquitoes that swarmed around his hut in Kabalo with their miserable humming; the Mai Mai advancing toward him singing, clapping their hands, laughing; the Rwandan commander who'd whispered, "Watch out—they may not have guns but poisoned arrows are just as deadly." The roar of MiGs and Antonovs still rang in his ears.

He was fighting Kabila, but there was no one to replace him. They were a great amorphous mass, advancing but directionless. He was a prisoner, a man who'd been swimming against the tide from the minute he was born.

He thought of the quartz alarm clock a Greek shopkeeper had given him long ago. It was set in a plastic wreath of flowers and red birds. He'd had to leave it behind when he fled Kinshasa, along with the stereo installation with the little doors, the most beautiful piece of furniture he'd ever possessed.

He was stuck in a deep pit and no one could pull him out. His friends got on his nerves within minutes. They wanted to take him out on the town, but what did he want with the noisy bars of Goma? He didn't drink and he didn't like the things people said when they'd been drinking.

The station TV5 screened a documentary about Kosovo. In the bush he'd followed the conflict on the radio, but now he saw them, the Albanians. They'd come back to find their houses looted and burned and had started looting and burning Serbian houses in revenge. If he were an Albanian, he'd murder Serbs, because they believed Albanians had no right to exist.

Halfway through the program the television went dead. The yellow lightbulb in the ceiling flickered. *This isn't a country; this is a forest.* He'd been so looking forward to falling asleep to music! He picked up his cell phone and called the man in charge at the electricity company.

But when the husky sound of Brenda's voice poured into the room later that evening and crept up the walls with their pale, washed-out bloodstains, he was so overwhelmed by the memory of his dead friend dancing that he reached for the remote control and turned the music off.

He got up and woke Boni. "Come on," he said. "It's Saturday. We're going to see how people in Goma party." At an intersection in the city center a soldier was harassing three youngsters. Assani stopped and looked out of his open window. He was in civilian clothes, but his imperious gaze made the drunken soldier stumble toward him as if hypnotized, gabbling excuses. The three boys stood at the side of the road, relieved, ready to tell their story. Assani said nothing. He listened to the soldier's confused explanation, then raised his finger sternly and drove on. "This country is bound to disappear," he said to Boni. "Mark my words. It'll be just like Yugoslavia."

He was hungry. He passed the garden of Restaurant VIP and walked down a side path to the indoor section, where he settled down at a table in a corner.

In the middle of the restaurant sat a particularly noisy group of diners. He knew one of the men—he'd once run a

travel agency and was now responsible for the rebel movement's department of transportation and public works. The
man was with some friends and three heavily made-up
women, among them a well-known *commerçante* who was
doing most of the talking.

The man's phone kept ringing and he answered it ea-
gerly and loudly, happy to show his friends how important
he was. So the whole restaurant heard that his assistant had
been caught with his hands in the till and arrested. The *commerçante* raised her glass and shouted "Happy New Year!"
—at which the whole table burst out laughing. It was a
shameful display. To think that civil servants in Goma hadn't
been paid for ages! Two rebellions on, Assani thought in disgust, and this country's still producing the same kind of politicians as in Mobutu's day.

It was busy at the disco Chez Nono, where Christmas
lights hung in the trees all year round. He slipped past the
people standing outside without brushing against anyone.
On the dance floor he saw a man he knew, who waved and
started to come over, but Assani pretended he hadn't noticed, turned around, and disappeared.

In the parking lot stood a tall, slim woman he'd driven
past earlier. Women in Goma seemed to know when a soldier had just returned from the front. She slowly walked
over to him. Boni watched from a distance, then opened the
car door and got in the back.

❊   ❊   ❊

As soon as he felt better he drove to Kigali to visit Aimée.
On the way he picked up a hitchhiker. He didn't look around

when the man got out. When he arrived in Kigali he discovered that the man had gone off with his bag of photo albums and notebooks. The Rwandans were right when they said the Banyamulenge were backward. He was still a naive villager, unprepared for the hazards of the city.

With Aimée he was safe. The relationship she'd had in Kinshasa was over. The day would come when she'd love him. He wasn't in any hurry—they had all the time in the world. They sat talking for hours in the small living room of the house she'd moved into with a girlfriend, where crocheted mats lay on the coffee table and over the backs of the chairs, just as in her parents' house in Lubumbashi.

One afternoon they went for a drive. Along the way Aimée wanted to call on an aunt she hadn't seen for some time. He refused to go inside with her and stayed in the car. When he felt the visit had gone on long enough he leaned on the horn and kept leaning. Annoyed, Aimée came out. Assani went on honking away, even though he could see she was coming.

"Have you gone crazy? What will my aunt think?" Aimée said as she got in. Assani merely grunted, but by the time they drove into Kigali he'd admitted that he'd misbehaved.

Aimée's family spent a year in the detention camp just outside Lubumbashi, then they were given asylum in the United States and put on a plane. Assani was afraid Aimée would want to follow them there one day and no matter how close they'd become he remained on his guard. She might be able to befuddle him somehow.

Aimée was very attached to her family. She wanted him to call her mother, to get to know her aunt, to go with her to visit her uncle, to . . . What did all those people have to do with the two of them? Families paralyzed you; everyone clung to everyone else and kept asking each other for advice. He was against that sort of dependence — it made you lazy.

On top of that Aimée was religious, another thing he objected to. Religion was alienating — he'd often noticed that with believers. God took care of everything; they surrendered themselves to him completely and were no longer in charge of their own lives. He couldn't accept that kind of submission.

Even though he sometimes stayed with her until deep into the night, they didn't sleep together. "I can do that with other women," he said. "I don't need you for that."

He'd barely had time to recuperate when he had to return to the bush. They were messing things up without him. His replacement wasn't taking proper care of his men and they'd made off with all the chickens for miles around.

He stored a few belongings at Aimée's place, in case he never came back. She heard nothing from him for weeks. No one knew she existed; no one would inform her if he was killed. With the help of a Rwandan soldier in Kongolo she finally managed to get through to him.

"I was worried," she said. "I thought . . ." "Thought what?" he asked. ". . . That something had happened to you." He shut off the call right away. It was bad luck to talk like that, he told her later.

The next time he got leave he was on his way to Kigali when a Rwandan officer in Goma phoned. "Where are you?" "I'm about to drive into Kigali." "Turn around immediately." "But I'm on leave," Assani protested. "I've got permission to leave Goma." There was an irritated silence at the other end of the line. "I expect you here in two hours," the officer said drily.

He obstinately drove on and told Aimée what had happened. "What do they want with me? Are they going to arrest me or something?"

"Haven't you heard?"

"What?"

She looked at him in disbelief. "Your friends in Kigali know what's going on and you haven't heard anything? It seems you've been promoted."

Two phone calls later he knew he'd been appointed the rebel army's chief of military operations. Aimée thought he'd be pleased, but he flopped into a chair and held his face in his hands. "This will be the death of me."

"What do you mean?"

"Up to now I was a soldier. At the front I sometimes disobeyed my superiors, didn't always follow orders. But this is a political function. From now on they'll really be keeping an eye on me." He searched feverishly for further reasons why this was bad news. "The others will be jealous of me. Can you imagine how many people want that job? It'll only bring me more enemies."

Suddenly he fell silent, as if something else had occurred to him. "How come I knew nothing about this? If everybody knows something I don't know, what else can they plot against me?"

KINSHASA
1998

The first few weeks were the worst; after that Mwepu got used to prison life. When they put him in solitary he had another difficult few days, but he got over that too. They let him have a Bible and he read all the books he could lay his hands on, mostly novels, although later he couldn't remember the names of the authors or even what they'd been about.

No one had told him why he was in prison, although it wasn't hard to guess. He'd seen the clash between Kabila and the Rwandans coming. The Rwandans knew that Kabila wanted to build a strong army and that he'd happily call on his enemies to help him if necessary. The only way they could legitimize their presence in Congo was by keeping the Congolese Tutsi in a state of uncertainty, ensuring they'd rally to the Rwandans' side if a new war broke out.

As soon as Mwepu caught on to this, he started doing everything he could to make the Congolese Tutsi feel secure, so they wouldn't start plotting as everyone feared. He knew that the day people like Assani started to feel truly Congolese would be a difficult day for the Rwandans—they'd be punished for their arrogance.

But Mwepu's Katangese brothers lumped all the Tutsi together. They couldn't imagine the Banyamulenge as allies and regarded anyone on good terms with the Tutsi as a traitor. So Mwepu, who'd done everything he could to prevent war, was accused of collaborating with the enemy.

After nine months Mzee Kabila summoned him. "I could have had you killed," he said. "But you're lucky; the God you pray to in your cell has spared you." Mzee wanted to know one thing. The decision to expel the Rwandans from the country had been made at a private meeting. Why had Mwepu let James Kabarebe in on it? Because he was on the Congolese side or because he supported the Rwandans?

"*Afande,*" said Mwepu, "there never used to be any Rwandans in the army. I worked with them because you brought them with you." They took him back to prison, but some time later he was freed.

For the first few months he stayed home; then Kabila ordered him to resume his work as presiding judge at the military court. One of his first assignments was to fetch Commander Masasu, who'd been amnestied by Kabila, from a prison outside Lubumbashi.

Masasu was now thirty. Physically he'd been seriously weakened by two and a half years in jail, as Mwepu saw when he shuffled toward him along the damp prison corridor, but mentally he'd held up well: he still had the proud, detached look he'd worn during his trial. That look disturbed

Mwepu. Masasu was still popular with the *kadogos* from the east he'd recruited years ago. It had given him strength in prison, but now he was free it could only bring him problems. Since the outbreak of the second war, all soldiers from the east were regarded with suspicion in Kinshasa.

On the plane Mwepu spoke to him in a fatherly manner, telling him the Katangese had strengthened their position while he was away and the climate in the capital would be far from favorable to him. Masasu looked out of the window—he was barely listening. Finally Mwepu said, "I just hope you make sure they don't put you on a plane to Lubumbashi again."

"What d'you mean?" asked Masasu distractedly.

"That'll be the end. There'll be nothing more I can do for you."

Masasu seemed not to understand. A few days later Mwepu visited Masasu's father and asked him to keep "the little one" in check.

Masasu was offered a post as deputy minister for internal affairs, but he declined. He wanted to go back to being a security adviser. Rumors were going around that people were calling him "general of the *kadogos*" and that he was convening secret meetings to plot the fall of Kabila.

One day he called Mwepu. "I need an audience with Mzee Kabila," he said peremptorily. "The soldiers from the east are disaffected; if he doesn't do something to improve their conditions I won't be responsible for the consequences."

Mwepu passed on his request to Joseph Kabila. Early in the first war Mzee had entrusted his son's military education to Masasu and they were still friends. "There's nothing

I can do," Joseph said apologetically. "Mzee's furious with
me because I gave Masasu a car and some money—he says
he's using them to prepare a coup against him."

Kabila's aide-de-camp let them know Mzee was prepared to receive Masasu, but he proposed the three of them
should talk first. Mwepu picked Masasu up at his house and
took him to his office, where the aide joined them. He asked
Masasu why he'd refused the job of deputy minister and how
he thought the war in Congo should be resolved. Masasu
looked at him as if he were made of thin air. "I only speak
about affairs of state with *papa* Kabila himself," he answered.

The atmosphere was tense and the aide-de-camp ordered Mwepu to keep Masasu there until the next morning. Mwepu sent out for food and that night they both slept
at his office. The tide turned against him and by morning
Masasu realized he'd walked into a trap. He asked to see
his wife, gave her all the money he had in his pockets,
hugged her and told her to take good care of the children—
at that point he started to cry.

Along with several officers and civilians from the east,
Masasu was put on a plane to Lubumbashi. Mwepu attempted to intervene even then, but was told he wouldn't
be presiding over Masasu's trial this time. The detainees
were tried in a village near the Katangese town of Pweto
and executed the same day.

Human rights organizations got wind of what had happened and before long the news was broadcast on the radio.
No one was spared, not even Mwepu, who was said to have
lured Masasu out of his house on false pretences and handed
him over to his executioners. It was Mwepu who had to

convey the sad news to Masasu's family. Since his own imprisonment it had become harder than ever to refuse to run errands like that.

The ship was drifting toward an iceberg — Mwepu could see the peak sticking out of the water in the distance, but none of the other Katangese wanted to look. They were partying, delighted to have eliminated another opponent.

THE EAST
2001

The village where Masasu was executed lay near the front line, so it wasn't long before word reached Assani. The radio said that Mwepu had picked up Commander Masasu at his house. So his friend was still alive, he was out of jail, and he'd immediately been sent to do a dirty job for Kabila. During the trial in Lubumbashi, Mwepu had done all he could to save Masasu's life. Masasu trusted him; he'd gone with him suspecting nothing. That was how it went with this kind of work: sooner or later you had to do things you didn't agree with. You were drawn farther and farther into the tunnel of evil — until you turned your best friend over to his executioner.

Joseph Kabila was said to have been present at the execution. Assani saw the hand of old Kabila in that too. Mzee knew that Joseph and Masasu were fond of each other; he wanted to show his son that friendship meant nothing in politics. He'd drawn Joseph into the tunnel along with everyone else.

Didn't Kabila realize he'd signed his own death warrant on the day of Masasu's execution? Did he really think he could kill Masasu without provoking an uprising among his *kadogos*? They'd left their families in the east to follow Masasu. He'd become their father, their brother—they would see his death as a threat to them all.

Barely two months later, Assani was driving from Uvira to Bukavu when he heard on the car radio that a bodyguard from the east had made an attempt on Kabila's life. He was so excited he had to park his jeep at the side of the road. Twiddling the knob on the radio, he searched for more news. The bodyguard was called Rashidi Kasereka—he knew him; Rashidi had said good-bye to him before he fled Kinshasa. "We're on your side," Rashidi had told him. He must have been watching Kabila from up close, just like Boni watched Assani. After Masasu's death his heart had become so full of bitterness that he'd walked into Kabila's office in the Marble Palace and shot him.

The Katangese didn't look ahead, Assani thought. They reacted impulsively. When the war started again, Mzee ought to have done all he could to guarantee the security of the Congolese Tutsi. If he hadn't forced them to flee, it would never have come to this. But Mzee had counted on the Katangese, thinking they'd protect him.

Speculation about who was behind the attack was already circulating, but that didn't interest him. Rashidi had been prepared to kill his leader and die himself—the radio was reporting that Rashidi had been shot by Kabila's aide-de-camp immediately afterward.

As Assani drove on, a great sense of calm came over him. It was good this had happened. Congo would never have another Mobutu, a president who ruled for thirty-two years and slowly wrung his people's necks. The rebellious spirit of the east had reached the capital. His battle had not been in vain.

In the weeks after Mzee's death, the young one, as Assani called Joseph Kabila, was never out of his thoughts. He remembered the time Joseph's father had sent him to the east to suppress a mutiny and the endless conversations he'd had with everyone, after which he'd decided to give Assani a free hand. The young one knew how to listen. He was aware of his own shortcomings.

And now he was president. Everybody was saying peace would come, that the door Mzee had held shut for years would finally be opened. Joseph made a trip to various western capitals. He promised to breathe fresh life into the Lusaka peace accords and not to obstruct MONUC,* the UN peacekeeping force sent to monitor implementation of the cease-fire agreement.

All those foreign heads of state who received the young president—they pictured Congo towering up behind him. But Joseph Kabila wasn't Congo. Didn't they realize he was only a man who'd gone to sit on the president's throne? The Congolese were making the same mistake; as soon as they saw the new president they started applauding, instead of trying to find out what kind of man he was.

Would Joseph remember him? Would he summon Assani, perhaps, to discuss the wedge his father had driven between them? If he had any courage Joseph would take a plane to Goma and talk to the rebels. That would surprise everyone. Or would he prefer to strike a deal with the Rwandans, over the heads of the rebels? Anything was possible — no scenario could be ruled out.

The UN was suddenly everywhere. The bars of Goma were full of foreign soldiers chasing girls. In the interior they supervised the Rwandans' withdrawal from frontline areas — territory they'd struggled so hard to take! Fortunately those UN guys had great jeeps, Assani thought grimly. If they fled the country they'd be forced to leave them behind, a whole fleet of them. They would certainly come in handy when he moved into the interior to take back lost terrain.

But after a while he realized there was no need to panic. Had he imagined everything would change overnight? They were still in Africa, where everyone was highly adept at getting around obstacles. He was in his own territory, whereas MONUC had yet to scout the place out — it would be years before the MONUC forces really understood where they'd landed.

Moroccans, Pakistanis, Egyptians, Canadians — they were all sweating in their uniforms and spent months furnishing their offices, enclaves of western comfort where the air conditioning produced such an icy chill it was like stepping into a fridge. They lived in groups in rented houses, where they hung colorful pagnes over the windows as curtains and ensconced themselves behind them. Ivory traders and diamond sellers stealthily made their way around to the back. Girls slipped furtively inside.

On a mission to Kisangani Assani saw white UN jeeps parked side by side in the nightlife district. In the bar of the Congo Palace Hotel, a Canadian was batting at mosquitoes with a badminton racquet. From a battery in the handle a current passed through the strings. The man was proudly demonstrating to the Congolese around him how to grill mosquitoes with it.

At a disco Assani came on a drunken Egyptian soldier with two women on his lap. A compatriot was trying to take him home but he was refusing to go. Assani looked at the scene out of the corner of his eye and was reminded of what a Ugandan soldier had once told him: *Congo is a big black hole—anyone who puts his foot over the border falls into it.*

The UN civilian personnel concentrated on human rights and child protection. They shook their heads when they saw the *kadogos* and tackled their commanding officers about them. "Those aren't children," Assani once heard a fellow officer protest. "Can't you see? They're pygmies."

The Rwandans had withdrawn from the front line, but in other towns their presence was no less obvious than before. Soccer teams in Kongolo and Kabalo had their own club strips, and even the balls came from Rwanda.

For several weeks Commander Benz and a team of experts, with the stationmaster Mwansa as technical adviser, had been working on the train that was to replace the pump trolley still trundling back and forth between Kabalo, Kongolo, and Nyunzu. Constructing a locomotive out of a fifty-two-ton wagon, a truck engine, and a bogie — if the Congolese really wanted to do something, they could, thought Assani. They attached a ninety-ton car to it and the makeshift train was ready to leave.

The rebels christened it Océan Pacifique, because they were close to the Indian Ocean and peace was in the air, but local people called it Ndombindo — a word with no known meaning for a vehicle they'd never seen before. The contraption chugged along the track with food for the soldiers, but it also transported paying passengers, a lucrative business for the rebels. It spewed an ugly plume of smoke and the driver had to brake six or seven miles before the next stop. At forty miles an hour the Ndombindo rode through a tunnel-like clearing in the forest. Sometimes Rwandans blithely sitting atop bales of rice were killed by overhanging branches.

Mwansa was still receiving the monthly rations of a Rwandan army officer and he earned a bit extra by transporting goods on the Ndombindo. If he was questioned by UN commissioners investigating the looting of state companies and raw materials in rebel areas, he could look them straight in the eye: the Ndombindo didn't belong to the railroad company; it was the soldiers' train.

❀   ❀   ❀

As head of military operations for the rebel army, Assani was once more stationed in Goma and he decided to buy the house he lived in there, in installments. Old Kabila had given him the idea back in Lubumbashi, he told Claudine by phone, and Mzee had given him fistfuls of dollars to help him along. He hadn't known what to do with so much money; he'd stuffed it into his breast pocket, his hip pockets, even the side pockets of his cargo pants, and when he counted it in his room it turned out Mzee had slipped him $13,200 with that offhanded gesture of his.

It wasn't the first time Claudine had heard this story. In Lubumbashi Assani had walked into her restaurant one evening and described the audience with Mzee to her with a mixture of ridicule and excitement. He was a good story-teller and she could see the whole scene before her: Kabila leaning back contentedly in his chair, his hands on his fat stomach, his Tanzanian tunic hanging from a hook on the wall; Assani sitting across from him watching the guards at the door distrustfully. Except that the sum Assani had mentioned that time had been $8,000 less.

He could get hold of a parcel of land on the other side of the border, in Gisenyi. A colleague gave him a French book with photographs of 300 villas. He leafed through it and chose one. Beneath each photo was a design—around here that was enough for a building contractor to get to work. It was good to have a house in Rwanda. You never knew how the situation might change.

The business instinct Assani had developed as a child by helping his mother manage his father's cows, and refined by selling gold in Burundi as a student, stood him in good stead. A Pakistani trader turned to him for protection. He was being blackmailed by customs; his trucks had been impounded for weeks at the border. Assani helped him and was rewarded with $2,000. He put the money toward his new house.

He managed to get hold of a car for a good price, then had the owner make out an invoice for a larger amount and pocketed the difference. He was discreet, but local dealers weren't, so people in Goma soon added his name to the list of big shots who were siphoning off the rebel movement's funds. Rumor had it he'd bought a plot in Goma, having already acquired building land in Gisenyi.

Aimée came to visit and he took her with him to Gisenyi. The foundations of his house had just been finished and he'd told the builders to put up a small shack nearby where he occasionally slept. Aimée was quiet that day, as so often lately. "What do you think?" he asked her expectantly. "You like praying so much—shouldn't you say a prayer to bless my future house?"

Aimée gave a faint laugh. There couldn't be a worse moment to tell him, but the way he was looking at her—she couldn't put it off any longer. "My family wants me to go to the United States," she said.

"So what?" They'd talked about it before. He didn't understand why she'd brought it up now.

"I've bought a ticket."

"What?" He stood at the edge of the building site totally baffled. He instinctively put his hand to his head, as if to protect himself from the news. *Around a woman lies your grave,* he thought in a flash. He should never have become attached to her. How had he let things get to this stage?

"My mother wants us all to be together again," Aimée said apologetically. But when she saw in his eyes the effect her announcement was having she started to back off. "It's not forever." She tried to soothe him. "I'm only going over there to take a look."

"No, don't say that. I know what this means."

In the weeks that followed he called Justine repeatedly, pleading with her to leave Aimée where she was. He called her aunt in Rwanda at such unchristian hours that she begged Aimée to calm him down. Aimée was so dismayed by his reaction that if she hadn't already bought the ticket she would have changed her mind.

Nevertheless he insisted on driving her to the airport. "If only I was still at the front," he complained on the way. "Then I'd be too busy to think and I wouldn't feel so alone."

❊   ❊   ❊

The Rwandans had grown used to depleting the wealth of Congo. The country was *nyama ya tembo,* the flesh of an elephant, they said: there was no way to eat it all up by yourself. With peace in sight and UN commissions investigating the looting, the wheeling and dealing was becoming increasingly secretive.

It worked just like the security service, Assani noticed. Everyone had fragments of information; no one knew everything. A message was sent by word of mouth to the agent of a small Congolese cargo company in Goma, requesting him to turn up at Kigali airport. In Kigali someone gave him $24,000 in cash and asked him to make three return flights to Manono. The agent thought of the young woman he'd recently married and the house they wanted to build, pocketed the money, and kept his questions to himself. He told the airport official in Manono that he'd flown in from Goma. Neither he nor the pilot knew what was being loaded onto the aircraft, although it wasn't hard to guess. These were ghost flights, not registered anywhere. Sometimes the minerals were flown, not direct to Rwanda, but to Bukavu, from where they were taken across the border in trucks, hidden under drums of gasoline.

Since Assani had been stationed in Goma again he'd witnessed more deals than ever before. The rebels, eager to hang on to their posts in the administration, were willing to sell their country down the river in return. They regularly visited Kigali, where they had themselves feted in luxury hotels and told their Rwandan masters what other insurgents were up to. "The current president of the rebel movement is in Joseph Kabila's pocket," they whispered. "Make me president and I'll be your man in Kinshasa."

The Rwandans came to Assani and told him everything. They were profiting from the situation, but ultimately they looked down on all those excellencies and five-star rebels whose ambitions were personal rather than national. They called them BMWs: *beer, music, women.*

Assani once railed so fiercely against the financial machinations between the rebels and the Rwandans that his Banyamulenge friends were shocked. He was the one with a reputation for doing the Rwandans' bidding! "You'd better watch out," someone warned him. "You know what they do to people like you."

During a meeting where the umpteenth underhand deal was made, Assani said he objected. The others glared at him, furious — they'd all decided before the meeting to go along with this deal; why had he suddenly taken it into his head to interfere? James Kabarebe, who'd been promoted to chief of staff of the Rwandan army, looked at him absently. Assani turned away in embarrassment. James despised the others for being subservient and opportunistic, but he felt even more contempt for Assani, who was unable to stop them no matter how strongly he disapproved.

Shortly after that Assani found himself out of the loop. He'd become a troublesome witness. They sent him off to a military camp in Rwanda, supposedly for training, but it felt more like a punishment.

From time to time he called Aimée. She was happy to be with her family again but was having a hard time adjusting to the small town on the east coast of America where she'd ended up. One morning she woke to snow for the first time in her life. As far as the eye could see, everything was white. She called him on an impulse. She suddenly felt very sad and lonely, she said, to realize she couldn't share this with him.

Every month he took a weekend off and drove to Gisenyi to supervise the construction of his house. He sometimes went to drink milk with a family who lived nearby. Devota, the daughter, was nineteen—no more than a girl. One evening they got to talking on the front terrace and since then he'd seen her quite often. He had to forget about Aimée, he told himself. And he must have one more child—he owed that to his mother. When Devota got pregnant he was satisfied. Now he could die in peace.

*   *   *

But he didn't die. Instead there were further peace negotiations in South Africa, and Rwanda was forced to withdraw from the remainder of eastern Congo. The news hit the town of Kabalo like a bomb—Commander Satellite's soccer club had just won the MONUC cup, under the inspiring guidance of their trainer Mutombo.

The Rwandans were bitter. One day they were shouting that they'd never leave Congo; the next day they were starting to pack. "What do you expect? This is politics," a Rwandan commander said to Mutombo. Old Kabila was an idiot, he laughed. Mzee had been proud that so many of the enemy had died here, but the number of soldiers killed by Kabila was more than matched by the number of children the Rwandans had conceived by Congolese women.

They dismantled a truck they'd seized recently, leaving only the carcass behind at the station. Mwansa stood watching in his shiny safari suit, hands folded at his back. He could tell that the officers were sorry to be leaving, but the ordinary soldiers were glad it was over.

They took all the soccer balls with them. Some even left with sacks of mangoes. Commander Satellite wanted to take Mutombo along—he saw a great future for him as a soccer trainer in Rwanda—but Mutombo didn't dare leave his family behind unprotected.

The administrator of Kabalo, a good, sensitive soul who'd come out of the bush to get help for his dying grandchild and been grabbed immediately by the Rwandans because he was educated, was left behind with a neon light a Rwandan officer had given him. He'd always recharged it at their headquarters. A lamp and a battery: that was all he'd managed to salvage from this war. Now he'd have to get friendly with MONUC—they had a generator.

❈   ❈   ❈

The South Africans have really gotten their act together, Assani thought as he drove the four-lane highway from Johannesburg airport to the congress center in Sun City, where the military commission preparing the reunification of the Congolese army was meeting.

They'd told him Sun City was a hotel, but it was a whole town, with mansions, swimming pools, bistros, discos, casinos, and playing fields. His compatriots promenaded the streets, dined in luxury restaurants, and generally made themselves at home, but Assani felt intimidated by so much perfection. Roads without potholes, buildings without dripping air conditioners, cars without rust—all this underlined the distressing decline of his own country. Earlier that year the Nyiragongo volcano had erupted in Goma and half the city had been wiped off the map. People had set about building right on top of the lava, their houses all jumbled together higgledy-piggledy. Someone had named his rickety wooden shop "Anti-Lava."

At the meetings of the military commission, Assani was right back in the middle of Congo. There they sat: the Mobutists who'd lost two wars and still hadn't learned what humility was, the Katangese who were behaving as if they had a permanent lease on wisdom, and the Mai Mai who'd saved all their skins and had come to reap their rewards.

For the first few days Assani merely listened, but when he saw that the government camp seriously planned to appoint some of the Mai Mai as battalion commanders and generals he requested permission to speak.

"The Mai Mai come from the bush," he said. "They're

not officer material. They have no discipline. It'd be better to assign them to the general staff, so they can learn how to behave."

"I don't come from the bush!" shouted a Mai Mai, pointing at Assani. "And that man there, he's a criminal; he's been fighting and killing us for years!"

A general from Equatorial Province shifted uneasily in his chair. "The Mai Mai are patriots," he said. "It's thanks to them that Congo still exists today."

"You don't know them like I do," said Assani. "They have no civilization. Mark my words, your next war will be fought against them."

"It's not the integration of the Mai Mai into the army that's irresponsible; it's the integration of the rebels," the general went on. "If they come to Kinshasa we're going to have to protect Joseph Kabila against them."

When they got outside Assani said to his colleagues, "You wait. If that general opens his mouth again tomorrow I'm going to say something that'll shut him up for the next two days."

The following morning the general delivered a eulogy for Kabila. Assani requested the floor again. "We've got a problem here," he said, looking around the table. Then he fixed his eyes on the general. "That man there, he's our problem — thanks to people like him we've got another twenty years of misery ahead of us." The general was shocked by Assani's audacity. "And why is he a problem?" Assani continued calmly. "Because he's only concerned about Kabila and the government side. We've come here to talk about the future of Congo. Kabila will die, but Congo will remain."

Then he addressed the general directly. "You're a boot-licker," he said. "Kabila's going to discover we're his best soldiers, because instead of fawning on him we'll point out his mistakes. People like you will kill Kabila. How do you expect a president to do his job if his soldiers shield him from everything? Better to have bodyguards from every part of the country. Your best protection doesn't come from a soldier belonging to your own people but one you drink Fanta with from time to time."

The general looked at him angrily. "I bet you went to a military academy," Assani said, undeterred. "But I'm convinced you've never been to war."

"See what I mean!" the general shouted. "I've always said they were arrogant!"

General Diallo, the Senegalese military commander in charge of the MONUC operation, had been quietly observing the clash. He took the two of them aside after the meeting. The general rapidly backed down: he hadn't meant what he said; that was simply the way people in Kinshasa talked about the rebels.

Diallo started to get interested in the tall, slender rebel soldier whose impetuous outbursts sometimes hit the nail on the head. In the months that followed they saw each other regularly at military gatherings and Assani took in the older Diallo's wise advice.

Assani had considered both the reunification of the army and the arrival of the UN peacekeeping mission a farce, but General Diallo calmed him down whenever feelings ran high and prepared him for the decision that was about to be made, a decision Assani was being dragged toward by forces beyond his control.

＊　＊　＊

The day the rebel movement submitted his name for appointment as general in the new united national army, Assani was seized with panic. This was it. They'd decided to sacrifice him. He wouldn't get out of Kinshasa alive a second time. But after a while he thought: I'm a soldier under Joseph Kabila. I'll never betray anyone who hasn't betrayed me first. If Joseph's father hadn't forced me out, he wouldn't have been murdered.

The Kinshasa government refused to endorse the appointment of some of the officers nominated by the rebel movement. They were accused of involvement in the murder of Mzee Kabila and convicted by default. Kinshasa regarded their nomination alone as a provocation: how could Joseph Kabila take men who belonged in jail and appoint them to the senior ranks of his armed forces?

One afternoon Assani saw a minister sitting on the terrace at Hotel Nyira in Goma. He'd just gotten back from Kinshasa, where the first few meetings of the transitional government had taken place. "Are you on vacation already?" The minister laughed, stood up, and proudly introduced Assani to some representatives of a cell phone company he'd persuaded to travel back with him from the capital.

"I hear you guys are busy making a deal about us over there," Assani said. "As long as you realize that either all of us will go for it or none of us will. Aren't those officers

Congolese? If the young one's planning to exclude people from the east he'll meet the same fate as his father. You tell him that."

The minister looked at his guests and laughed in embarrassment. "These folks will be the death of us yet," he said, slapping Assani on the shoulder to mollify him. "You'd better not talk like that when you're in Kinshasa."

"Why not? I'm not a diplomat—that's your job. I'll say whatever I think, just like I do here."

But the rebels were forced to come up with new names. Some of the soldiers whose nominations had been accepted in Kinshasa responded by refusing to go. Rwanda would be all too eager to stoke this smoldering conflict into flames—didn't Kinshasa realize that? Rumors of a third rebellion hung in the air.

Assani's phone didn't stop ringing. Kinshasa wasn't really interested in peace, the dissidents said. Didn't he know how dangerous it was to go there? They'd hang him out to dry at the first opportunity. "You people are giving me gray hairs," Assani sighed. "Do you think I have any choice? This train's moving ahead; I can't stop it on my own."

Soldiers weren't pebbles you could toss down wherever you liked. After five years of civil war you couldn't just fly them over to the other side of the country as if nothing had happened. He decided he'd have to risk going to Kinshasa. When they'd seen how he got on over there, they might have the confidence to follow him.

The day before he left, Assani walked into his living room to find that his uncle Rutebuka had come all the way from the high plains to speak with him. He'd grown old. Sitting there in his faded pants and ancient suit coat, clutching a felt hat in his lap and fiddling with it continually—was this the man he used to fear so much?

Rutebuka told him about Esther, his wife, who'd been sick recently, about one of old Rumenge's sons who had died, about a new kind of medicine for the cows—the sort of stories men from the high plains filled their days with and Assani had absolutely no time for. His cell phone kept ringing. He paced up and down the room nervously, sometimes disappearing into the garden as he talked on the phone. Rutebuka stared shyly at his shoes. The baked-on dirt of the journey was slowly drying out, crumbling in grainy lumps onto the clean floor.

It was only after Devota, little Moshe, and the newborn baby were in bed that Rutebuka posed the question he'd come to ask: "Why have you decided to go to Kinshasa? It'll be the death of you."

"What else can I do?" Assani sighed, flopping exhausted into a chair facing him. "Join the men who've fled to the mountains?"

"Why not? You've got everything here: cows, land, houses. What's Kinshasa got to offer you?"

Assani looked at him. His uncle wasn't thinking about his country; he just wanted to live with his own people up in the high plains. He hadn't intended to mention it, but it slipped out before he had time to think: "None of you ever understood me," he said. "If it was up to you I'd never even have gone to school; I'd still be walking behind the cows, like a semiliterate."

Rutebuka tried to say something, but Assani held up his hand, fending him off. "Perhaps you've forgotten but I haven't. You never gave me any help, I always had to do everything myself—as if I were an adult, not a child. If it wasn't for my mother I'd never have gotten this far. And now you're trying to give me advice?"

"I never realized you saw it like that," Rutebuka replied hesitantly. "Why didn't you say anything about this before?"

Assani rubbed his forehead. "Sorry. I'm tired. It's been a difficult time. You shouldn't imagine it was an easy decision to make."

Rutebuka insisted on staying the night at his house so they could go on discussing the matter the next day. But there was no time to talk in the morning either—the phone kept ringing, Moshe cried, Devota was upset. All the same, it was good to see his uncle sitting in the living room, surrounded by all the other guests who'd come to say good-bye.

I never wanted to be a soldier, Assani thought on the way to the airport. I had no ambition for any of this. I'd rather disappear into thin air than go back to Kinshasa. But the plane was waiting for him and he dragged the UNICEF tents out of the jeep and handed them to his bodyguards.

KINSHASA
2004

On the morning of the third anniversary of Mzee Kabila's death, Assani accompanied the army general staff to the memorial gathering at the mausoleum, followed by a guided tour of the Marble Palace. The guide showed them the chair in which Kabila had been sitting when his bodyguard came to whisper something in his ear and took the opportunity to shoot him in the neck. Assani could see the fat, self-satisfied Mzee sitting there, arms folded, staring at the ceiling. He'd heard people say that the door at the back of the study opened onto a cold store where Mzee kept fish and that he often used to walk around in there, laughing, rummaging in the boxes of fish that reminded him of his glory days as a smuggler on Lake Tanganyika.

The last words Mzee had said to him resounded in his ears: *I'll send the Simbas after you. They'll bring me your head on a plate. I'll display it in the museum!* Instead it was Mzee who'd been murdered. No, there was a God and he was great. This evening he would call Mwepu. His friend wouldn't like it, but Assani had to tell him how he felt: he was cheerful; nothing could spoil his mood now.

*　　*　　*

None of the rebels from the east had brought their families with them to Kinshasa. The situation was still too unstable, they had no confidence yet, and the Kinois were inevitably suspicious in return. As long as the rebels' families were still in the east they could always walk out and slam the door behind them.

Assani had been here for almost five months now. His wife was afraid of Kinshasa, but he managed to persuade her to visit. Along with the two children they'd had together she would bring Chief, his son from his first marriage. He notified Mwepu, who sent an escort to the airport to pick them up. For days after Devota arrived, calls from his colleagues poured in: was it true that madame and the children were here? They congratulated him. He could tell they felt reassured.

Assani quickly signed all the documents at his office that day and hurried home. As soon as he drove through the gate, the door to the terrace opened and Chief and Moshe threw themselves onto the hood of his car. What had he got for them? Chocolate! They pulled him inside, where Devota was sitting in the living room with the baby.

It wasn't good to have been away from them for so long. When Devota asked Moshe where daddy was, he pointed to Assani's photo instead of to him. Chief was fourteen. He'd lived with Elias in Bukavu for several years, but after marrying Devota, Assani had taken him in. Chief was a shy boy from the high plains, very different from the energetic Moshe, who managed to break all the photo frames in the room within a few days. But when Assani drove through the city with them, Chief talked incessantly about the tall buildings, the four-lane highways, and the lively streets, so that he began to look at Kinshasa with fresh eyes. On weekends he went swimming with the kids at the house in the hills. Chief would have liked to move to Kinshasa right away.

At night the baby slept in bed with Assani and Devota. That little creature against his back — he'd never imagined that something so simple could make him so happy. Chief and Moshe, who slept in the room across from theirs, were up and knocking at their door by five in the morning.

His wife didn't really know him at all — she couldn't get through to him and he did his best to keep it that way. He watched her. He wasn't familiar with all her different faces yet. Had the Rwandans sent her to spy on him? He hid things from her, so she went looking. One day he forgot to fasten the combination lock on the leather case in which he stored documents and got home to find her poring over the notebook where he kept lists of his friends and his enemies.

They stayed for ten days; then Chief had to go back to school and Assani drove them to the airport. When they'd gone the house was uncannily silent. He walked from room to room, looking for traces of their presence, and sat for some time staring at a broken photo frame he'd found under the boys' bed. Then he turned on the television, picked up his new cell phone, and worked through all the ring tones until he heard the voice of his crying baby.

It was a perfect little gadget. He'd gotten it from a government minister who'd just arrived back from a mission on which he'd made some money. They'd run into each other in the lobby of the Grand Hotel. "Anything you need?" the minister asked. "My cell's been acting up lately," Assani said, so they went into a shop in the chic lobby. In a lighted showcase, between gold bracelets and French perfumes, lay the tiniest mobile phone Assani had ever seen: a Samsung with a claret cover. He was shocked by the price, but the minister counted out the $400 with a steely look.

Devota called to say she'd arrived in Goma. He pretended to be busy. It was an instinctive reaction—as soon as she got too close he withdrew and became a stranger to her again. You had to keep a woman in the dark about what was going on inside you; otherwise she'd have you under her spell. A man never knew what deep water he was getting into by falling in love with a woman.

❊   ❊   ❊

Every evening after work, Assani went swimming at the house in the hills. As he swam lap after lap the stress would fall away and by the time he drove back down into the city he felt balanced and calm. One Saturday he invited Mwepu to join him and after their swim they sat on the steps to talk. No one could see them but they could look out over the entire city. The guard had withdrawn to the back of the house with his family.

When Devota and the children were around, everything had seemed normal for a while, but that didn't last long. More and more soldiers were being sent from west to east and vice versa, winding up the tension to a high pitch.

A Munyamulenge who'd been appointed battalion commander had arrived at a small town in the west with his men. Local people started calling around in panic: the rebels were back in town, they'd stepped off the plane fully armed and were walking along the main street!

Mwepu confided in him that the president wasn't at all happy that the soldiers who'd been convicted by default of the murder of Mzee were still able to move around freely in the east.

"You know as well as I do the trial was a sham," Assani said sullenly.

"But why are they refusing to come to Kinshasa if they've nothing to feel guilty about?"

Assani shuffled back and forth impatiently on the stone steps. "To be thrown in a cell? How can you expect them to have any confidence after what you Katangese did to Masasu? Anyone who ends up in prison here is a dead man, innocent or not."

"Staying there and allowing themselves to be manipulated by the Rwandans looks like an admission of guilt," Mwepu went on.

Assani stood up, fetched a watering can, and walked over to the gardenias, which had recently come into bloom. Every day when he went swimming after work the white flowers gave off a sweet, intoxicating scent. Mwepu watched him. "Can't you see why Joseph has a problem with those dissidents?"

"Pfff!" Assani blew through his teeth. "I'm on the road to peace while my president cries like a child over his dead father. My father's dead too. Am I supposed to spend my whole life mourning for him? A man in power should be able to swallow anything that comes his way, but Kabila does the exact opposite: he spits everything out."

Assani's cousin Jules had recently been appointed second in command to the general sent to Bukavu by the Kinshasa government. The former rebels were convinced the general had come to crush them—Jules was having a hard time restraining them and he called Assani regularly.

Assani stood still for a moment and looked at Mwepu. "Do you know what Joseph should do? He should give those boys an amnesty. If he goes on hounding them they'll make alliances with other dissidents. Before you know it the third rebellion, the one everybody's so afraid of, will be a reality."

He started irritatedly watering the other plants as well. "If Joseph goes on like this I'll head back east again," he said. "What does Congo mean? Why should I want to be Congolese? A century or so ago some Belgian drew up the borders. We can create new borders, starting in the east, and if necessary we'll make a pact with the devil to defend them."

"Your future lies in the nation of Congo," Mwepu said patiently. "What are you people planning to do in the east, all of you huddled together? It'll only make you more vulnerable." That was something he was continually trying to drum into the heads of the Katangese around him: the Tutsi needed to find their place in Congo. But most Katangese were still villagers at heart and wouldn't listen. In their eyes every Tutsi was an agent of Rwanda. "Just you wait," they told Mwepu. "That so-called friend of yours will surprise you yet." They said it with such conviction that Mwepu began to have doubts. He'd learned that if everyone was wrong, then everyone was right.

The president knew things were more complicated than that, but he couldn't send his critics away without endangering his own position. Stories that Joseph wasn't really Kabila's son but the child of a deceased Rwandan friend, adopted by Mzee as a baby, were already going around.

"Tell me something: why is it that whenever you people have a problem you always flee to Rwanda?" Mwepu asked. "I'd be more likely to flee into the interior of Congo than across the border."

Assani had refilled the watering can. "We can only start bothering about borders when we've solved our other problems," he said. "Can you imagine what it's like to look in the mirror in the morning and realize you've got the face of a condemned man? Have you forgotten I wouldn't be alive now if I hadn't fled Kinshasa in 1998? Just because I'm a Tutsi. By the time James Kabarebe dredged me up out of Lower Congo I looked like an animal."

"But James is a Rwandan; he doesn't have the same plans for Congo that you have. Why should you want to sacrifice your ideals for him?"

Assani shrugged. "You shouldn't think I always agree with James. OK, he saved my life, but later, when other interests came into it, he didn't hesitate to sacrifice me. I don't owe him everything. But how can I put my fate into the hands of the Congolese without knowing what I'm likely to get in return? Who can guarantee they have anything good in store for me? The insults and accusations haven't stopped. Even yesterday . . ." He hesitated a moment but decided to go on. "The chief of staff showed me a document in which I'm accused of smuggling weapons into the country from Brazzaville."

They continued arguing until it got dark, the guard switched on the light on the terrace, and Mwepu began playing with the keys to his Mercedes as a signal that it was time to leave.

At home later that evening, Assani sat in front of the television and felt angry with the whole world. In the middle of the night he called Mwepu. It was a few moments before he answered, sleepily. "You guys in intelligence," Assani said without any introduction. "Don't you ever switch off your phones? Don't you ever need time to catch your breath?"

Mwepu laughed. "If I'm not mistaken it was you who called me. I was asleep. You sound wide awake to me. Which one of us is really the intelligence guy?"

*   *   *

Assani now had three cell phones, and when the crisis in the east erupted they all started ringing at once. The new general in Bukavu had found unregistered weapons at the home of one of the dissident soldiers. Instead of disarming and arresting him, he'd quietly put the offender on a plane to

Kinshasa, without telling either MONUC or his second in command, Assani's cousin Jules.

Jules was furious. "Kabila's soldiers don't want peace; they only came here to arrest us and drag us off to the capital," he shouted. "What am I supposed to tell my men now? They think I handed one of them over to you!" Later Assani would say he'd tried to calm Jules, but Jules's *kadogos*, who'd watched their commander striding back and forth through the garden, claimed Assani had incited him to act against his superiors.

More and more soldiers thronged around Jules's house. The familiar drums of war sounded, and the soldiers sang a song they'd learned in the Protestant church: *We rejoice in doing what we've been called to do.* That same evening they set out for the general's house and shot dead two of his bodyguards at the gate. To their disappointment the general jumped over the garden wall and fled to the local MONUC headquarters. They looted the general's house and that night they drove his jeep through the streets of Bukavu.

In Kinshasa Mwepu and Assani argued heatedly on the phone. "Why shouldn't a soldier who's committed an offence be brought to the capital for interrogation? What's wrong with that?" Mwepu asked.

"I told you Kabila should give those boys an amnesty instead of rounding them up!" Assani thundered. "Otherwise they'll stash away weapons to defend themselves — what else do you expect? But the young one won't listen to strategists, only to people on the street, and they're out for revenge. What was he thinking? That the soldiers would

take the arrest lying down? When someone's carrying a jug
of water on his head, he shouldn't start throwing stones or
he risks getting a stone thrown at his head in return. The
jug will be smashed in no time."

At first Mwepu tried to calm his friend, but then he
decided to let him rage. "We're sliding, we're sliding . . ."
Assani said. "We don't know what sort of ditch we'll end up
in. People like Jules have escaped death so many times they're
capable of anything. He'd have killed the general if he'd found
him home, you do realize that, right? He wasn't acting as a
soldier anymore; the man had become his personal enemy."
Assani sounded more and more disconsolate. "Our leaders
have to look beyond those dissidents. They should be helping them."

"The president has been hurt himself," said Mwepu.

Assani sighed. "I know. His father was killed. He can't
get that image out of his head. That's precisely our problem: we don't have a leader who can rise above us."

❊   ❊   ❊

From Lubumbashi, Bukavu looked like a dangerous city,
but her sister had sworn everything was quiet and Claudine
was glad she'd talked herself into coming. She'd forgotten
how beautiful it was here. In the early mornings, with the
fog lingering over Lake Kivu, she walked down through the
dewy garden and listened to the singsong voices of the fishermen echoing across the water. Sometimes a pirogue would
appear out of the mist and she'd catch sight of a lone man
paddling, humming softly as he cast his net, at peace with
himself and the world.

After her Greek brother-in-law Jannis left for the office and the children had been taken to school, Claudine sat on the terrace drinking coffee and talking with her sister. Later her sister would drive into town to shop while Claudine lay reading on a lounge chair in the garden. It had been busy in the restaurant over the past few months. She was glad of a break.

Peace had one merit at least: you could phone anywhere in Congo for the price of a local call, so she was able to keep up with things at La Paillote. The terraces of cafés and restaurants in Bukavu had been furnished with new umbrellas from the cell phone companies Vodacom and Celtel, which had recently set up offices in the east.

One morning she called Assani in Kinshasa. "You'll never guess where I am," she said.

"Tell me."

"In Bukavu."

He ought to be at work by now, but she could tell she'd gotten his attention. "So what's it like there?"

"Quiet, to my surprise. My brother-in-law has an import-export business. He says the situation's getting back to normal." She didn't tell him what else Jannis had said: that his business could really thrive only when they put a stop to all the hassle with insurgent soldiers. Under pressure from MONUC and the politicians from the east, the arrested soldier had been freed and flown back to Bukavu, but the leader of the dissidents was now a pariah. His house was heavily fortified and his men were patrolling the surrounding streets, moving in a cloud of dust and noise. Jannis said that when the general first arrived in Bukavu he'd been

greeted with cheers from the residents. They expected him
to teach the dissident soldiers a lesson and chase out their
Rwandan bosses, who were still in evidence on the streets,
once and for all.

Assani seemed to swallow a remark at his end as well.
"You wait," he said after a pause. "It may seem peaceful, but
things can turn around from one day to the next."

Claudine gazed at the water through her sunglasses.
The fog had cleared now and she could see a long way out.
Some pirogues were moving in a tight group, as if for mutual support. Jannis had said there was a lot of illegal traffic on the water; even the weapons recently confiscated from
the rebels had probably already been smuggled back into
the city via the lake. "If you know anything," she said to
Assani, "I hope you'll tell me."

"No, no. But I wouldn't stay too long in Bukavu. You're
safer in Lubumbashi."

That very afternoon there was gunfire in town. Jannis was
two miles away, in Rwanda, getting a truck through customs, and he called to see if everybody was home. "Some
kind of incident between the new general's men and those
of his sacked number two," he said, sounding exasperated.
"Stay indoors just in case." The border was closed immediately. Jannis was barely able to nip across in time and he
had to leave his truck behind.

"Does that happen often?" asked Claudine, noticing
how calmly her sister was taking it. "Yes, it does," she said.
"No need to worry." The children went to school as usual

the next day but an hour later they were back. The youngest ran up to Claudine in his blue-and-white uniform and snuggled tightly against her. She could feel his little heart thumping. The soldiers were shooting, he said, and people tore off in all directions. One *maman*'s oranges had rolled all over the road.

The next day they stayed indoors, relying on the reports Jannis brought them after sporadic trips into town. The city had been divided into sectors, he said. The general's soldiers were searching for weapons in the districts they controlled and they'd dragged some Banyamulenge citizens —whom they regarded as accomplices of the insurgents— out of their houses, herded them together, and killed them. The dissident soldiers had occupied the border area and there were rumors of Rwandan reinforcements.

One afternoon Jannis came home and reported that a Tutsi commander from Goma was on his way to Bukavu with his men to put an end to the genocide of the Banyamulenge, as he called it. There were said to be 1,000 of them and they were creating havoc in the villages they passed on their way. "I'll have to get you all out of here," he decided. "Before we know what's happening the whole of eastern Congo will go up in flames again. MONUC is trying to mediate, but they've no idea who they're up against. Until they get a mandate to open fire they won't be able to do anything." For the first time Claudine could see that Jannis was nervous. There was already looting in town. It would only get worse when yet more irregular troops arrived.

They hurriedly packed a few things. When they drove out of the gate Claudine was astonished by the change that had come over Bukavu. On her arrival from Lubumbashi it had struck her how busy the town was, but now the streets were almost deserted. The district they were driving through was held by the Munyamulenge commander, Jules, but not all his men were Banyamulenge, Claudine noticed. They had red eyes for lack of sleep and some were not in uniform but in mismatched clothing with weird accessories. The children, sitting in the backseat of the jeep with Claudine, couldn't believe their eyes and pinched her arms with excitement. From the city behind them they could hear gunfire.

"Where are you going?" A boy wearing a woolen hat, with a large fake gold cross hanging from his neck, stuck his head through the open car window. He'd knotted a towel at his shoulder the way Tutsi chefs traditionally wore their pagnes.

"Where d'you think?" said Jannis, smiling, pointing to his family in the car. They drove on at walking pace. They weren't the only ones fleeing the city; the closer they got to the border the more Banyamulenge they saw — men, women, children — all walking in the same direction with household goods on their heads. "That's what you get if you don't dis-associate yourself from the rotten apples in your own com-munity," Jannis sneered. "When zero hour comes you have to run."

He'd booked two rooms at Hotel des Chutes, which had a view of the border. After checking in, Claudine went out onto the terrace. From the city across the water she could hear mortar fire. She tried to call Assani but couldn't reach him. A while later he called her.

"Are you still in Bukavu?"

"No, no."

"Thank God. What did I tell you? It's safer in Lubumbashi."

"I'm not in Lubumbashi. Bukavu airport's closed, as you probably know. We've just crossed the border."

He sighed. "If you'd called me before you left Lubumbashi I'd have told you not to travel that way. It's only a matter of time before I lose you too in all this insanity." He was silent for a moment, as if trying to get his bearings. "Are you at the Hotel des Chutes?"

"How did you guess?"

"I know every square inch of that damned region."

"I assume you're not indifferent to what's happening here."

"Me?" he laughed scornfully. "I'm a dead man. The rebel leader's a cousin of mine. Of course people here think I support him. Everyone out there's phoning to ask if I've written my will yet."

"But you don't support him?"

"No, no, I'm done with war. I've taken a different path. Eastern Congo is full of Mai Mai, Interahamwe, and deserters. I'd only go out there if I was forced to."

Claudine heard him walking through the house. "No one listens to me," he said. "The featherbrains are in charge here; mud slinging is the fashion. I'm beginning to ask myself if I'm crazy. It seems I've got it all wrong. I can't find more than a handful of people who agree with me."

It was Sunday afternoon. Why wasn't he with his friends? What was he doing there alone? "Are your friends in Kinshasa aware that you don't support the rebels?" Claudine asked.

"They'd never believe me. Anyhow, it's the weekend. People won't be talking to each other."

"Yes they will!"

He continued striding through the house and Claudine heard a door close. "When I have time off I usually go swimming," he said. "But I'm not in the mood right now. The time for me to try to explain things is over. We're already hiding in each other's houses." He told her about a guest who'd been with him for several days, a Munya-mulenge colonel who'd fled his own home because he no longer felt safe there. But the man had really started to get scared only since he'd been around Assani, convinced he'd be the first person they'd come for if the situation deterio-rated. "Staying with you only brings my death even closer," he'd said that morning when he got up, and he'd quietly disappeared.

The tension was rising by the minute, Assani told her. The radio had just reported that Bukavu airport was about to fall to the rebels, who were descending on the city from Goma. "At the start of the second war I had weapons and troops but now there's nothing I can do—I'm as defense-less as an ordinary citizen. I've told my people in Bukavu to take revenge if anything happens to me over here."

Claudine's sister walked up to her, an inquiring look on her face. Claudine waved her away and went up a flight of steps into a leafy arbor. Neither her sister nor Jannis would appreciate her talking to a Munyamulenge at a moment like this. And a soldier too! She was reminded of the nervous conversations she'd had with Assani in Lubumbashi, when he was still on the other side of the front. This is war, she thought suddenly. From one minute to the next we're at war again.

"You still there?"

"Yes," she whispered. "I was just finding a quiet spot where they can't hear me."

"That's good. Discretion sets man apart from the animals." He needed to talk to her, she felt.

"What do the rebels actually want?"

He sighed, as if tired of having to explain everything to her. "They probably don't even know themselves what they want any more. My cousin had his back to the wall. He was afraid of being taken to Kinshasa. MONUC, the European Union, the Great Lakes Conference—none of that stuff means anything to people out there. They're going back to the village. You can only understand what makes them tick when you've fallen into a hole yourself."

The president was behind all this, he said. He was provoking the conflict. Kabila could start a war, but did he know how to end one? He wasn't acting like the leader of a nation. "This country's going to the dogs; you'll see. There aren't any analysts here; they thought it was a matter of fifty dissidents at the most, but pretty soon there were a hundred and now it's more than a thousand. They're driving us into each other's arms. At first I didn't agree with the others, but it's become a matter of self-preservation, just like during the war." Suddenly he laughed. "Even Banyamulenge soldiers who went up into the high plains years ago are calling me. I've no idea how they managed to get hold of a phone out there but they've got one. I fought them for years, they cursed me all the way, and now they're ringing me to ask if I'm in danger here in Kinshasa!"

Jannis' premonitions proved correct: rebel soldiers from Goma were approaching the city and MONUC was unable to stop them. At the brewery on the edge of Bukavu, crates of beer were standing ready; the brewery security service was afraid that otherwise soldiers would force their way in, as they'd done during a previous looting spree. That time the brewery staff had found spent cartridges at the bottom of the premashing vats when it was over.

Now hyped-up soldiers stormed the city, plundered shops, smashed their way into houses, raped women, girls, even infants, and made off with money, jewelry, and cell phones. The general had killed their wives and children, they said. They'd come to avenge their families.

Claudine followed it all on Radio Okapi, the station run by MONUC. The general and his men were said to have left the city. Frightened civilians were hiding in churches, jumping into the backs of patrolling UN pickups, and pouring onto the MONUC compound.

The Banyamulenge guests at Hotel des Chutes sat in edgy groups on the terrace, staring at the border and making endless phone calls. A young Munyamulenge sitting alone at a table gave Claudine a worried look as she walked past. "Our people in Kinshasa are going to die," he said. He looked so desperate that, impulsively, she went over to sit with him.

He worked for an international organization in Bukavu, he told her, and for the first few days he'd done all he could to stay at his post, but his colleagues were increasingly hostile. They told his boss he sympathized with the insurgents and that they'd seen him near the border in uniform. He became so afraid he decided to leave with his family. "Now of course they'll say, See, he supported the rebels, that's why he fled. But what else could I do?"

Claudine looked around. Her sister had gone into town with the children. Jannis was down at the border — she could see his parked car. The young man peered past Claudine at the Banyamulenge sitting at one of the other tables. Her pale skin seemed to reassure him.

"I'm against the mutineers," he said, almost inaudibly. "They're being manipulated by the Rwandans. When Jules went to Kinshasa a while ago for his official appointment as number two, the Rwandans were unhappy and complained he wasn't 'positive.' That's a fashionable word in Rwanda nowadays; if you don't side with the regime you're not positive. As soon as Jules got on the wrong side of the general, the Rwandans said, See, what did we tell you? They were delighted to have gotten themselves another dissident."

He discreetly pointed to the table where the Banyamulenge were sitting. "A lot of people are secretly backing the mutinous troops," he said. "They're afraid reunification will cost them their jobs. If the region secedes, they might get a chance to become ministers instead of minor civil servants at ministries in Kinshasa. Rwanda's playing on that very cleverly."

Claudine saw Jannis's car creeping up the hill. She excused herself. It was time for her to be off.

The whole of Bukavu was now in rebel hands. Jannis had managed to get over there and he was full of stories that evening. His own company hadn't been looted, but the soldiers had set fire to some of the warehouses near the market. They all had cell phones hanging around their necks and they looked pretty wild. He'd seen a Tutsi soldier herding three cows down the middle of the boulevard with a stick, and he'd passed a convoy headed by a pickup with two dead soldiers in the back. Here and there men stood talking in groups at the side of the road. The mutineers had killed several people, including a well-known *commerçant*.

"What's happening in Bukavu?" Assani asked on the phone that evening. "I hear so many rumors I don't know what to believe."

Claudine told him what Jannis had seen and heard in town. "The soldiers are making mistakes," she said, suddenly defiant. "They're looting, raping, burning warehouses — they won't win any friends that way."

"What else have they done wrong?" Assani asked caustically.

"They killed an innocent *commerçant*."

"That man wasn't as innocent as you think," said Assani sternly. "He was financing all kinds of shady enterprises. I'd have done the same myself. It's good they killed him. How many Tutsi did the general kill?"

"Fourteen, they say, but that's no reason to . . ."

It was as if something snapped at the other end of the line. "Fourteen innocent civilians and you find that normal? Are they dogs, or what? If the general kills fourteen, the others should kill twenty-eight. An eye for an eye, a tooth for a tooth."

"But . . ."

"You just shut up now, madame," he said scornfully. "Fortunately I wasn't there, otherwise I'd have taken revenge. I've had enough damned moralizing from you people; it doesn't get us anywhere. We're not priests. Until they exterminate us, we'll carry on taking revenge. Now I'm going to start killing in earnest."

He sounded melodramatic, like an actor onstage, which only made Claudine more defiant. The way they trafficked in corpses here, using them as political weapons . . .

"Don't call me madame," she said angrily.

"Mademoiselle, then."

Before she had a chance to respond, Assani had shut off the call.

Claudine stood in the arbor, her heart thumping, her phone in her hand. Darkness had fallen; the waiter had turned on the lights on the terrace. As she walked down the steps she felt a chill creeping over her. She shivered in her thin sweater.

As soon as Claudine turned on her phone the next morning, Assani called. "Sorry," he said. "I don't know what got into me last night. I was beside myself with rage and at last I'd found someone I could take it all out on."

"Don't worry," said Claudine, who'd slept badly and was relieved that he'd called her. "It takes its toll on all of us. I wasn't my usual self either."

"I'm not normal any more; I'm afraid of losing my head. Jules wants to know why I'm still here." Again she could hear him walking through the house. His footsteps sounded hollow—it must be a high-ceilinged villa without much furniture. "What should I do?" he asked. "Should I go to work? I didn't sleep a wink last night. My ears hurt from phoning all the time. I normally call the chief of staff in the mornings to ask how things are, but I haven't done that yet."

"Of course you should go to work." She could hear another phone bleeping, but he made no attempt to answer it. "Someone's calling you," she said.

"Let them call," he responded, sounding tired. "I'm talking to you now. You calm me down; you're . . . I don't know how to put it. You've become like a sister to me. You must help me. I'm in danger. The only thing stopping me from sliding over to the other side is . . ." He hesitated a moment. "The weight of the decision."

❀   ❀   ❀

Kabila loyalists had called on the citizens of Kinshasa to protest against the occupation of Bukavu. Assani was afraid the demonstration would turn against the politicians and soldiers from the east, so he divided up the sixty soldiers they had at their disposal between the four most sensitive buildings: the residence and the office of Vice President Ruberwa, the headquarters of Ruberwa's party, and his own villa on the boulevard.

But things didn't go the way he expected. Once they got out on the street, the Kinois vented their anger and sense of impotence on people of every stripe. Demonstrators made for the headquarters of MONUC, which they accused of handing the citizens of Bukavu over to the Rwandans, and attacked UN workers, destroying their cars and setting their houses on fire. They carried portraits of Mobutu, burned the Congolese flag, and sang, *Mobutu — we know his father. Mzee Kabila — we know his father. But Joseph Kabila is a Rwandan.*

While state television broadcast clips of the singer Koffi Olomidé and his scantily clad dancers, a private station set up a fund for the victims of the attack on Bukavu and offered viewers an open microphone. A succession of street children and foul-mouthed riffraff came on the screen, interspersed with parliamentarians and ministers, creating a burlesque piece of theater. The rebels were Tutsi, they said, supported by the Rwandans — so they were going to kill all the Tutsi and occupy little Rwanda. Occupy Rwanda! On television!

Assani stood in uniform in front of his house as the crowd marched down the boulevard. A short distance away an angry mob was trying to destroy a bronze bust of Mzee, and there was a rumor that the mausoleum was under attack. At this point nothing was sacred. His fifteen *kadogos* scouted out the route. They didn't have much ammunition. He'd ordered them to shoot if they felt threatened: not in the legs, in the head.

"Watch out, they're Tutsi, they'll shoot!" he heard someone shout from the crowd. These people weren't afraid; they were too excited for that and they'd seen too much on

their odyssey through the city. This was their day and no
one was going to take it away from them. To his surprise
they began talking to him: Did he know Jules, the rebel
everyone was talking about?

"Sure I do; he's my cousin," Assani said.

"Why are you over here if he's over there?"

"He was here too, but he went back. His job was there."

"So what went wrong?"

"One of his men was arrested and put on a plane to
Kinshasa. He refused to accept that."

It was Mzee Kabila's fault, they shouted. They'd never
had any trouble with the Tutsi before he came along. Would
Assani go with them to find Tshisekedi, the opposition leader
who'd been sidelined during the peace talks, and take him
to the Palace of the Nation, Joseph Kabila's working palace? "As a soldier I can't get involved in politics," Assani
told them. They went on their way laughing.

That afternoon two people from MONUC came to see
if everything was all right. Assani pointed out a house where
a new neighbor had moved in, Erik Lenge, a Katangese confidant of the president. He was an army major, but his stock
of weapons exceeded his rank by a long way. "He's got mortars with a range of five miles," said Assani. "What does he
want with those in the city? Did he come to live across the
street from me so he could blow my house to pieces?"

One of the UN employees was a Malinese. His accent
reminded Assani of General Diallo, who'd been like a father to him. He studied the calling card the man handed him.
"Colonel Mamadou, you come from a real country," Assani
said. "I'd like to retire there when I'm old."

Later Assani got into his gray Mercedes with tinted windows and drove into town. Several party buildings had been destroyed but none of the places he'd protected had come under attack. He drove into the Kinshasa hills, passing the police who'd closed off the street where Vice President Yerodia lived, and sounded his horn outside his second house.

The guard kept Assani waiting before timidly sticking his head around the gate. Earlier that day he'd been threatened by military police farther up the street. "You're done for," they'd told him. "You work for a Rwandan. Soon we're coming to live in this house."

Assani gave the boy some money to buy food and went down into town again. Nothing here was the way it seemed. His people were leaderless and unpredictable. It frightened him.

※　　※　　※

For years he'd been invisible. People knew his name but had no idea what he looked like, or knew his face but not what he was called. But that Sunday when he drove into the *cité* to fax a letter he heard someone call out abruptly, "*Mon général!*"

He was standing in an open shop doorway, wearing a track suit and a red baseball cap—anonymous, or so he'd thought. He slowly turned to find himself looking into the excited faces of a group of street kids, gaping at him as if he were a famous pop star. "What d'you mean, 'general'?" he asked. They made him cross the busy street with them to a little shop where photos of all the officers of the general staff were on display, with their names underneath.

He stared at his photo as if at a "Wanted" poster and broke into a sweat. So that was it: they'd dragged him out of the darkness into the light and hung him on the wooden door of a shop in a densely populated neighborhood of the capital city. Just when he was thinking of disappearing again.

Congo wasn't a country and the Congolese weren't a people. There was no cohesion. The Belgians with their eternal optimism — why were they still trying to stick the pieces together? Wasn't it obvious this country could turn into Yugoslavia overnight? They were the ones pulling the cart; couldn't they see that if their attention lapsed for a second it would come to a halt and all the corncobs would fall off?

Everyone here was living in his own republic. For the average Kinois the country stopped at Masina, a neighborhood on the way to the airport. Beyond that everything was incomprehensible. His own republic was nearly 1,000 miles away, in the border area between Congo, Rwanda, and Burundi. Nevertheless here he was. Or was he really here at all?

On the way back from the *cité* he drove straight past his house on the boulevard, just as he'd done earlier in Goma before the doctor prescribed painkillers. When he got home he went into the living room and stretched out full length on the floor beneath the picture of young Kabila, lying the way he used to in the bush, one long arm around his head as if to protect himself. He fell asleep immediately.

He dreamed he was on a tour of inspection somewhere near Kabalo. He'd erected his tent under a tree that was full of wild parrots. The birds were making a tremendous racket, chattering and arguing, shitting on the tent, and flying back and forth. Boni wanted to shoot them, but Assani said, Leave them alone; they were here first.

The screeching above his head wouldn't stop. It woke him up. It was his Samsung cell phone on the coffee table — he'd programmed a rain forest tune into it. It shone brilliant blue in the falling darkness. "*Allô?*" The voice at the other end was Jules, who'd been forced out of Bukavu by MONUC.

He couldn't bring himself to stand up, so even after he'd finished talking to Jules he stayed where he was, lying on the carpet, huddled up with his eyes shut. Suddenly he remembered the title of an essay he'd been asked to write for the state exam in high school. In big letters on the blackboard in the study hall it had said: *If you go forward, you die; if you go backward, you die.*

When you had to choose between a friend and a brother, in Africa you always chose your brother. Even if you didn't, no one would believe you. A few days ago he'd been late for a meeting of the general staff and when he finally arrived the rumor that he'd fled was already buzzing through the corridors. Some people were surprised he'd had the nerve to come at all — the traitor. Others were friendly, so friendly that he grew suspicious. Meanwhile his friends in the east had raised the alarm because he'd failed to answer his phone, instantly assuming he'd been arrested.

After the meeting the chief of staff asked why he didn't call him anymore. "Why would I?" Assani said. "I'm in trouble. Does Kabila still regard me as one of his men?"

Every time he got into his uniform in the mornings, lacing his high black boots and straightening his green cap in front of the mirror, he asked himself, Am I still one of Kabila's men? How can I serve Kabila if Jules is in trouble over there? He couldn't be loyal to an army that was killing his people, couldn't serve his country and betray his own people.

In the midst of it all, his mother, who'd always lived far away in the safety of the high plains, had come down because she was sick. His sister had taken her to a hospital in Kigali. He called her every day. She was tired and refusing to eat. She said it was time to die.

Her voice had changed; she sounded like a little cheeping bird. "Didn't you know that old people have less and less breath?" she said when he remarked on it. "Until they stop breathing—then they're dead."

She was always teaching him to be tough, even now. "What do you think?" he asked Mwepu. "Would they give me permission to go visit her and say good-bye?" His friend looked worried. Several weeks earlier Assani had said he wanted to go to Goma to see his children. "I'm afraid this isn't the right moment to put in that kind of request," he said.

Assani groaned and stood up, turned on the light, and went into the storeroom to look for something to eat. He could hear his bodyguards talking in the UNICEF tent behind the house. They were discussing the general and his men, who had marched back into Bukavu as soon as Jules left. Sometimes it was instructive to listen to what they were saying when they were together, but he didn't feel like it this evening. Maize meal, onions, dried fish . . . He took some potato chips and a carton of milk out of a box and a piece of cheese from the fridge and installed himself in front of the television.

On the Odyssey channel a deep-sea diver was swimming with giant turtles. Look at that: he seemed perfectly relaxed! Assani tore open the bag of chips and cut the rind off the cheese with a large knife. In a state like this he didn't eat hot food; even if his *kadogos* had cooked a meal for him he wouldn't touch it. As he put the carton of milk to his lips a sour smell came from his clothes. It was the smell of fear.

Devota called. She'd been calling him continually over the past few days, even though he couldn't help her and she certainly couldn't help him. Sometimes she begged him to come home because he was in danger in Kinshasa; at other times she was glad he wasn't in Goma, where he'd inevitably be drawn into the new rebellion.

"Why the silence?" she complained.

"I'm listening."

"What did I just say?"

"That you went to the hospital with Moshe. That you saw AIDS patients."

"They were in a terrible state. I hope you're being careful over there."

She was leading him into an argument. Bickering — she enjoyed that. He was too tired to bicker.

"Why don't you say something?"

"What am I supposed to say? Do you think I have time for other women?" While he was talking he walked through the house. He'd started sending his things to Goma as soon as the situation in Bukavu became unstable: the photo album from the day of his appointment, the uniform James Kabarebe had sent him. It was a reflexive response — he'd so often lost everything in the past. At the same time, with an effort that ran contrary to it yet was no less reflexive, he continued furnishing his house. He'd had an extra bathroom built, bought furniture for his study, and hung up a calendar from the defense company Norinco: tanks gleaming cold and metallic in a Chinese sunrise.

Devota had shut off the call. He tried to call her back but she'd turned off her phone. His instinct had been right: she wanted an argument. Now he wouldn't contact her for a while, so she'd think he was angry.

The electric clock in the living room gave nine interminably slow chimes. The battery needed changing, but he'd lost interest in that kind of thing. He pressed the bell. "Take that away," he said to the soldier on duty, pointing to the remains of the food on the table. "And bring me some water." He had a stock of small bottles he drank in one go — it was safest that way.

He tried to call Jules but couldn't reach him. "That's it; we're going into the bush," Jules had said. Now the *kama mbaya mbaya* — come what may — would begin in earnest. Killing, looting, rape — he'd seen it so many times before. The thought oppressed him so much that he tried the number again.

"I'm already camping over here," he said when Claudine called. "My rucksack's packed in case I have to get out fast, but I'm not running away any more. They'll have to come and get me. I don't have much ammunition, but I'll defend myself right down to the last bullet — the last one's for me."

"I don't understand this," Claudine said. "MONUC persuaded you to go to Kinshasa. Aren't they responsible for your safety? Why don't you call them if you're in danger?"

"MONUC, pfff . . . They're in danger themselves!" He sighed grimly. "I'd better not call you any more; you talk like the wind in the desert. Can a baby survive in a burning house by shaking its head back and forth? If I talk to MONUC . . . Who knows what they'll do with the information? They don't have a clue about our old wounds — they've no idea what happens when they're opened up again."

Mwepu called on another phone. "I'm in your neighborhood," he said. "I'm coming over."

The last time he'd seen Mwepu was at the trial of a colonel who'd hired a contract killer to get rid of someone. Assani had been assigned to the trial as a lay magistrate. The press had made a lot of fuss about the case because the colonel had been close to Joseph Kabila. Assani was convinced the man had done some kind of dirty work for the president too, but of course they weren't investigating that.

The trial had been held in an open hangar where people could walk in and out. From the platform Assani saw a man he thought he knew shuffling through the crowd. He was wearing a nondescript pair of pants and a T-shirt and he had come in not through the main entrance but from the side, where there was standing room for the public. Assani lost sight of him for a while, then realized the man had been lurking behind a truck people were using as a urinal or for shade from the sun.

It was Mwepu. Assani couldn't take his eyes off him. If he'd had a camera he'd have filmed him. The ease with which Mwepu played the role of an inquisitive listener, his ability to make himself invisible — Assani was starting to lose those instincts, but his friend was a master of them. It was like watching himself, the way he used to be: a submariner, a man drowning. Their eyes met for an instant but Mwepu had shown no sign of recognizing him.

The gate opened and he heard a car come through. There was his friend, Mwepu, who'd already posted two soldiers a few houses away to watch everything that moved in the vicinity of the house. Chasing shadows again — military intelligence was afraid someone would take advantage of the chaos to kill the president.

Mwepu pushed open the tall glass door and saw Assani sitting on the couch in a track suit and T-shirt, legs pulled up under him, a bowl of grapes in his lap. The sour smell of sweat hung heavily in the room. "Isn't the air-conditioning working?"

Assani batted away a mosquito as it sailed sluggishly across the room. "I'm in the bush again — you don't need air-conditioning there." He pointed to the curtains, which had been shoved beyond the ends of the rails. "What do you think the idiot I brought with me from the east does with the runners? Throws them away!" He put the bowl of grapes down on the table and looked distractedly at Mwepu. "You guys are going to have a problem with me," he said. "First you'll have to kill me and then you'll have to bury me."

Mwepu sat down in an armchair facing him. "You're dead already," he said cheerfully. "What are you afraid of, decomposition?"

Since Devota and the children left, Assani had been using two bedrooms. He kept his army uniforms in one, his civilian clothes in the other. That night he decided to sleep in the civilian room at the front of the house, his pistol under his pillow. The hate campaign on local television had started again — there was pastor Ngoy, a little man whose shoulders barely showed above the tabletop and who was capable of only one thing: cursing Rwandans.

Recently, after recording a show, pastor Ngoy had seen a Tutsi soldier standing outside the entrance to his apartment house. He began sweating profusely: the Rwandans had found him. He called the police, who came immediately. The soldier turned out to be a bodyguard protecting a politician from the east who was too scared to stay in his villa and had taken refuge in one of the apartments. The incident ended in a shootout and Assani had been called in to calm things down.

From time to time the gate opened and he heard the stifled voices of the soldiers on watch. "Let's go back," they'd been saying more and more often over the past few days. "Why are we still here?" Some had girlfriends. Their reflexes were the same as his: they wanted to get out and at the same time they were building lives for themselves.

Mwepu had brought a message. Someone had said, "Assani must be able to jump." Mwepu refused to say who

it was from or what it meant—he'd have to work that out
for himself.

Was the person who'd sent him the message an enemy
or on his side? Did he mean that Assani should jump over
the garden wall when they came for him, or that he had to
choose between Rwanda and Congo? Assani turned the
words over and over in his head. They began to torment him.

On an impulse he called his friend. "I've jumped already," he said. "But I'm having difficulty landing; the
ground's full of land mines. The only safe place is the garden of your house."

"Anything's better than hovering in the air," Mwepu
answered.

In the middle of the night a soldier called from Uvira.
"*Afande*," he said, "your people have fled over the border into
Burundi and now Kabila's soldiers are looting their houses.
The furniture, doors—they steal everything. They turn on
the taps; the water runs out of the doors into the street." The
man was a Fulero who'd grown up in the hills near Uvira.
He wasn't telling Assani anything new. "Leave them to get
on with it. What can we do to stop them?" "I don't agree,
afande." He shut off the call but the man called back. "They're
even dismantling the roofs, *afande*!"

Assani lay on his back in the pale light from a lamp
outside, his hands folded at his chest. He'd called his
mother earlier that day. He tried to imagine her lying asleep
in a hospital bed well over 1,000 miles away, snuggled between white sheets. I should never have come to Kinshasa.
The words reverberated in his head. I've walked into a
trap.

In his mind he drove from his house on the boulevard to Camp Tshatshi in the hills—the tunnel from one prison to another. Before he reached the gate to the camp he was asleep.

Two men were lugging a body, trying to throw it at him. He deflected it but it fell back against him with its full weight. He woke up whimpering and grabbed his phone. Where was Jules? *The person you are trying to call is outside the zone covered by your service provider. Please try later,* a woman's voice said.

Someone called to say that 500 people from Kalemie were moving up into the high plains. A biblical caravan of men, women, children, and cows were fleeing the fury of people in the valley. Escorted by their own warriors they were heading back into the mountains they came from.

❊   ❊   ❊

There were some people in this country, Colonel Mamadou thought, who needed to be protected against their own despair, and General Assani was one of them. The way he'd talked that afternoon during the demonstration about his Katangese neighbor who supposedly had it in for him— Mamadou had immediately recognized the combination of bravura and fear. Sometimes a man who was frightened stepped out into view, inevitably becoming a victim.

Mamadou had been in Congo for the past two years as a milobs, a military observer for MONUC. He often went on missions into the interior and he'd gotten to know the explosive mixture of conflicts in the east at close hand. Most people had selective memories. They did terrible things to each other and then screamed for help when the time for vengeance arrived. Each leader had his own agenda and Congo always came second. He'd seen no sign of a figure like Mandela or Malcolm X here.

General Assani used to be an intelligence officer, or so he'd heard. That was a dirty job in the Great Lakes region, where human rights abuses had been the order of the day for many years. He must have seen and done horrible things.

In his experience people like Assani were damaged for life. You couldn't tell by looking, but it was as if parts of them had grown numb. Unable to trust anybody, they became afraid of their own shadows. Someone might know a certain thing about them, another person something else, but only they themselves knew the whole truth. Their secrets oppressed them and made them fearful.

Mamadou knew it hadn't been easy for Assani to come to Kinshasa and when he saw him that time in front of his house—tall, lanky, the hollow eyes in his narrow face restless and alert—he'd understood why: his Tutsi features made it impossible for him to merge into the crowd. The Kinois would always associate him with Rwanda, and probably not without reason; once a man had worked for their security service, would the Rwandans ever completely let him go?

In the days that followed, Mamadou called him several times to see if everything was OK. They spoke only briefly—he could tell Assani was tense. Everyone suspected the politicians and soldiers from the east of having encouraged the rebels. If that was true, then after Jules's defeat Assani must feel guilty about sacrificing his cousin.

Assani could play an important role in the peace process, General Diallo had told him, since he had come to

Kinshasa not for money or personal gain but because he wanted to change things. If he backed out he might drag the whole transitional government down with him — they'd do well to keep Assani's mind on the job. Mamadou tried to arrange to see him, but Assani didn't seem interested. He relented only after Mamadou told him he'd recently spoken with General Diallo.

Mamadou was sitting under an umbrella by the pool at the Greek Club when Assani arrived. There was a hint of uncertainty in his stride, as if he'd been spending too much time indoors and was no longer used to the fierce afternoon light. He was wearing black pants with a bright blue shirt, and leather shoes with square toes the color of coffee creamer. It wasn't difficult to imagine the mountain boy he'd once been.

"And how's General Diallo doing? He must be happy to be out of this land of barbarians." Assani sank into a plastic chair next to him. His eyelids were swollen from lack of sleep, but he smiled and gave Mamadou a slightly challenging look.

"No, no, not at all. He's keeping close track of developments."

They exchanged a few generalities about the events of the past few weeks. Children climbed out of the swimming pool and trotted over to their mothers, who were lying in the sun on the far side. No matter how fiercely war raged in the hinterland, at the Greek Club in Kinshasa it was always holiday time.

When their drinks had arrived and the waiter had left, Assani said to Mamadou, "Protect us. Even the gorillas are protected — why not us? Kabila ought to go on television and say that anyone, soldier or civilian, who lays a finger on a Munyamulenge will be punished, but he does exactly the opposite: he sets up loudmouths to rant against us." He was silent for a moment, looking around to be sure no one was listening. "They're killing our soldiers in the interior, did you know that?"

Mamadou discreetly took a pen and notebook out of his pocket. "Can you tell me exactly what happened?" he asked. "Can you list specific cases?"

Assani told him about nine Banyamulenge soldiers who'd been disarmed and shot in Walunga by the general's men shortly after Jules's revolt, about two soldiers who'd died in Kalemie, about civilians who were being threatened: "They feel unprotected, so they turn to Rwanda for help — then everyone brands them as traitors!"

Vice President Yerodia — who'd declared at the start of the second war that the Tutsi were vermin to be eradicated — had just arrived back from a visit to France. On arriving at the airport he'd said, in front of the cameras: *We'll chop them into little pieces, limb by limb.* "We know what that means, we recognize the signs. But the UN . . . You guys will only sound the alarm when you see our gravestones."

Assani pointed to the high wall around the swimming pool. "When you look at that you see only a wall, but I immediately think of the danger lurking behind it."

"Was Yerodia speaking French at the airport?"

"No, no, Lingala."

"What were his exact words?" Mamadou gave him the notebook and Assani wrote in capital letters: TO KOSOKOLA BANGO MA SOKO.

"I wish I hadn't come to Kinshasa," he said. "I want to join the others. We'll create a pure state in the east. Anyone who's against us will have to go live somewhere else." He slid the notebook back toward Mamadou. "My ancestors are buried in the high plains of South Kivu," he said. "But every night when I turn on the television I hear I'm not Congolese." He sighed. "Why can't the UN give us a state where we can live in peace?"

Mamadou sat leaning back in his chair, looking at him. The way Assani was lashing out in all directions—he suddenly understood the fatherly tone in which General Diallo had spoken about him and was glad he'd followed his instincts and pressed for a meeting.

"I promise I'll follow up on this," he said, pointing at the notebook.

"The boys who died were innocent. They had nothing to do with the mutiny," Assani said, suddenly quieter, as if the simple fact that Mamadou had written down his complaint made him feel calmer. "I'm in mourning. Every death reawakens the memory of other deaths. People who've often been hurt in the past react differently from normal people— they turn as vicious as wounded game."

Back at his office Mamadou checked up on the information Assani had given him. His colleagues in Bukavu confirmed the report about the executed Banyamulenge soldiers. The case was under investigation.

To kosokola bango ma soko—Mamadou wrote what Yerodia had said on a piece of paper and asked his driver what it meant. The man laughed. "That you're going to spank someone's bottom."

"Is that all? Doesn't it have a double meaning?"

"I don't think so, no."

Over the next few days Mamadou asked all the Kinois around him. They assured him the words threatened a thorough dressing-down, but no one mentioned chopping people to pieces.

❊ ❊ ❊

Assani had been sitting on the couch all evening watching war films, drinking milk, and eating cookies. He finally managed to contact Jules, who'd fled to Rwanda with his men. That wasn't good news, but at least Jules would be safe there.

After midnight he couldn't stand to stay in his house any longer. Wearing his track suit he went out and got into his car. "No, no, I'm going alone," he snapped at the bodyguard who walked up to him, Kalashnikov slung over his shoulder. The boy opened the door and muttered, "At least take this with you," throwing Assani's pistol onto the passenger seat.

He hadn't talked to his soldiers for days. What was there to say? The atmosphere was heavy with departure. "Just make sure you get out of here," they said. "We'll follow."

The voice of Rafiki, a singer from the east, thrummed through the car. *Your friend is your enemy; treachery is based on trust.* Quite a change from the frenzied blaring of singers in Kinshasa, who never uttered anything but meaningless catchphrases.

He had a premonition that something was about to happen. Very soon, too—he was rarely wrong about these things. Following his usual routine, he drove past Vice President

Ruberwa's heavily guarded residence, then his office, to check everything was normal. Outside party headquarters two Banyamulenge guards were sitting peering down the quiet street. They looked so vulnerable, their young faces distorted with fear. If he stopped to talk to them they'd be reassured for a while, but he drove on without so much as a nod.

A white military intelligence car went by: Mwepu's boys, just cruising around. He'd recently tested out his Mercedes on the boulevard at night. It had far better acceleration than their cars — if they tried to come after him they'd never catch up.

A couple of girls were standing by the roadside, on the lookout for clients. At this time of night they'd be starting to get desperate; all the bars in the neighborhood would be closing soon. On the terrace of Le Surcouf, a Congolese clown in a Texan hat playing a cheap guitar was singing "Ancien Combattant," a hit with aid workers and other gullible types: *Pourquoi la guerre, pourquoi la guerre? La guerre, ce n'est pas bon, ce n'est pas bon.* (Why war, why war? War's no good, no good.) Souvenir vendors followed a white man who was walking to his jeep, proffering finely-tooled wooden boxes, black-painted men holding spears, and models of Tintin in Congo. "Good price, sir, good price!"

Assani was driving more slowly now. A skinny girl in a miniskirt lifted her blouse to show him her breasts. In the rearview mirror he noticed that the UN jeep behind him had stopped. Soldiers were the same the world over, he thought: they pick up their women on the street. This was pleasant, roaming around the city at night; it helped him relax. He took a turn at random and soon didn't know where he was.

That morning he'd stood talking with a group of fellow officers at work. "What are you people after?" someone had asked him. "You've got so many posts in the transitional government. Why aren't you satisfied?"

"Someone ought to take a proper look at the problems in the east," Assani answered. "It's a mistake to think that the situation in Bukavu has been resolved just because the general's back in charge. Kabila is creating dissidents; they're all getting in touch with each other and if things go on like this I'll join them."

At first he'd always protested if they tried to get him to put his name to dubious documents, but now he signed everything blindly. His colleagues knew there was nothing he could do—he'd lost any power he once had. They kept him in the dark as far as possible, but some things they couldn't hide. He discovered that one so-called reserve company in the east he was responsible for supplying was composed of Interahamwe and Mai Mai who'd been mixing with government troops. Sooner or later the situation would become so threatening for the Rwandans that they'd have to take action.

Didn't Kinshasa understand that old ties came into play at moments like these? A general in the Burundian army had called him. He'd worked with Jules in the past and wanted to know if there was anything he could do for him. It was easy enough to get a few untraceable crates of munitions delivered to a friend in need.

"Our strategy and our diplomacy are failing," he'd told his colleagues. "You claim Rwanda is involved in the revolt in the east. Rwanda says it's afraid of the Interahamwe. Why don't we make sure Rwanda doesn't have any pretext to attack us?"

The streetlights went out. Did that happen even in residential districts like this? Assani drove more cautiously. Somewhere he heard a generator start up.

His phone rang. Two-thirty. Who would call him at this hour?

"Where are you?" Mwepu sounded agitated.

"Umm . . . Somewhere. Why?"

"Aren't you at home?"

"Not yet, no."

"There's . . . It looks like there's been a coup. Check everything's OK at your place. I'd stay right away from there for a while. Try to find somewhere to take cover."

Mwepu's calling to warn me, he cheered inwardly; he's looking after me! But the next moment he thought: he's watching me — of course he'd want to find out where I was at a time like this.

"Did you know this was coming?" Assani asked

"No. It's someone in the presidential guard. He's taken the television building. It seems he just broadcasted a statement."

See! Exactly as he'd predicted: the cordon around Kabila was so tight that even people like Mwepu didn't know what was going on inside it. "If you didn't know this was coming, maybe you're a target as well. I'd lie low if I were you, even if it's only in the scrubland behind your house."

He stopped to look up his bodyguard's number. Two soldiers on guard duty at the other side of the square walked toward him hesitantly, two terrified shadows in the night.

They conferred for a moment, then the braver one crossed the street. "You'll have to drive on, you can't stop here," he said. Instead of answering, Assani fixed the soldier with a stern look. It worked—the boy felt intimidated and slunk away.

It was quiet at his house, his bodyguard said, except that the neighbor across the street had left a few hours earlier in a convoy of eight jeeps. Major Lenge. Of course. He was a member of the presidential guard. If he'd read out a communiqué on television, then Kabila was dead, or at least a prisoner.

Assani called the president's number. Busy. But when he tried again he got him on the line. "*Afande* . . . Is everything all right with you?"

The reply sounded feeble. For a moment their old intimacy returned. "Do you know Erik Lenge?" the president asked. "Do you know who he is?"

"No, *afande*, not personally, no."

"Are you safe? Make sure you're in a safe place." Joseph sounded weak and disappointed. Lenge had been his friend—he'd given him everything and now Lenge had betrayed him.

"That's what happens when you play with children," Assani said the next time Mwepu called. "Sooner or later they fling mud at you." He was driving again. His phone kept ringing; people were calling from all over the country; everyone was wide awake.

Suddenly he felt insecure in his track suit, without a bodyguard. He should take cover, but where? What kind of a coup was this anyway? A major who went to the television building with eight jeeps to read out a communiqué announcing the fall of the transitional government while the whole city was in bed? It looked like a diversion, a dress rehearsal.

The chaos was total. All the messages he received contradicted each other. Some people said that there was artillery fire around the presidential residence; others said that Lenge was driving across the city with his convoy, the military police giving chase, or that he'd gotten out to make a speech in a café, or was being shot at as he tried to cross the Congo River to flee to Brazzaville.

Everyone had been sitting around complaining about Rwanda, but the danger came from within — now that idiot was driving across the city creating havoc! Assani decided to go home after all. All his men were awake; they'd been worried about him. He took a shower and put on his uniform. By the time he was ready it was light outside.

He walked along the street. The sky was milky white, the boulevard deserted. Today people would stay indoors, turn on the television, listen to the radio, and keep up-to-date with all the rumors by cell phone. It would be a bonanza for the phone companies.

Close to Vice President Ruberwa's office he picked up several spent cartridge cases. The guards at the gate had heard gunfire in the distance, they said, and immediately rushed out into the street to answer it.

He was calm — his bush instinct had kicked in. He didn't look like a man who hadn't slept all night. They aren't even capable of mounting a coup, he thought bitterly. This place will fall apart of its own accord; they'll eat each other up — that was something they wouldn't be able to pin on him.

❊   ❊   ❊

His mother was dying. In the Kigali hospital they couldn't do any more for her, so his sister had taken her to his house in Gisenyi. When he raised the subject the chief of staff looked at him regretfully. "I can't let you travel out there right now. You understand that, don't you?" Mwepu avoided Assani's eyes when he mentioned it, as if he didn't really believe him. He'd brought this on himself by repeatedly telling people he was going to join the dissidents. Perhaps he'd said it on purpose—so that they'd stop him.

He called his mother every morning. She was lucid but her voice was getting weaker. Devota and the children crossed the border every day to visit. His mother understood why he couldn't be with her.

"You know I often have tough decisions to make," he said to her one morning. "Advise me what to do when you're no longer here; tell me something to help me live on after you."

She didn't need much time to think. "You must stay in your own country," she said, her voice barely audible. "Respect your boss and keep your door open to others."

She died that evening.

The chief of staff was moved when he heard. Permission from the president came almost immediately and by the following afternoon Assani was on a plane to Goma, where Devota was waiting for him with the children. As he drove through the gate to his house he saw that his garden had been turned into a parking lot. The mourning had begun.

His mother was lying in an open coffin in the living room. Her diminutive stature matched the birdlike voice she'd had these past few weeks. How small she'd become; how little was left of the strong woman that he'd known as a child and that she'd still been right up to their last meeting.

Every time Assani was in mortal danger during the war, he'd thought of his mother, wanting at all costs to spare her the task of burying him. But now he was standing here he felt so desolate that he no longer understood why he'd wanted her to go first. His mother knew all his secrets; she would never let anything slip. Whereas Devota . . . Before you knew what was happening she'd told her girlfriends everything.

Moshe threw his arms around Assani's legs. He'd grown heavy over the past few months and Assani had difficulty lifting him up. His little son seemed to understand the solemnity of the moment and looked down at his grandmother in silence.

The days that followed passed as if in a dream. There was no end to the procession of family and friends that over ran the house. *Keep your door open to others.* That was the hardest part of the advice his mother had given him. She knew him; she knew he was intractable and stubborn, a loner inclined to close himself off with the pain people had caused him. Now that she was no longer there he'd have to take care of them —was that what she'd meant?

People wanted to talk to him about the rebellion, which had gone quiet for the time being but might break out again at any moment, like the Nyiragongo volcano on the edge of Goma that steamed, smoked, and hissed if you got close.

He remained noncommittal and didn't contact anyone. It was so easy to say the wrong thing. Mwepu always understood when he had a bad day and came out with things he shouldn't have said, but people around here thought differently. And Kabila's men were in town, keeping an eye on him.

"Kinshasa won't listen to us. They want us dead, not alive," one of the insurgents said. Assani agreed, but he no longer believed war was the solution. "Stay out of it," someone whispered to him. "You're already in Kinshasa—you're safer there than here."

Mwepu called him daily. He'd vouched for Assani and the nearer the end of his leave came the more uneasy he sounded. Mwepu's friends had laughed at him when they heard Assani had left for Goma. "We won't be seeing him again," they said.

"I'm not ready yet," Assani told Mwepu one day, sounding evasive. "You know what it's like after a funeral; people turn to stone in your yard and refuse to leave until they've presented you with all their problems."

It was quiet at the other end. "I only hope you're not going to disappoint me," Mwepu said.

Along with Devota, Assani drove one of the last guests home. On the way back they passed a little shop where he'd once stopped to buy milk and chocolate for his mother. Instead of being pleased she'd protested, "Why buy me chocolate? Have I got so old that you're starting to treat me like a child?" When he thought back to that scene it was as if a heavy weight were pressing on his chest. A wave of fear engulfed him. Suddenly he burst into tears.

He was so upset he had to park the jeep at the side of the road. Devota had never seen him cry before. "I no longer exist," he said, laying his head on the steering wheel. "It's as if I stopped existing when she died." He was surprised at himself—he hadn't felt this coming. When he got home he had to sit in the car for a while before he could face the remaining guests.

When the visitors had stopped coming and the people staying in his house had gone, Assani went with Devota and the children to look at the parcel of land he'd bought on the shore of Lake Kivu. He'd gotten the builders to erect a fence around it. Early that morning the sky had been gray, but gradually it grew so hot that Devota and the baby had to shelter under the lean-to roof of the one little structure on the plot.

What am I doing in Kinshasa? Assani thought as he paddled in the rippling blue lake with the boys. Uncle Rutebuka was right: everything I need is here; what am I looking for over there?

Devota drove back while he walked home with the boys, Moshe on his shoulders, Chief next to him. If he were to walk half a mile in the other direction he'd be in Rwanda. That was a pleasant thought—close to the border he was safe. But if he stayed here he'd have to do bad things again. As soon as the drums of war sounded he'd be drawn in, irrevocably.

He forced himself to think of the good things that had happened since his arrival in Kinshasa. He'd made friends — after five years at war he'd thought he was incapable of that. At first he'd felt exposed without weapons or soldiers in a city where there was so little security, without a single unit under his command, but he'd gotten used to it.

Mwepu hadn't called him yet today. He was holding his breath over there. He owed Mwepu. Abandoning him would be like abandoning a friend at the front. He'd promised himself they'd never part as enemies. If he ever made a decision Mwepu didn't like, he'd have to be able to explain his reasons.

That night he dreamed that someone came to tell him he'd been appointed brigadier general in Goma. "No, no," he said, shocked. "I'm leaving for Kinshasa tomorrow; they're worried about me over there; I'm already late."

On the plane he felt alone for the first time in his life. Not like before, solitary, an orphan, unfairly treated by his uncles, but as a man who, on his own, without a mediator of any kind, had come to a decision. Devota was sitting next to him with the baby, Chief and Moshe in the seats in front.

They'd just arrived in Kinshasa and were driving into the city from the airport when Mwepu called.

"Where are you?"

"In Goma."

"Still? I thought your leave was over."

"I'm not coming back. There's nothing for me there."

His words fell like a hammer.

Assani wound down the window and the honking and shrieking of Kinshasa surged in. The smell of palm oil, dust, and putrefaction made him gasp for breath. Someone shouted something in Lingala.

Mwepu laughed. "But . . . there are children in the car!"

"You said I had to jump, didn't you? I've brought my family with me." Assani leaned back and looked at the billboards for Vodacom and Celtel that hid the *cités* from the road. "You Katangese are the ones who do the killing here," he said. "If anything happens to my family, I'll hold you responsible."

HISTORICAL
BACKGROUND

In 1994 the plane carrying the Hutu president of Rwanda, Habyarimana, is shot down on its approach to the capital, Kigali, and the power struggle between the Hutu majority and the Tutsi minority that has smoldered for decades erupts. In the three months that follow, Hutu militias murder 800,000 Tutsi and moderate Hutu.

After the genocide an estimated 2 million Hutu flee into eastern Zaire, present-day Congo. Among the many different peoples living there are Hutu and Tutsi. The crisis in neighboring Rwanda has already exacerbated tensions between the two groups, but with the influx of Hutu refugees the conflict spills over the border.

The Mobutu regime, undermined by corruption, is unable to control the Hutu army arriving along with the refugees. From within the camps the Hutu engage in armed resistance to the Tutsi regime that has taken power in Rwanda.

In 1996 Paul Kagame, the new strongman in Kigali, decides to invade Zaire with the help of Zairean Tutsi refugees in Rwanda. Once inside Zaire they are joined by other dissidents and the invasion turns into a widespread rebellion against the Mobutu regime. Under the leadership of Mzee Kabila the rebels cross the vast country of Zaire in seven months and topple Mobutu. This is usually referred to as the first war.

Kabila proclaims himself president, changes the name of the country from Zaire to Congo, and appoints James Kabarebe, military leader of the rebels and a Rwandan, as commander in chief of the Congolese army. By 1998, however, relations between Kabila and the Rwandans have soured to such an extent that Kabila orders his former allies to leave the country. The Congolese associate all Tutsi with Rwanda, and across the country they are hunted down, arrested, and executed.

The second war begins. In the east the Rwandans, supported mainly by Congolese Tutsi rebels, again invade Congo and create an air bridge to the Kitona military base in the west, from which they attempt to seize the capital, Kinshasa. This attempt fails because neighboring Angola has sided with Kabila and is helping to defend the capital.

Congo lies at the heart of Africa; nearly all its neighbors become involved in the war. Rwanda is assisted by Uganda and Burundi, the Congolese government side by Angola, Namibia, and Zimbabwe. The conflict soon becomes known as the First African World War.

This time the war lasts five years and claims millions of lives. In November 2000 Kabila orders the execution of

Commander Masasu, who fought alongside him during the long march to Kinshasa in 1996. Soldiers recruited by Masasu feel threatened. Two months later Kabila is assassinated by one of his bodyguards from the east.

His son Joseph takes over and peace negotiations, begun under Kabila but hopelessly bogged down, gain momentum. The existing Lusaka peace accords are followed by accords signed in Sun City and Pretoria; the UN peacekeeping mission, MONUC, gradually grows into the UN's largest current military operation.

Under the terms of the peace accords the rebels arrive in the capital in 2003 to form a transitional government headed by the young Kabila. In 2006 Congo holds its first democratic elections in over forty years and Joseph Kabila is elected president.

CHRONOLOGY

1885
Congo Free State becomes the private property of Leopold II, king of the Belgians.

1908
Congo becomes a Belgian colony.

1960
Congo gains independence, with Kasavubu as president and Lumumba as prime minister.

1965
After a turbulent period of revolts, mutinies, and secessions, Mobutu seizes power following a coup.

1971
Mobutu renames the country Zaire.

1973
Mobutu nationalizes all private companies and hands them over to his cronies.

1990
After the fall of the Berlin wall and the end of the Cold War, Mobutu can no longer count on support from his western allies. During the National Conference his position as president is challenged, but he manages to hold on to power.

1996
In the east of the country the former rebel Laurent-Désiré Kabila, supported by Rwanda and Uganda, wages war against Mobutu.

1997
After a march of seven months from east to west the rebels conquer the country and topple Mobutu. Kabila proclaims himself president.

1998
Kabila turns against the Rwandans who helped him to power and orders them to leave the country. A new war breaks out.

1999
Signing of the Lusaka accords. The Congolese commit themselves to national dialogue; foreign powers promise to withdraw from Congo within an agreed period. The first members of the UN peacekeeping mission MONUC arrive

in Congo to monitor the implementation of the cease-fire agreement.

2001
President Kabila is assassinated; his son Joseph takes over. Peace negotiations gain momentum.

2002
Signing of accords in Sun City and Pretoria intended to pave the way for free elections.

2003
A transitional government takes office, comprising all parties to the conflict; the army is officially unified.

2006
First Congolese elections in more than forty years. Joseph Kabila is elected president of the Democratic Republic of Congo.

HISTORICAL
CHARACTERS

Jef Van Bilsen
Belgian professor who suggests in 1955 that Congo should
become independent within thirty years. His plan is considered absurd and meets with fierce resistance.

James Kabarebe
Chief of staff of the Rwandan army; previously aide-de-
camp to Kagame, military leader of the rebellion, and commander in chief of the Congolese army under Mzee Kabila.

Joseph Kabila
President of Congo; succeeds his father in 2001.

Laurent-Désiré Kabila
Known as Mzee; former rebel leader who topples Mobutu
in 1997 and proclaims himself president; murdered in 2001.

Paul Kagame
President of Rwanda; previously vice president of the RPF,
commander in chief of the Rwandan army, minister of defense, and vice president of Rwanda.

Patrice Lumumba
Charismatic prime minister of Congo immediately after independence; murdered in 1961.

Masasu
Member of the RPF and later a soldier in the Rwandan
government army. In 1996, along with Laurent-Désiré
Kabila, he fights against Mobutu and is appointed military
security adviser; executed on Kabila's orders in 2000.

Joseph-Désiré Mobutu
President of Congo/Zaire from 1965 to 1997. The longer he
holds power the more corrupt he becomes. When toppled
by Kabila's rebels he is forced to flee to Morocco where,
universally vilified, he dies of cancer less than four months
later.

Azarias Ruberwa
Vice president of the transitional government that comes
into being in 2003 after five years of war; Munyamulenge.

Etienne Tshisekedi
Political leader, several times prime minister under Mobutu,
despite repeatedly colliding with the president; regularly

jailed under both Mobutu and Mzee Kabila, he remains a major opposition figure.

Abdoulaye Yerodia
Vice president in the transitional government formed in 2003; representative of the old guard around Mzee Kabila.

GLOSSARY

afande	(Swahili) commander
bami	(pl.) kings, traditional chiefs
Banyarwanda	(pl.) people of Rwanda
Banyamulenge	(pl.) people of Mulenge
cité	populous district
Great Lakes region	Uganda, Rwanda, Burundi, Eastern Congo; the region around Lake Victoria, Lake Tanganyika, Lake Kivu, Lake Edward, and Lake Albert
Interahamwe	Hutu militia largely responsible for the genocide in Rwanda
Inyenzi	(Kinyarwanda) cockroach. Name given to Tutsi fighters who fought against the Rwandan Hutu regime in the early 1960s; later used as a term of abuse for all Tutsi.

ISP	Institut Supérieur Pédagogique (Institute of Higher Education)
kadogo	literally: little one; child soldier
Kikongo	one of the four main languages of Congo; aside from the provinces of Lower Congo and Bandundu, it is spoken in parts of Congo-Brazzaville and Angola
Kinois	resident(s) of Kinshasa (fem. Kinoise)
Kinyarwanda	official language of Rwanda
Lingala	one of the four main languages of Congo; aside from the capital, Kinshasa, and a large area of northwestern Congo, it is spoken in parts of Congo-Brazzaville and Angola
maman	(French) literally: mother; used to refer to any mature woman, especially a market trader
Mai Mai	(Swahili) literally: Water Water. People's militia, or members of such a militia, who see themselves as defending ancestral territory in eastern Congo. They resort to superstitious war rituals. Bullets are said to glide off them like water.
Mobutist	person who is well-disposed toward Mobutu or who enriched him or herself under Mobutu's regime

MONUC	UN peacekeeping force: Mission de l'Organisation des Nations Unies en République Démocratique du Congo
Munyamulenge	(sing.) person from Mulenge
Mzee	(Swahili) wise old man, elder; nickname for Laurent-Désiré Kabila
OBMA	Office des Biens Mal Acquis (Office of Ill-Gotten Gains)
pagne	rectangular strip of fabric, usually printed in bright colors, or the article of clothing made from it
palaver	talk, parley, or discussion
pirogue	canoe or open boat, dugout
RPF	Rwandan Patriotic Front, Tutsi-dominated party that seized power in Rwanda in 1994
transhumance	seasonal transfer of grazing animals to different pastures, often over substantial distances
Swahili	one of the four main languages of Congo; aside from eastern Congo, it is spoken in much of East Africa
Zaire	name given to Congo by Mobutu in 1971, changed to Democratic Republic of the Congo in 1997 by Kabila